two new languages, English and Navajo, very fluently. Even more interesting is how Miguel was unselfish and trusting enough to give some Navajo men a chance to silversmith alongside him. Miguel gave others opportunities just as he was given an opportunity.

When Dr. Edgar Hernández, the writer, enlisted me to help translate some text in the book into Navajo, it facilitated an even deeper connection between me and this book. Also, it brought back some of my own memories growing up on the Navajo reservation. The most challenging and fun part of the book in terms of translating was when Sampson, Miguel's godson, who is also a Navajo, speaking in Navajo, makes a reference to the moon during his eulogy. This quote in Navajo has a very deep, rich meaning, one that is nourishing to the soul and gentle at the same time.

Carol Benally, RN, MSN

Dr. Edgar Hernández captivates our minds, hearts, and souls in his third book, *Miguel Hernández—Mystic*, a memoir about the unique and inspiring life of his beloved older brother and father-figure. In this book, Dr. Hernández expertly illustrates Miguel's love and compassion for helping anyone in need become the best they can be.

One of Miguel's core beliefs was the following, as he himself explained it: "As I see it, all people are related though most of us just don't know it. So, we all need to do all we can, especially those of us with means, to help others." Miguel took the time to meet all people he encountered, whether it be as simple as greeting people in a restaurant or talking to people with whom he had business. He was able to influence an incredible number of people people to do the right thing for the betterment of mankind. In particular, Miguel helped many Mexicans living and working in the US illegally to become legal, productive residents. In outlining Miguel's unusual and heroic life, this book imparts a message to all of us to help fellow men, women, and children to truly make our world a kinder, gentler place.

Put this book on the top of your must-read list! I laughed and cried while reading it! And most of all, it made me want to be a better, more caring person!

Gretchen A. Boyer, BFA, MA, EdD

In *Miguel Hernández—Mystic*, my father, who is the author, clearly illustrates the greatness of my uncle and my namesake—Miguel Hernández—a man we were so fortunate to intimately know. As depicted in these pages, Miguel championed the core values of generosity, trust, sympathy, dignity, and self-sacrifice. Anyone reading this book will be motivated to engage with these forces of good in an effort to better the world as did Miguel over and over again.

I can recall the evening in my childhood when my father arrived home from work a touch earlier than usual. Without many words, he gathered our small family together, and with a deep, heartfelt breath he exhaled the news to us. Miguel was no longer with us. My father wept.

In that moment, as a six-year-old, I felt a part of me attach to Miguel's soul. I didn't understand it then, and even now it remains a mystical sensation to me. Looking back, this was my introduction to spirituality and an early awareness on my part of something bigger than any one of us. Because, while Miguel was no longer with us, his influence continued. In fact, it felt greater than it ever had before. This is another testament to Miguel's mysticism.

I've always believed that energy combined with good will is among the most valuable resources a human being could ever possess. And here, in this careful telling of Miguel's life story, I am shown this to be true again and again. Why? While most of the world recognizes opportunity as a chance to gain, Miguel believed the most golden of opportunities lay in moments to give, "to do something unique, that satisfies, that stands out and lasts forever."

Miguel E. Hernandez

In *Miguel Hernández—Mystic* we read about Miguel, a self-made man with limited education—in terms of schooling. However, as it relates to his worldly knowledge and vast caring, we find Miguel to be highly educated. He is compassionate, loving, and caring not only for his family, which is large indeed, but also for his circle of friends and members of his community, some of whom he has met only briefly. Miguel is an embodiment of divine-like features who walks the talk and has dedicated his life to others. This memoir will encourage you to reflect on the true meaning of life. It will leave a deep impression in your life. It will make everyone better human beings.

I hope one day this book, along with the writer's two previous memoirs, are made into movies, so even more people can appreciate the people featured in them—seemingly regular people who, in fact, are giants in their service to humanity.

Parvinder Khanuja, MD

Captivating and immersive. Edgar Hernandez brings to life the stories and challenges faced by his elder half-brother, Miguel, through the immigration process. While this process is known to be long and arduous, Edgar enchants the reader with personal accounts of his family members' journey, all the while gifting the reader with a style that is optimistic and filled with gratitude. His unique style of writing has the reader bouncing down the road in the back of a truck, traveling with him and his family while making necessary preparations for immigration. While the stories are inspiring, the greater undertones of gratitude, positivity, personal influence and destiny make this book a joy to read and self-reflect. As his previous writings have done, the book had me question what influence we can have on others, how we can elevate those around us and alleviate some of the burdens of life while accepting our individual gifts and purpose. Fantastic read.

Jeff Owens, MD

As we live our life on this earth, we cross paths with a few people who have truly shaped our character and our destiny. Miguel Hernandez was this person, an inspiration to so many who were merely existing, but not living as they searched for ways to improve their life. He saw the best in those who thought so little of themselves and were struggling to survive. He had a keen understanding of the human spirit, and could see into the soul of others. When reading this beautiful book, I felt that Miguel could see me, and through the author, allowed me to reflect upon my own life, prompting me to take every moment and live it to its full capacity.

Dr. Hernandez has provided us with an outstanding portrayal of his brother; an honorable man with relentless determination and courage. A truthful visionary with compassion for those making the journey to the United States, and an anchor for those floundering within its boundaries. This book encourages us to reach out to those around us, to connect and look beyond others' shortcomings, as we have all been affected by the pain in our life and our own personal struggles.

Hooked within the sixth paragraph of the introduction, I could not put this book down as my inner desire was to know this man- the mystic. If we could only have more of Miguel's spirit, vision, and desire to bond with humanity. Imagine what this world could be!!

Denise Sorget Kulesha, M.D.

Such a delightful, touching, well-written story! As described by Dr. Edgar Hernandez, his brother Miguel was truly an altruistic, charismatic, self-less, hero who touched the lives of so many. Living out his vision that he was placed on this earth for a reason, Miguel's magnetic personality leaves you with the longing that you too had met him. Knowing Dr. Hernandez for years, he demonstrates many of his brother's characteristics: genuine compassion, presence, charm and nobility. Dr. Hernandez's obvious love and respect for his older brother is eloquently captured with every written word. Captivating, emotional read!

Debbie Rosati, MSN, RN, Manager Recovery Room
Patrice Rosati, BSN, Intensive Care Unit RN, CCRN

Dr. Edgar Hernández's memoir, *Miguel Hernández—Mystic*, is the inspirational true story of a man who lived a simple and transformative life. A Mexican immigrant who believed in and shared the American dream. You will be drawn into the telling of a life well-lived. A life uncontrolled by fear. A life of doing what is right and just. A humble life without power, riches, fame, or prestige, yet more powerful than any world leader. Be prepared to see the ways that truth triumphs over evil. Discover how one man can make the difference in hundreds of lives, both for current and future generations.

Published in a time when the USA is fractured with immigration propaganda, this book reminds us that we are all brothers and sisters. We have different coverings but share the same heart, dreams, and needs. This page-turner is better than any self-help book written to encourage a purposeful life.

Judy Steele-Beckett, BSN, RN, MHSA

Miguel Hernández—Mystic is an inspiring, loving tribute to a great man, the older brother and father figure of the book's writer, Dr. Edgar Hernández. Along with Miguel's unstoppable drive to help his family immigrate to America, he also finds redemption in everyone he meets. He has a magical way of turning acquaintances into family and empathizes with their stories. This memoir will touch your heart.

Venessa Thompson, MSN, WHNP

Miguel Hernández—Mystic is a memoir about the writer's incredible older brother, who inspired many people with his magnetic personality. Miguel Hernández was a true servant of people who always saw the best in everyone. In describing Miguel's many investments in people and the great legacy he left behind, this book is an inspiration and demonstrates what a tireless servant of God Miguel was. I highly recommend this memoir, as well as the writer's previous two memoirs, because these books demonstrate the great opportunities for the disadvantaged that the United States has to offer and elegantly describe why many of us immigrants have come to this country for a better life.

Alberto Urbieta, Director of Electrical Engineering

MIGUEL HERNÁNDEZ

MYSTIC

IN SEARCH OF A GREEN CARD SPONSOR

MIGUEL HERNÁNDEZ

MYSTIC

IN SEARCH OF A GREEN CARD SPONSOR

BESTSELLER
BESTSELLER
BESTSELLER

EDGAR H. HERNANDEZ
M.D., M.S., F.A.C.S.

CARTWRIGHT
PUBLISHING
Visibility • Authority • Legacy • Clients

First Edition
First Printing 2019
ISBN: 978-1-7321736-4-4 (paperback)
ISBN: 978-1-7321736-5-1 (hardbound)

Library of Congress Cataloging-in-Publication Data is available.

This work was designed, produced, and published in the
United States of America by

CARTWRIGHT
PUBLISHING
Visibility • Authority • Legacy • Clients

3495 Lakeside Drive, #270
Reno, NV 89509

www.CartwrightPublishing.com
415-250-6343

Cartwright Publishing is a publisher of business and professional books. We help entrepreneurs, business and community leaders, and professionals share their stories, passion, and knowledge to help others. If you have a manuscript or book idea that you would like us to consider for publishing, please visit Cartwright Publishing.com.

Cover photo: Edgar H. Hernández
Cover design: Robin Vuchnich
Interior design: Robin Vuchnich

Other Books by the Author

———◆———

*On the Border of a Dream: One Mexican Boy's Journey to
Become an American Surgeon*

*Earth Angel with a Green Card: A Mexican Mother's Journey of
Faith, Hope and Dreams to Join her Children in the USA*

A Note from the Author

———◆———

I have tried to recreate events, locales and conversations from my memories of them. In order to maintain their anonymity, in some instances I have changed the names of individuals and places, and/or I may have changed some identifying characteristics and details such as physical properties, occupations and places of residence.

To the Hernández family from
Michoacán, Mexico.

———◆◆———

To American immigrants, legal or otherwise, and to your families—you have contributed greatly to our country.

To my grandchildren—Elisa, Sophia, Lucy, Francie, Eva Rose, Juliana, the little one, my only grandson Miguel, and the future twins to be born later this year—your hugs give me strength.

To Native Americans, especially Navajo Indians—in recognition of your tremendous contribution to the arts and for embracing my brother, sharing your talents in jewelry crafting with him, and giving him a place in life. Thank you. A'hééh'.

Next time you really want to challenge the goodness of people around you, do this: when you find yourself dining at a restaurant, approach the folks at nearby tables. With a big, sincere smile and a friendly, hearty handshake, introduce yourself to them and wish them a great meal. Their response will be a true testament to human kindness.

Try it sometime—it's an eye-opener!

—Edgar Hernández

Table of Contents

FOREWORD

Miguel Hernández—Mystic is an affirming, encouraging, and inspiring memoir about an amazing man. The stories and experiences the author, Dr. Edgar Hernández, relates about his older brother Miguel Hernández reflect on a man of the highest moral character, integrity, and honesty. Through Miguel's numerous selfless deeds and his massive idealism, we readers are encouraged to open our hearts—and possibly even our homes—to our fellow man, no matter how "other" they may seem to us at first glance.

Miguel never met a stranger because, to him, we are all one big family—all brothers and sisters. And because Miguel saw everyone as family, he made it a priority to get to know people and to help those in need. Readers will be astonished at the dozens and dozens of people that Miguel helped to get green cards in order to live and work in the United States without fear of deportation. All anyone had to do for Miguel's help in getting a green card was to simply know him and follow his four guidelines, as recounted in this book, and Miguel would assist them in any way possible.

It happened on several occasions that when someone met Miguel for the first time, that person had the impression of having met Miguel previously. In this way manifests a dimension of Miguel's unexplainable but apparent mysticism. His ability to look deep into someone's eyes and be able to put that person at ease was a gift from God that few people possess or make the effort to engage with. By reading this book, I expect many readers will be inspired to engage with "strangers" (not Miguel's word though!) in a sincere and heart-felt way, as did Miguel.

Readers will also be moved and astonished by Miguel's persistent effort to bring his entire family from Mexico to the United States. Miguel's eventual accomplishment of this monumental goal is a testament to his boundless love for his family. If only everyone could have a relative like Miguel Hernández, or better yet—if we, ourselves, could embody even a small portion of his ideals and practices—then all humanity would benefit. You see, as it played out in this book, Miguel's kindness, compassion, and assistance had a magnificent multiplying effect.

It has been my pleasure to know the author, Dr. Edgar Hernández, for over thirty-five years. I have never met a more generous, hard-working physician or person. Even though Dr. Hernández's schedule for the day may have been full, if I called about a patient, I always got the same response—"I am just sitting here with my feet up on the desk. Send them right over." Or it may have been—"I am heading to the hospital. Send them to the ER, I will see them there." Never once did he say, "Sorry, I am too busy."

It is apparent from reading this book how greatly Miguel acted not only as older brother but also as father figure to Dr. Hernández, as Dr. Hernández's character traits are certainly similar to those of Miguel. This comes out in his love for his family and his work ethic. Dr. Hernández's generosity reminds me of Miguel as well. Many times when out to dinner with Dr. Hernández, he has quietly asked the waiter to pay for the meals of other patrons that he didn't know. And as a doctor, he does the same, donating his services to patients whom he realizes cannot afford life-saving surgeries.

Upon reading *Miguel Hernández—Mystic*, I realize now that Dr. Hernández's optimism and vast generosity are legacies of his influential older brother: Miguel Hernández, a silversmith and Mexican immigrant with a third-grade education who possessed a degree of wisdom that the rest of us can only attempt to aspire to.

I saw the mysticism of Miguel Hernández when traveling in the Greek Isles with Dr. Hernández and his wife, Lupe. We were visiting the Home of Mary, mother of Jesus, when suddenly Dr. Hernández became ashen, sweaty, and very upset. Dr. Hernández related to us that he had just had a vision of Miguel, his brother, in the home of Mary. Even today when talking about this experience, he breaks out in a cold sweat. Only a true mystic could create such a vision and such a reaction.

In reading this wonderful book, allow this mystic's undaunted valor, compassion, and persistence to inspirit you, so that, like him, you can take advantage of life's golden opportunities to make positive differences in the lives of our brothers and sisters. If all of us enact even a small part of Miguel's magnanimity, our world will be a kinder, safer, and happier place.

Merle C. Turner, DO
Family Physician

INTRODUCTION—THE POWER OF A HANDSHAKE

Hand in hand, Miguel and I walked under the arches spanning the driveway entrance to Bob's Big Boy on Central Avenue in Phoenix, Arizona.

It was 1959. I was nine years old and had only been in the US for a month. It was my first time in the diner with its billboard-like neon sign flashing: "Bob's Famous Fine Foods." Outside stood a Big Boy statue in red-and-white checkered pants with whirly hair and holding a tall hamburger above his head. He seemed to be beckoning us in.

Inside stretched a long counter as well as tables and booths with shiny surfaces featuring both the red-and-white checkered pattern and alternating black and white panels. People sat in the booths and at tables, enjoying the food and talking, as restaurant staff traversed the floor.

"Wait until you taste the sauce inside the burger," Miguel told me.

As would become our custom, upon taking a seat, Miguel announced, "Let's wash our hands." First, I went. Next, Miguel. Upon his return, we selected our meal: two of Bob's famous cheeseburgers with fries and two vanilla milkshakes.

Continuing the custom, Miguel took a panoramic view of the restaurant, surveying the people to the left and right of us. Miguel notified me, "Edgar, I am going to greet these wonderful people."

While I watched, Miguel approached the family at the table to our right. The children's bright red hair contrasted with their pale skin that was dotted with freckles, freckles their mother had too though her hair was strawberry-blonde. The father had the classic all-American good looks of the actor Troy Donohue.

With a smile on his face and a hand extended to the young father, Miguel began, "Good afternoon, sir. My name is Miguel Hernández."

The two children giggled. While the mother's eyes showed bemusement, her lips turned up in a small smile.

The young father, after a beat of hesitation, extended his arm to shake Miguel's hand. "Happy to meet you. I'm Burt." Pointing to his wife and the children, he continued, "This is Sandra, my wife, and Troy and Emily."

In turn Sandra, Troy, and Emily shook hands with Miguel, who observed, "You are a very polite family."

To the little girl Miguel stated, "Emily is a lovely name. I know an Emily who is beautiful as well. She has red hair and freckles just like you. She has a diner in another part of Phoenix."

As he was wrapping up the greeting, from his peripheral vision Miguel noticed that the four folks sitting at a nearby table had begun squirming. Their discomfort seemed directed at Miguel, suggesting their thoughts: "Hope he doesn't come here. Hope he doesn't bother us. Maybe he'll sit down and leave us alone."

"You all have a good afternoon," Miguel told the family and then turned to make his way to the squirming group at the nearby table. Upon his approach, the two couples repositioned themselves as if in a huddle over the table. Their conversation became more energized with noticeable gesticulations to emphasize the intensity of their communication, all an obvious act to dissuade Miguel from speaking to them. As Miguel neared, they refused to look his way and instead upped the volume of their discussion.

Miguel was not discouraged.

To clarify, though Miguel was persistent, he was not at all aggressive in manner, speech, or appearance. He stood five feet, eight inches tall. Long eyelashes framed his warm brown eyes. Moderately thick eyebrows paired easily with his dark black hair that he wore combed straight back. He wore an easy smile on his *café-con-leche*-colored face. He loved wearing a single-colored short-sleeved shirt—with the sleeves rolled up a bit and his biceps partly exposed—often royal blue, green, or red, with a *cuero* brown belt. To hold the belt in place Miguel wore an intricate belt buckle of turquoise, silver, and gold that he had crafted himself.

Sporting this tidy and unpresuming appearance and with his face cast in a calm and welcoming smile, Miguel stood before the table of four, all of whom maintained their crouched defensive huddle, pretending he wasn't there.

"Good afternoon. I'm Miguel Hernández, and that is my younger brother, Edgar, over there"—pointing to me—"and I'm here to say good afternoon and exchange a handshake of greetings and best wishes," he told them.

Miguel extended his hand to one of the party, a short, chubby fellow. The man hesitated but, after a moment, straightened himself up out of the huddle and reluctantly accepted the handshake.

While shaking hands, Miguel maintained an unflinching eye contact, like he was looking right through to the man's very soul. This was Miguel's trademark gaze, one that he didn't just use when meeting new people. He looked at me, our siblings, his coworkers, really everyone, with this sincere yet intense eye contact when he was listening to or communicating something heart-felt and significant. Often people were taken aback by his direct and piercing trademark gaze.

"What's your name?" Miguel inquired with a gentle sincerity.

Again after a slight delay the man answered, "Glen. Glen Miller. Pleased to meet you."

The others' faces had begun to relax. Their lips curved into slight smiles. Warmth began to emanate from their eyes.

Indicating the pretty brunette lady sitting next to him, Mr. Miller told Miguel, "This is my wife, Diane," and Miguel gave her a friendly handshake.

"These two folks are our long-time friends, Lloyd and Carol Krafft," Mr. Miller said, and Miguel proceeded to shake their hands too.

The ladies wore deep pink lipstick, making their eventual smiles appear bigger and their teeth whiter.

In total contrast to their original stance, the group became sociable and asked Miguel, "How do you like the food at Bob's Big Boy?"

"I love this diner. It's a special occasion because it's Edgar's first time here."

Mrs. Krafft questioned, "So he's your little brother?"

Miguel clarified, "Yes, my younger half-brother. We're originally from Mexico, and we have the same father. Edgar has only been in the US for four weeks now."

"That's wonderful," she observed.

At Miguel's prompting I came over to meet the two couples.

"My name is Edgar. It is very nice to meet you," I told them, careful to look each person in the eye as I delivered firm handshakes.

"Your English is good," Mr. Miller commented.

"Thank you. I practice, and I have good teachers," I replied.

Miguel concluded the greeting, saying, "Hopefully all of you, nice people, will have a great meal and a wonderful day."

Once at our table, Miguel commented, "Aren't they terrific? They have fine handshakes and excellent eye contact. They are sincere. And the younger couple and their children—their handshakes had a gentle but slightly firm grip that lasted a few seconds. Also good eye contact. You see, Edgar, this is how you should conduct yourself. You can tell a lot about someone when you touch

4

their hands. You can tell a lot about their sincerity, especially when shaking hands and making direct eye contact. I hope you learned something here today."

I smiled, nodding in agreement.

Midway into our meal, as we savored our food—and that unforgettable sauce!—Mr. Krafft, one of the gentlemen in the group of four, neared our table.

"Can I tell you something, Miguel?" Mr. Krafft asked with his small Don Ameche-like moustache twitching and his thick raised eyebrows, setting off a few ripples of wrinkles on his already wrinkled face.

"Yes, sir. Please sit down," Miguel responded.

After sitting down, Mr. Krafft explained, "My friends and Carol and I watched you greet that young family, and we thought it odd. We even considered walking out in order to avoid you. But after you greeted us and we talked, I realized it's not odd at all. In fact, I think it's kosher. It's original and unique. And it's not every day we have an opportunity to greet total strangers with a handshake. Furthermore, I don't even look at you and your brother as strangers. I don't know how to describe it, but it seems like we've met before. I don't know. It's a different feeling—like I know you."

I was stunned by his words.

Miguel replied, "Mr. Krafft, you are correct. We have known each other before, but it was a long time ago."

Miguel and Mr. Krafft ended up talking longer. Miguel learned that Mr. Krafft and his wife were from New York City, and they invested in businesses all over the country. Mr. Krafft even piloted a small plane to visit the businesses with his wife.

Mr. Krafft learned that Miguel was a silversmith, crafting original pieces of Navajo jewelry in silver, turquoise, and even gold. He learned that Miguel was laser-focused on earning enough income to immigrate Nena (my mother) and all of our siblings to Phoenix from

Mexico and that Miguel was also refurbishing a house for the whole family to live in. He learned of Miguel's effort to aid Mexican workers in getting their green cards, so they could live and work in the United States with ease and pride.

During their conversation, Emily, the young red-headed girl, came to our table and gave me a Bob's Big Boy paper placemat that had cartoons on it. She even signed her name on it. I was touched.

After exchanging contact information, Mr. Krafft and Miguel stood, shook hands again, and said their goodbyes.

Miguel looked at me and explained, "Edgar, my main goal in life is to make friends. We just made eight new friends today. And it's only lunchtime—no telling what the rest of the day will bring!"

When Miguel asked for the bill, the waiter informed him, "There is no bill. In fact, there's no need to pay a tip either. Mr. Krafft, the gentleman you were talking with, he paid your bill and said we should take care of you every time you come here."

Bewildered, Miguel asked, "He said that? But why?"

"He's one of the owners of this business."

At that Miguel turned to me and declared, "Aren't they wonderful?"

This is a memory from my past that I've never forgotten, and sixty years later I can still taste the exquisiteness of that sauce I first encountered at Bob's Big Boy with Miguel.

Let me add that Mr. Krafft ended up visiting Miguel several times when he was in Phoenix. He gave Miguel a specially made gabardine coat from New York City. He and his wife commissioned Miguel to make them pieces of Navajo jewelry. When Miguel asked Mr. Krafft if he would sponsor and employ two hard-working, kind Mexican workers who'd been living illegally in the Phoenix area, Mr. Krafft agreed.

Tragically, the Kraffts died in 1960 when their small plane crashed. Miguel and I treasured the strong but short-lived friendship.

6

I begin this book with this incident at Bob's Big Boy because it aptly depicts my older brother, Miguel Hernández, in all his mystical glory. Miguel was gentle, yet bold. Humble yet, charismatic. A man of passion. A man of good will, sincere generosity, and concern for others. Over the course of this book, you too will come to view Miguel as the super human being he was. A true superstar. A mystic.

For all the years my siblings and I knew Miguel to the last day of his life, he would introduce himself to people, as he did to those people at Bob's Big Boy, with an unabashed soul-penetrating eye contact, a sincere smile, a firm handshake, and a friendly greeting. Really, it seemed like he was greeting old friends. While I never saw anyone ridicule or reject him, it wasn't unusual that some people were confused, hesitant, puzzled, or just hoping to avoid the interaction. But Miguel was persistent, so people returned the greeting, some more warmly than others. Mr. Krafft was among many who, at first skeptical, came to respect and adore Miguel.

When someone asked Miguel why he greeted random people like that, he explained, "Actually, I know these people. I've known them since long ago. Therefore, this should be the norm, this is the way we all should greet our brothers and sisters." Miguel believed that we, human beings, are all family, no matter our age, gender, race, economic status, religion, nationality, or other grouping. He believed that we are all one big family, and he acted on that belief in his interactions with others.

I, for one, found it entertaining and loved to see people's reactions to these spontaneous greeting by this mysterious stranger, Miguel Hernández. All of my family regularly witnessed Miguel initiate these spontaneous greetings, and to us it was Miguel's natural act of human kindness. People simply were not accustomed to such a novel act.

Miguel would say to me, "Edgar, it makes me feel so good to think that maybe these people will extend these kind of greetings to new folks who are outside their home and circle. Just think, if everyone did this in life, we would have no fears!"

Whenever he talked like this, it made me think more about life, about wanting to know more about the people around me and to recognize everyone as individuals trying to do their best. That's the thing about Miguel, what he said and did—it made people think more deeply about everything and everyone, and not so much about themselves. Miguel's words and deeds energized people to do better and be better. To believe ever more goodness was possible and act on that belief.

Miguel was born in 1919 in rural Michoacán, Mexico. He had only a few years of elementary education, about the equivalent of an American fourth grade education. He immigrated to the United States in 1951 to work as a silversmith—a craftsman of traditional Navajo jewelry—until his death in 1984. From 1951 to 1966 Miguel often spent sixteen hours a day working alongside seventeen fellow silversmiths, all of whom were Navajo except Miguel. They were hard workers, working on weekends as well. As silversmiths, they did not work for hourly wages, but instead by piecework. "The more pieces you make, the more you earn," Miguel often said.

Because Miguel spent so much time with his Navajo colleagues, Miguel became fluent in the Navajo language. Sam Tso, Miguel's colleague and friend, once said, "Miguel speaks Navajo like a silk whisper, smooth and soothing."

Miguel was acknowledged as a giant in the art of Navajo jewelry craftsmanship. He brought his Mexican Indian talent into the brilliance of the fine art of traditional Navajo jewelry making. He introduced gold into the silver and turquoise crafting, a practice never before considered until Miguel came on to the scene in 1951. Miguel did not stamp his initials on any piece of jewelry he created because he saw that as disloyal and unjust to the creators of the fine art of the Navajo Native Americans.

Miguel mastered the English language too, both written and spoken, a feat necessary for him to become an expert navigator of the green card process, from start to finish. He not only could guide people through the lengthy process, but he was also adept at pursuing alternate pathways to reach solutions in even the most complex documentation entanglements.

The first person Miguel helped immigrate was in 1954, and the last was six months before he died. A primary reason Miguel worked so hard crafting jewelry was because of his goal to immigrate fifteen people in our immediate family, a process both time-consuming and costly. Miguel also helped many distant relatives navigate the green card process. He aided eighty acquaintances, most of whom were working illegally in the US, to get their green cards as well. He connected illegal immigrants with sponsors (and vice versa), and he invited many illegal immigrants to live as guests in his home for the days, weeks, or months they needed to gather their papers and get back on their feet. Miguel also opened his home to anyone in dire circumstances looking to restart their life, no matter their gender, race, religion, age, or nationality. In total, Miguel hosted about one hundred twenty guests in our 206 N. 9th Street home.

Miguel was all about hard work and kindness towards all around him. Miguel never took credit for any of what he did.

For my family and many, many others, Miguel was a mystic and remains a legend. For me, personally, he was my strength, my guide, my inspiration.

This is his story.

Chapter 1

Winning La Lotería

"It's a boy," Nellie said.

"How do you know?" Miguel asked.

"He's strong—I can tell—and muscular. He wrestles a lot, kicking and elbowing my stomach like a punching bag."

Miguel smiled and asked, "What are you all going to name him?"

"Sampson," answered Nellie, "Like in the Bible."

"Yes, that's a good name. A strong name. A scripture name with spirit," observed Miguel.

"We expect he'll be born next week, and my husband and I would like it very much, Miguel, if you'd be Sampson's godfather."

After acknowledging the responsibility that comes with the role, Miguel accepted. He would be Sampson's godfather.

———

About six weeks later, Miguel was on the road, driving his 1954 Ford Fairlane northeast from Phoenix to Window Rock for Sampson's baptism. Window Rock is the capital of the Navajo Nation, and Nellie and much of her family were Navajo Native Americans.

Though Miguel hailed from Mexico where he spent the first thirty-two years of his life, when he came to America in 1951, he immediately started working at Silver by Lambert—Indian Jewelry, alongside seventeen Navajo silversmiths. That's how he became good friends with many people of the Navajo Nation, including Nellie and her sister Grace. Together, they worked as front-of-store attendants at the jewelry shop, working closely with customers, taking orders, and translating customers' jewelry specifications so the silversmiths could craft their designs. It's also how he became fluent in the Navajo language and familiar with Navajo culture. Miguel felt honored to be considered a brother of the Navajo.

Phil Stone, a fellow silversmith, Navajo, and good friend, accompanied Miguel to Sampson's baptism in Window Rock. Phil was in his mid-forties and had spent most of his life roaming from place to place. He had been a longtime alcoholic and could never hold down a job. He said he just couldn't concentrate and his desire to work would fade away. After a few months at one place he'd move on to another, and on and on.

A year earlier, in 1956, Phil was at a restaurant where he first met Miguel. Actually, they met when Miguel was doing his customary meet-and-greet with fellow patrons at the restaurant, similar to how he ended up meeting the Kraffts.

When Phil and Miguel met, Phil was in the midst of a major life change. For several weeks he'd stopped drinking and had joined a support group. Phil religiously attended their meetings and continued to do so for as long as I knew him as well. He communicated all this to Miguel, as well as his one current need: work. Phil was looking for work.

"I think you should try out crafting Navajo jewelry at Silver by Lambert. There are eighteen craftsmen there. Except for me, they are all Navajo Native Americans, just like you. The Lamberts run an orderly business, so as long as you stay clean, I believe they'd welcome you to join the team."

"I'd like that, Miguel. And with my support group meetings and your help, I believe I'll be able to stay away from alcohol," responded Phil.

"My father is a drinker, so I know how destructive it can be. The other silversmiths know I don't drink, and some of them even come to me when they need help avoiding the temptation. I promise to give you my support. And I'll talk to the Lamberts about hiring you too."

Because they trusted Miguel's recommendations, the Lamberts were happy to give Phil a chance to try his hand at being a silversmith. After three weeks, it became clear to everyone that Phil was gifted. He was a rising star. Unfortunately, about six weeks into the job he badly injured his left hand when using a very sharp file to shape a bracelet. The filing required taking a bladed, one-inch wide, one-foot long file and raking it back and forth, quickly and forcefully, over a metal surface. While doing this, Phil accidentally raked it over his left hand and ended up shredding a deep cut into his hand, partially severing a tendon. It was a serious injury, requiring thirty stitches, in addition, he'd need several months of daily therapy for the hand and arm to heal and regain function.

As he'd only worked at the shop for a few weeks, he'd have to be let go. On top of that, Phil had no relatives and really no place to stay. He'd been rooming with another transient in a shack. So not only would he be without work, he'd have no place to stay. That would greatly hinder the healing of his hand and limit his access to getting the rehabilitation he needed.

This is where Miguel stepped in. First, he pleaded with Margaret Lambert to allow Phil to live upstairs since there was plenty of room there for him. You see, Miguel was living in a small apartment above the jewelry shop, in the building owned by the Lamberts. Once Margaret agreed, Miguel contacted the medical team that treated Phil and found out how to change the wound dressings and how to perform the physical therapy. It was a special technique that typically only an occupational therapist would perform, manipulating the hand and fingers in certain ways to revive its dexterity and functionality. Miguel actually became so adept at the technique that Phil's surgeon offered him a job.

After three months, Phil regained almost full functionality of his hand and arm and began to work again. He became the eighteenth Navajo silversmith at the jewelry shop, and he and Miguel also became good friends. To others Phil would introduce Miguel as "my brother." Around most people Phil was very quiet, the kind of person that didn't speak unless spoken to, though once he became comfortable around you, he became a motor-mouth. That's how he was around Miguel and eventually around me as well..

As the two men had three hundred miles to cover to reach Nellie's parents' in Window Rock, there was plenty of time for conversation. The language used to carry out their conversation was, of course, Navajo.

"That's an interesting letter I see peeping out of your shirt pocket, Miguel. It's got little zigzag lines in red, white, and green. You've been carrying it with you for two weeks now," Phil noted.

"Actually, I received it three weeks ago. It's from Mexico. From a close friend of the family," Miguel explained.

Phil smiled, nodding his head, and said, "Yes, you and your big family in Mexico, that I hear about so often. My only family is you and all the silversmiths at the jewelry store. Tell me more about the letter."

"It's from Chucho. I don't recall that I've told you about Chucho, which is a nickname for Jesús. Chucho is like a brother to me. I've known him since I was a child. He writes me on occasion to let me know how my coconut grove is doing or to give news from the pueblo."

"La Mira is the name of your pueblo, isn't it?" Phil asked.

"Yes, La Mira in Michoacán. Because Chucho has always been a man of few words, I'm quite struck by this letter," Miguel stated.

"Why? What's it say?"

"He wrote that my father is sick. That he has bloody coughing episodes, worse than normal. Chucho admitted that he's worried," answered Miguel.

"That's just awful. I remember you once told me that you hope to drive to La Mira someday. Drive this very car down there and visit all your family and friends. And what about Pedro and Olivia? Will they go too?" Phil offered.

"They're in a tight situation with their jobs. It's a big deal for them to make it to one of my Sunday barbecues, so them taking two weeks off, that probably won't happen. But maybe by the time I'm ready to go to La Mira, they'll have different jobs and more options."

Olivia, our sister, and Pedro, our brother, immigrated to the United States in 1954. Olivia had been living in Mexico City with an abusive and dangerous husband. To get away from him and start a new life, she moved to Arteaga in Michoacán. That's where she first started designing and creating dresses for weddings, baptisms, and confirmations.

Miguel, who'd immigrated to America in 1951, had the idea that Olivia should immigrate as well. In order to live and work legally in the US there is more required than just filling out an application and paying some money at the border. It's a more involved process than that—even in the 1950s.

Back then, one key part of the process for someone looking to immigrate and work legally in America was to find an American business owner willing to sponsor them. As a sponsor, the business owner was not only making a promise to employ the immigrant but was officially vouching for their skills, character, and education. Though some business owners would be hesitant to make such a pledge, when Miguel found someone that he wanted to help—in this case, Olivia—there was no stopping him.

Miguel had some good friends who were able to connect him with one of their good friends who owned a bridal shop in the Phoenix area that was in need of a dressmaker. Miguel persuaded the business owner to both sponsor Olivia on a work visa and to act as principal sponsor for Pedro, our brother, who would enter on a student visa. While their applications to immigrate, lodged at the American Consulate in Nogales, went smoothly, after six months the bridal shop closed due to a death in the owner's family. Fortunately, Olivia and Pedro were able to find another sponsor, a family in need of caretakers for one of their family members who had polio. Olivia worked as the primary caretaker, and Pedro went to school and worked part-time assisting Olivia. Because the family needed Olivia and Pedro on call, in case an emergency arose, in their limited time off they were required to stay close to their sponsor family's house. As the house was located in Cave Creek, about thirty miles from downtown Phoenix, this made it difficult for them to attend the barbecues Miguel hosted, one Sunday each month, much less go to Mexico for two or three weeks.

"Yes, that's right. Olivia and Pedro work very hard," Phil agreed.

As they drove, the conversation expanded, making the five-hour drive seem like a quick errand run. There was Phil, with his black eyes opened wide and his heart full of curiosity as he listened and exchanged words with Miguel.

"Miguel, I'm jealous of you," Phil declared.

"How's that?" Miguel asked.

"You've got family thinking of you, missing you, depending on you. And, sure, that means you gotta work really hard to get a good savings going—doing those sixteen-hour days and remodeling that house. You have a lot of responsibilities. On the flipside, I'm alone in the world, no knowledge of who my parents are or where they are or where they're from . . . No family to connect and convene with. But instead of feeling sorry for myself, I'm proud to call you my friend. That's a blessing. You are a man with a heart of gold, and I know of no one more loved than you. I know everyone agrees with me."

Miguel responded, "Thank you. Phil, you too are my brother, just like Chucho."

"I know you've got a lot of brothers and sisters in your family. How many?"

"Phil, I have eight full siblings and nine half-siblings. My full siblings are Alberto, who is the oldest, then me, Ruben, Avisac, Raquel, Ruth, Rebeca, Olivia, and Neftali. Our mother died after giving birth to Neftali. Then there's Lionel from my father's second wife. She too died after childbirth. In rural Mexico it's not uncommon for women to die of an infection after they give birth."

"That's a terrible shame," Phil noted.

"Actually, a few years ago, in 1954, my brother Ruben wrote me a letter to see if I could help immigrate his three children— Daniel 'Bolivar,' Luis, and Blanca—and I ended up meeting them in Hermosillo, Mexico. And *gracias a Dios*, I was able to help them immigrate with relative ease. And then there's the children of my father's third wife, Nena. Luckily Nena's still alive and well. She's in La Mira with my father and their children: Edgar, Lupe, Asunción, and baby Reyna. Jorge is in Vera Cruz with Alberto. Surama is with Avisac in Zamora."

Miguel went on to add, "Out of all of my adult siblings, meaning the kids from my father's first two marriages, everyone is married and has their own families except Olivia, Neftali, and me."

"Miguel, I thought you were getting married. What was it, six months ago or so that you and that lady in New Mexico were considering marriage?"

Miguel smiled and admitted, "Yes, that was Pancha. It's true—I was on the razor's edge. But I had cold feet. I've been preoccupied with my younger brothers and sisters in La Mira. I promised to help them immigrate. It's a promise from my heart. So, if I get married and have children now, it will create a problem fulfilling that promise."

"You mean getting them green cards?" Phil asked.

"Yes. It's expensive to gather all the needed papers and pay the fees. It's time-consuming. Plus, I'm refurbishing the house on 206 N. 9th Street for them to live in. Don't get me wrong—it's my greatest pleasure to bring my brothers and sisters to the USA. Once they're here and settled in, that's when I can look into marriage." Miguel paused and then added, "What about you, Phil?"

"Me and what? Marriage? Well, I've only just settled down for the first time in my life. It's almost two years now that I've been settled. But I've been thinking about it. We'll see," Phil acknowledged.

Phil returned to the original topic, the letter, and asked Miguel, "So, what are you planning to do based on what Chucho told you about your father? Instead of waiting, you could take your Ford Fairlane and go to Mexico real soon."

"Phil, I've been troubled ever since I received the letter. My heart tells me yes, go, but my wallet tells me to wait a little until I'm more secure, until I've saved more money and gotten further along with the house. But then I worry that right now my father may be in worse shape than I can imagine. I need to decide. Soon."

"Can I give you my two cents?" Phil asked.

"Yes, tell me."

"I would go if I had your wealth," Phil advised.

"Wealth?" Miguel asked.

"Yes, 'wealth.' It's a treasure to have a family, something I never had. If I were in your shoes, I'd leave and see what's going on with your father. Wealth is a measurement of love for your family, brothers, sisters, and all relatives. It's not monetary. There are many rich people who have no one to love. Wealth is what you have."

Miguel looked at Phil and said, "That's one of the kindest things anyone has ever said to me."

Phil continued, "Now that I've been with you and everybody at the jewelry store for about two years, for the first time in my life I have a tight-knit community and strong friendships. When I look back on my years drinking and roaming, I think I know why I was doing that. It's because I felt so alone. Lost and worthless. While the folks at my support group help me, Miguel, really, you are the one who's provided the most constant and solid friendship that I've ever had. You are the reason I've been able to change and become a new and better person. I thank you for that."

Miguel took a moment to let Phil's words sink in. Then he replied, "It's an honor to call you my friend and brother, Phil. From my perspective, you are the one putting in the daily effort to fulfill all the new responsibilities that being a new and better person requires. I admire you for that, and I, without a doubt, believe in your strength and continued success."

Nellie had already told Miguel and Phil to expect a small gathering of mostly family members and a pastor for the baptism. Nicholas, Sampson's father, wouldn't be present because he was away, doing military service. He hadn't been there for Sampson's birth either.

Nellie had already explained that her parents spoke very little English. Her father, Benjamin, spoke Navajo, and her mother, Grace, spoke Navajo, Apache, and Spanish. Miguel understood how important communication in the Navajo language would be to Benjamin and Grace Begay and that his ability to communicate with them in Navajo would act as an important bridge for building a strong relationship between himself and the Begay family.

———

Later, when I came to America to live with Miguel, go to school, and come to know the fellow silversmiths, Miguel would encourage me to pick up as much of their language as I could while also becoming fluent in English. For several years, from seventh grade to the end of high school, daily I would spend hours at the jewelry shop. Because Navajo was the primary medium of communication there, I learned words and phrases in Navajo and became proficient in the Navajo language. In turn, this allowed me to have a stronger connection with my Navajo uncles, as I called the silversmiths, and the Navajo community.

Later on, as a practicing general surgeon, there were several instances when it wasn't just my expertise as a surgeon and physician that solved a crisis. Through my familiarity with the Navajo language and ability to apply it to connect with certain patients, I was able to provide them with greater relief from their pain and confusion.

I remember one particular occasion in my early-thirties when Miguel and I had lunch together. I described to him an experience I had had with a seventy-eight-year-old patient by the name of Daniel Pablo, a Navajo Native American whose only language was Navajo. The following is the scene I described to Miguel over that lunch.

———

I was in the ER treating another trauma patient when I heard an elderly man desperately hollering, "*Háájih t'łool? Háájih t'łool? T'łool shaanołééh!*"

The elderly man was beside himself, gazing around, his face contorted with confusion and fear. He appeared as if he wanted to talk to someone or like he wanted to leave. He was pacing the halls and looking at a baby boy in another patient bay. The baby boy was badly burned. The man himself needed treatment: his jacket was half burned through to his back, and he smelled charred. He trembled and kept reaching to touch his back, which by now was exposed and, I noticed, clearly burned.

He could not stay still and kept repeating, "*Háájih t'łooł? T'łooł shaanołééh!*" and pointed at the little boy whom my junior resident and a nurse were attending to. Because they could not communicate with the elderly man, they could not calm him or even understand him. However, I understood that he was saying: "Where's the rope? Get me the rope!"

Before this man and the boy were moved to the burn unit, I made a point of speaking with him the best I could. While it had been years since I was immersed in the Navajo language at the jewelry shop, I could still understand much of what the elderly man was saying, but was only able to conjure up a few words and phrases in reply.

"*Shíééh* Dr. Hernández *yinish ye'* [My name is Dr. Hernández], and I am here to care for you and the baby," I told him.

Hearing me speak even pieces of his language brought him a bit of calm. He replied, "*Shíééh* Daniel Pablo *yinish ye' Háá jih shi ye.'* [My name is Daniel Pablo. Where's my son?]"

I did my best to communicate that we had telephoned his son, who we assumed was the father of the baby, and that Mr. Pablo's son was on his way to the hospital.

While one of the nurses was carefully cleaning the burns on his back, Mr. Pablo held my arm and then my hand. He was hanging on to me with a very frightened look. His droopy, bushy, long eyebrows were wilted by sweat since the burn room was kept warm as part of the burn treatment protocol.

While holding on to me, Mr. Pablo would scream out, "*Shi'ye'! Shi' ye'!* [My son! My son!]" and also "*T'łooł dóó, t'óh dóó!*" While I understood that he was again calling for rope and water, I didn't understand why he was repeatedly asking for those things.

Eventually, Mr. Pablo's son and his son's wife—Tom and Fatima Pablo—arrived.

First, I explained to Tom and Fatima, "Mr. Pablo is fine, and he will make a full recovery from his physical trauma, but his mental trauma will take longer, but that too will be fine. He looks traumatized and puzzled."

I continued, admitting, "We too are puzzled as to what happened. He keeps yelling out for rope and water. Also, he was brought in by a neighbor, and there's a baby, who we assume is Mr. Pablo's grandson and perhaps your son."

"Yes," Tom quickly confirmed, "That's our son, our baby boy, Roy. Where is Roy? Is he okay?"

"Yes, both the baby and Mr. Pablo are fine," I relayed.

Tom went on to explain, "The neighbor that brought them in— that's George. He's our neighbor and friend. Please, Dr. Hernández, please know we are good parents. I had to take Fatima to the doctor. It was unexpected. We normally wouldn't leave Roy alone with my father, but this time we figured it would be fine because we'd would only be away for thirty minutes to an hour . . .

"It was our neighbor George—he spotted smoke and ran over. Our son was lying on the ground in front of the house, wailing. The front part of our house had caught fire. My father was running about outside behind the house, screaming, 'Water! Water!' and then he'd point to the water well and scream, 'The rope, the rope! Water, water!'

"George told us that when he went to the well, he found the bucket separated from the rope, and the assumption is that my father was not able to retrieve water because of this. It was George that drove my father and our son here to the hospital."

Later after Mr. Pablo explained to Tom and Fatima that I could understand and speak some Navajo, Tom told me and the team in the burn unit as he left with his family, "*T'áá áánoł t'soh nit'saago a'hééh.*' [A big thank you to everyone]"

I ended my explanation of the case, admitting to Miguel, "Miguel, thanks to God, our burn unit was able to save those patients. But I wish I'd paid more attention to learning Navajo or retained what I learned better over the years."

Miguel, always so positive and compassionate, assured me, "Edgar, sometimes only a word or two makes people feel more comfortable. Because of the Navajo you spoke to Daniel Pablo, you provided him with that extra bit of comfort he desperately needed. You did good, Edgar. I'm proud of you, and I bet Nellie, Grace, and Sampson will be proud of you too when I tell them about you and the Pablos."

Back to 1957—the Ford Fairlane turned down a driveway surrounded by tall pines and boulders. Soon thereafter Miguel and Phil made out a wood-framed cabin surrounded by towering pines. Next, they heard the bellowing of dogs and shortly afterwards, three barking hounds surrounded the car.

Miguel and Phil arrived at the Begays'.

A gray-haired man emerged from the cabin. As he approached the car, they could make out his stone-like face and deeply sunken eyes. A trickle of hair grew from his chin, and his sideburns were lightly formed. He wore his graying long hair in a well-kept low ponytail.

Miguel turned off the engine, and he and Phil stepped out of the car.

Miguel immediately approached the gray-haired man to make an introduction, saying in Navajo, "*Shi ééh* Miguel *yinish yééh, dii ééh* Phil *jolyééh.* [My name is Miguel, and this is Phil.] *Nishééh* Nellie *bi'zhéé áhnit'íính.* [You must be Nellie's father.]"

Upon hearing that Miguel could speak his language, the gray-haired man's face softened just a bit. He responded, "*Aoo, shi ééh áhnisht'íính.* [Yes, I am.]"

23

Soon after, a woman stepped out of the cabin. Her dark hair fell in a long braid down her back. She had glistening eyes and wore a turquoise choker and a bracelet of silver and turquoise.

First, she called out to them in English, "Come in!"

As they neared, she asked, "You speak Navajo?"

When Miguel and Phil both confirmed, "*A'oo* [Yes]," her manner at once became more relaxed. She pointed to her husband, saying in Navajo, "That's Benjamin, my husband and Nellie and Grace's father, and I'm Grace, Nellie and Grace's mother. Nellie and Grace will be here soon with Sampson. Please come inside."

On the way into the cabin, Miguel asked Benjamin, "*A'wééh ninol nin*? [Have you noticed how the baby resembles you?] I think there's a strong resemblance between you and Sampson."

Four weeks earlier after Nellie had given birth to Sampson at the Phoenix Indian hospital, Miguel, Phil, and everyone at the jewelry store visited her there and met Sampson.

Upon hearing Miguel's observation, a small smile appeared on Benjamin's lips, and he responded, "*A'oo. T'áá'á'ko'h.* [Yes, I guess.]" When he turned to his wife, he displayed an even wider smile of pleasure at Miguel's observation.

Phil commented, "I heard that Sampson has an uncle who was a code talker in World War II. Is that true?"

Grace answered, "It is true. That would be his Uncle Ray. He was stationed in the Pacific when he was a code talker."

"'Code talker'—what's that?" Miguel asked, intrigued.

Benjamin explained, "A code talker is someone who speaks a language that is so little-known that their language can be used as a secret way to communicate. Navajo is considered just such a language. In World War II, Uncle Ray and other Navajos worked as intelligence officers, using the Navajo language as a kind of 'secret code language' to communicate important intelligence messages, which other countries couldn't decipher."

"Incredible. Absolutely incredible," Miguel commented, in awe of the Begay family.

After a brief stop in the cabin, they moved through to the backyard where more family members were busy preparing for the celebration. Some were carrying tables. Others were digging what appeared to be a trench in the ground. When Miguel saw the goat carcass, he knew immediately what was happening—*cabrito enterrado*. They were going to cook the goat in the ground underneath a fire, a method he'd learned years earlier in Mexico. They had vegetables and spices that would go into a big galvanized basin, about three feet in diameter. After the goat was skinned and cut, they'd place the pieces of meat into the basin, then bury the basin in the ground, cover the top with an aluminum sheet, place logs across the top of the trench over the buried basin—and light a fire. This method allowed the meat and vegetables to cook slowly in the ground underneath the fire.

When Nellie and the baby arrived, along with Grace, Miguel spoke again to Benjamin, "*Na'h k̓óó nih t'soi.* [Here is your grandson.]. *T'áá' yíisíí ninol nin?* [Don't you agree that he looks like you?]"

Benjamin opened up, replying, "*A'hééh* [Thank you], Miguel, and thank God. I prayed while the moon was half for a grandson. Thank God for a great moon's gift."

At the mention of the moon, Miguel immediately thought of Andres Maldonado, my grandfather on my mother's side. Miguel grew up with my grandfather in La Mira and loved him as if he were his blood grandfather. My grandfather often spoke of the moon as a guide to our destiny and to our success in life. A moment later Miguel's hand moved to touch the letter protruding from his shirt's breast pocket, for he recalled the line in it where Chucho wrote, "Andres and I are concerned that your father is ailing badly." Miguel's brow wrinkled with worry, and his eyes got a faraway look.

Benjamin's words called Miguel back, "Our pastor will be here in two hours, the goat will be done in three, and then we'll celebrate my grandson's baptism. Don't worry, Miguel. You will be a great godfather. He will have two fathers—you and me." Benjamin's eyes were no longer sunken; they were puffed with loving tears. He was referencing the fact that Sampson's father was not present.

Miguel hugged Benjamin and the baby.

As Nellie had explained, it was a small gathering. A total of fifteen people: the pastor, Nellie, Benjamin, Grace, Roger (Nellie's half-brother), Phil, Miguel, and some cousins and colleagues. Miguel became a godfather. He eventually would be the godfather of seven children, in both America and Mexico.

The ceremony was delightful, the food tremendous in taste and flavor, and the people kind, congenial, and interesting. When Phil and Miguel presented the gifts they brought—from Phil a small turquoise child's necklace that he crafted himself and from Miguel a pair of tiny Levi Strauss overalls—everyone oohed and aahed with delight, especially Nellie.

As night fell, the pastor and a few others departed, and the remaining celebrants moved to the cabin's interior. After enjoying a second portion of the succulent *cabrito enterrado* with vegetables, beans, fried bread, and grapes, the group sat in a circle atop several layers of colorful Navajo carpets. A low table stood at the center of the group on which sat a number of lit candles casting a warm glow in the room.

Conversation shifted from silver crafting to friends, family, and community. Nellie turned to Miguel and said, "I find it amazing that you are far from your family and community in Mexico, yet over the six years you've been here, you've managed to build up a very strong community. So many people consider you a member of their family."

Miguel looked at her, smiled, and offered, "I'm blessed that the Lamberts found me in Nogales, sponsored me, and placed me among such wonderful people."

"I've never heard the whole story. How is it you came to the United States?" Nellie asked.

Benjamin joined in, "Yes, I'd like to know more about you. Tell us something about yourself, Miguel."

After more urging from the others, Miguel told them a bit about his life in Mexico and how he came to the United States of America. The following chapter tells that story.

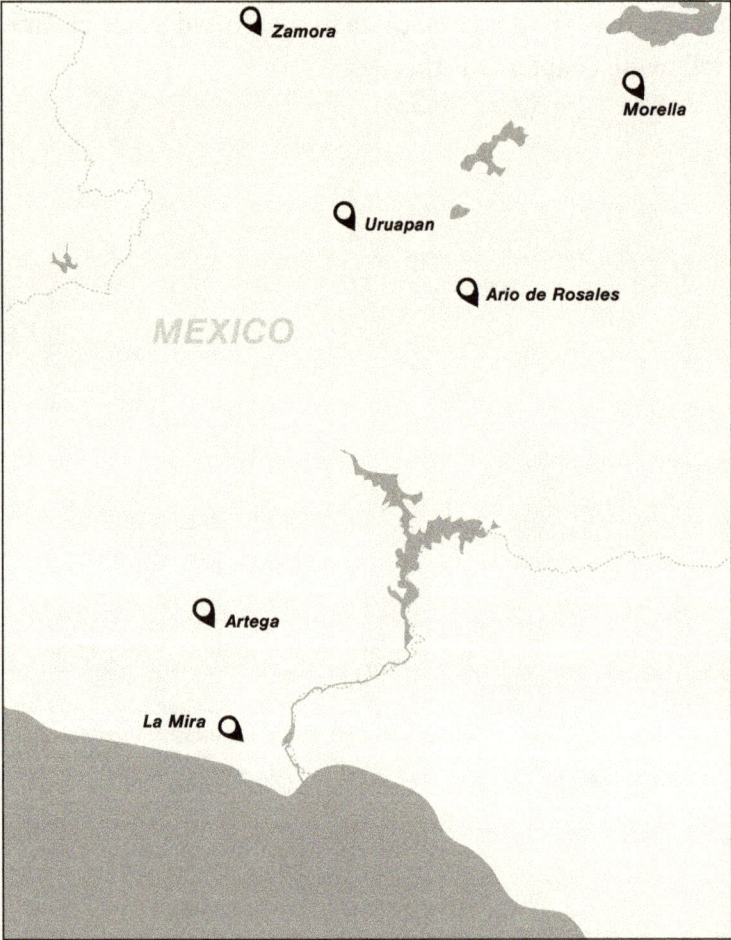

Chapter 2

FROM RURAL MEXICO TO THE USA

In 1919, Miguel was born in rural Michoacán in a pueblo called Arío de Rosales between Arteaga and Uruapan [see map on page 28]. He had one older brother though all the rest of his siblings were younger. Our father was an almost-licensed doctor and dentist (he didn't complete his studies, but that's another story), and an excellent and dedicated practitioner even though not a medical and dental school graduate. Like Phil Stone, he liked to roam. Therefore, he moved frequently from clinic to clinic, and village to village, and the family moved with him. They were in Morelia, then Zamora, then Uruapan, then Arteaga. Finally, La Mira—his last stop.

Miguel stopped going to school after the fourth grade, which Papá wasn't totally happy about, and soon after he started working in an ornament and jewelry factory. By the time he was twelve he was able to do most, if not all, that jewelers did. He could make Mexican ornaments and different types of silver and gold pieces, from rings and earrings, to pendants, bracelets, and necklaces. The jewelry was quite different than that of the Navajos'. It had more of an Aztec and Toltec influence. There was no turquoise. Actually there were no gems. The pieces were either exclusively gold or silver, or a combination of both.

When Miguel was fourteen, he met a gentleman with blond

hair. The man explained that he was in Mexico to buy textiles to take back to the United States. He talked about the United States of America, how it was a pillar of wealth and opportunities. "No matter your background, with focus and hard work, you can achieve anything in the USA." Miguel never forgot this man's words.

At the age of twenty, Miguel decided to invest in a generator, microphone, and speakers. He used the equipment to conduct functions—weddings, birthday parties, baptisms, community fiestas, and such—around Uruapan, Zamora, Arteaga, and La Mira, the village where our father finally settled. This was the 1940s, so these places didn't have electricity. La Mira still didn't have electricity in the 1950s when I left there.

As emcee of the celebrations, Miguel learned how to energize guests, to get them laughing, dancing, singing, and having a great time. He also did the catering, supplying food and drinks. Miguel found the most amazing piñatas for birthday parties. When he earned enough money, he bought thirty-acres of coconut-producing palms near La Mira. This coconut grove was to be his nest egg for the future.

Around the age of thirty Miguel decided it was time for a change—it was time to pursue the American dream that the blond-haired gentleman had first told him about sixteen years earlier. However, he was nervous about approaching our father. Yes, Miguel was a grown man, so you would think our father's approval wouldn't be important to him. That was not the case. For Miguel, the family—our father, my mother (Miguel's mother had died over twenty years earlier), and his many siblings—were important to him. He wanted to remain close. And he wasn't asking for permission. He was asking for our father's support. His blessing.

Getting our father's blessing was crucial for Miguel to feel at peace in his heart before pursuing such a huge life change. The reason Miguel didn't know how to approach the subject with our father was because Papá wasn't the warmest and friendliest person. He was a brilliant healer and devoted to the family, but he could be a bit distant too.

To help figure this out Miguel decided to visit a close family friend, Chucho. Ten years earlier, when Miguel was twenty-two, he and our father got in a disagreement. The disagreement was about a man named Gilberto, whom Miguel partnered with in a popsicle business. Our father advised Miguel to avoid Gilberto because he had a reputation as someone with little integrity. Miguel disagreed, saying, "Papá, I look at everyone with positive feelings. Yes, Gilberto has been dishonest in the past and not always honorable. But I think he's changed. He's now a good man. Maybe I'll be proved wrong, but I'd like to try."

This dispute caused a two-year split between our father and Miguel. Miguel's two-year absence came to an end when Chucho brokered a reconciliation. It should also be noted that after Miguel settled in the United States, our father and Gilberto ended up becoming friends.

Chucho agreed to be present when Miguel spoke to our father.

The meeting took place at Miguel's coconut plantation. The three ate fried bass they caught themselves. Miguel did the cooking. As was normal for him, our father had tequila and plenty of cigarettes at hand to smooth out the conversation. (Something I haven't yet mentioned is that our father was a prolific and longtime drinker and smoker, also the reason he didn't complete medical school.) Chucho and Miguel did not touch alcohol or cigarettes, not at this meeting, not ever.

The ocean breeze was soothing, and the food plentiful and delicious. Envision a hot pan with oil. You fry the bass until it is crispy and golden brown. You slap it onto a hot tortilla and slather it with lime, cilantro, and salsa. Using your hands (no forks or knives) you eat this fabulous *ranchero* fish taco.

When it was time to talk, Miguel began, "Papá, I want to leave to *los Estados Unidos de América* and make something of myself. It's stagnant for me here, and I can't advance much. I want a future, a big future. However, I don't want to go without your blessing."

"Okay," our father replied. "When do you want to leave?"

Both Miguel and Chucho were stunned by this quick acquiescence.

Our father went on to say, "You know the children are attached to you very much, and Nena will be heartbroken to see you leave."

"I know," admitted Miguel, "but I will make you a promise: as soon as I get set up and have a good job, I will work hard and save the money to bring all of you up there with me."

My father replied, "Miguel, you can exclude me and Nena. We are here to live and die in La Mira."

———————

When Miguel left La Mira, our father accompanied him on the voyage to the border town of Nogales, where Miguel would have to provide the papers necessary to get his green card to enter the USA legally. It would be a five-day journey to reach Nogales, taking pickup trucks and buses through several Mexican states to reach it.

The first leg of the journey was on a dusty dirt road in the back of a pickup truck from La Mira to the tiny village of Los Coyotes. Really, Los Coyotes was just a few buildings dotting either side of a main road. Because the dirt road was in such bad condition, it took around two-and-a-half hours to complete this fifty-mile ride to Los Coyotes.

Among the few establishments Los Coyotes had to offer was a gas station-cantina-restaurant that people passing through typically visited to take a rest in their journey. Miguel and our father entered this establishment and came upon a husky-looking man who had big, bushy hair and a distinctive Emiliano Zapata-like mustache—one that was wide and thick.

While a girl, likely the daughter of the owner, took our order, a Tecate for my father and some *horchata* for Miguel, the husky man walked over and greeted them, saying, "My name is Benjamín Contreras and I own the store. That's my daughter, Sylvia, waiting on you. Do you want any food with your drinks?"

Papá told him, "We are both Miguel, Miguel, Sr., and Miguel, Jr., father and son." Papá invited him to sit with them.

In the meantime, both Papá and Miguel noticed the man's right hand was poorly bandaged and the elbow obviously swollen.

"Where are you headed?" Señor Contreras began.

Miguel answered by explaining his plan to go up to Nogales and engage in the green card process in hopes of going to the United States of America.

Meanwhile our father continued to smoke and drink beers. He made drinking and smoking look elegant, like he was an actor playing a part in a bar scene, coolly styled in a clean, but worn-out double-breasted suit and occasionally winding his pocket watch. Even if Papá appeared elegant, Miguel hated to see him drink and smoke, but he had become accustomed to it, having witnessed it over the course of his entire lifetime.

They talked leisurely, like they were in no rush. As Miguel didn't know what his future would look like in the coming weeks, months, or years, he was particularly enjoying Papá's company.

"What happened to your hand?" our father inquired.

"Well, it's a tricky thing," Señor Contreras replied and went on to say, "but I can tell you it hurts and throbs a lot. It feels hot inside it. Just this morning, I went to the priest. I confessed my sins regarding the incident. And I prayed for forgiveness and perhaps even a cure. Now, it's in God's hands."

Papá faced Señor Contreras and announced sternly, "Señor, you have a severe infection, and you'll need more than a confession. You need surgery and antibiotics. Otherwise, you will lose your hand."

The man's face quickly became ashen.

Papá continued, "Let me ask you, sir—from the tracking and

33

puncture marks, this looks like it was an injury from a blow to something you hit. Is my diagnosis correct?"

Señor Contreras looked down and acknowledged sheepishly, "Yes, sir, it is."

"Do you have a doctor here that can care for you?"

"There's a doctor that comes around now and then. Or we have to travel to Arteaga or Uruapan. Some people go to La Mira to see a doctor who practices out of his home and does dental work too."

At these words, Miguel looked at our father. He looked back at Miguel and said to him, "Let's go outside for a bit. Excuse us for a minute, Señor Contreras."

Outside Papá stated, "Miguel, his infection is so bad that he'll lose his hand and then perhaps his life."

Miguel, stunned, remained silent. His face set with concern.

Our father took his hat off and brushed his hair back. Then he decided, "We need to help him. I think this man's morning prayer has been answered."

This was the plan: a bus going to La Mira was coming in ten minutes. Miguel would take this bus back to La Mira to retrieve our father's medical instruments and supplies. He would then take that same bus back on its return trip to Los Coyotes. Our father would treat the man's injury, and then he and Miguel would continue their journey north.

When Papá shared the plan with Señor Contreras, he told him, "Of course, I'm going to ask something of you in payment for taking care of your hand."

"*Claro que sí.* I have money, and I will happily pay you," Señor Contreras answered.

"In return for the medical care, I ask that you promise that whatever—or rather, whoever—you hit with your fist will never be hit again."

Dipping his head, the man whispered, "I hit my wife and broke one of her teeth, and that's how I injured my hand. An alcoholic rage. I promise never to hit my wife or anyone ever again. *Gracias*, doctor."

"My whole name is Miguel Hernández Cabrera. Just call me Miguel, not 'Doctor.'"

Because our father never completed the medical program, thus never got his diploma, he wouldn't allow anyone to address him as "Doctor."

The man raised his head and asked, "Miguel Hernández Cabrera— so you are the medicine man from La Mira?"

"Yes, I am. And please call your wife out. I'd like to look at her mouth and treat her too," responded our father.

In the meantime, Miguel made the two-and-a-half-hour trip back to La Mira. Upon reaching our village, he had to move quickly so as to be able to catch that same bus on its return trip to Los Coyotes. It would leave in about forty minutes.

When people saw Miguel running through the village back towards our house, about a mile in distance, they were astonished. Hadn't he said his goodbyes and just left to *los Estados Unidos de América*? Nena was astonished when Miguel stormed into our small house. Swiftly he explained what was happening and what he needed. Nena moved quickly, gathering instruments, bandages, and bottles.

"Nena, do you think this is everything?"

"Yes, Miguel, I have been preparing this tray for these types of procedures for your father since 1940."

Miguel smiled, gave her a kiss on the cheek, and said a second goodbye, "Nena, you will always be in my heart and mind. I will come back. Please take care of my father. He needs you very much."

It was a long day for Miguel and Papá, but a lucky one for the Contreras family. Miguel, having made the two-and-a-half-hour return trip to Los Coyotes, watched on as Papá treated Señor and Señora Contreras. He left them with ten glasses of antibiotic mixes and instructions on when to drink the medicine and how to reapply the clean dressings. He told them he'd be back in about five days to check in on them.

Papá and Miguel departed to continue their journey to the border town of Nogales in the Mexican state of Sonora. Since they needed to take a series of vehicles to get there, first they went to Arteaga, then to Uruapan, Morelia, Guadalajara, Mazatlán, Los Mochis, Culiacán, and Hermosillo. Finally they would arrive in Nogales.

Miguel would stay on in Nogales while Papá would immediately retrace the route back to the Contrerases in Los Coyotes and back to our family and community in La Mira.

Together, on this journey north to Nogales, father and son moved from city to city, from bus to bus, and from cigarette to ashes. They discussed family unity and the importance of staying in contact despite the inadequacies of the postal delivery system. They talked about faith, hard work, honesty, and respect for everyone because you never know what others are going through. Our father told Miguel to be kind, respectful, and appreciative to everyone who helped him. To be resourceful and apply the many talents he had acquired during his years of working in various industries to find good work. And to practice the highest integrity at all times.

In Nogales, Miguel stood before our father while the two watched the people boarding the bus to Hermosillo, the bus our father would board to start his return journey.

It was time to say goodbye.

With the many passengers on the crowded bus watching from their individual windows, Miguel took a knee before Papá. Papá then blessed him, making the sign of the cross over his bowed head. Despite Papá's general disinclination to hug, Miguel then quickly stood and embraced our father. Just as quickly he took Papá's hand and kissed it. For Miguel, this significant farewell would not have been complete without this embrace and kiss on the hand.

Before stepping onto the bus, Papá pointed to a shop up the street.

A jewelry store. "*Mijo*, while you are getting together your papers, try that place to get some work. A starting point."

———————

After checking into a hotelito in Nogales, over dinner Miguel reviewed the papers he'd gathered for the immigration process—birth certificate, municipal letter, three references, a clergy letter, a three-page summary about his doings in the past ten years including the kind of work he'd done and the places he'd worked. All seemed to be in order.

When the waitress asked if he needed anything else, Miguel asked, "Actually, yes. I am new to Nogales, and I have some papers that need to be notarized. Do you know of a good public notary?"

"There's a man that comes here for breakfast every morning, and he's a notary. You can meet him if you like."

"Thank you, I'll do that," replied Miguel, "Tell me, what's your name?"

"Celia, Celia Montes," she answered, "And you?"

"*Me llamo* Miguel Hernández. I just arrived from Michoacán and will be immigrating to the USA and may need help doing so."

"*Sí, es mucho trabajo*," responded Celia. "Come in the morning at about 7 am. I'll be here and I can introduce you to Aurelio, the notary. He's a nice and respected notary."

And that was how Miguel's relationship with Aurelio began. Aurelio not only helped Miguel successfully navigate the immigration process, he helped me, as well as many, many other people seeking to get their green cards. Aurelio taught Miguel so much about the intricacies of the immigration process that Miguel was then able to guide many others through it. Not only did our family members benefit, so did many people outside our family, each attaining a green card and a life without fear as proud citizens of the United States of America. These inspiring stories will unfold later on. For now, know that it was through the kind suggestion of Celia Montes that Miguel met Aurelio, a man who made a huge impact on the Hernández family as well as on many others.

Aurelio's appearance and manner were truly distinctive. Unforgettable. He was well over six feet, five inches tall, very skinny, with noticeably long arms, neck, and torso. His arms were so long that his shirt and coat appeared two sizes too small. He resembled a praying mantis of sorts. He seemed like he lacked energy in that he moved and spoke very, very slowly. Painfully so. Plus, his voice was very, very soft. You had to strain to hear him. Every interaction with him took three to four times longer than you would expect it could possibly take.

When Miguel first met Aurelio, he was taken aback (although he didn't show it) at how slowly their conversation moved. Miguel was always patient and respectful, so the added time wasn't problematic. He was simply surprised. Aurelio, though incredibly lethargic in speech, manner, and movement, was competent in helping people gather the papers and solve complicated documentation issues in order to get their green cards. Plus, he was devoted to his clients. Together Miguel and Aurelio made a great team and ended up becoming lifelong friends.

I met Aurelio myself when I came to Nogales. I was a little over nine at the time, and I too was struck by his appearance and sedate-like manner. Years later when I was in medical school, I learned about Klinefelter's syndrome, a not uncommon chromosome disorder that only affects men. From the symptoms I had observed years earlier, I realized that Aurelio likely had Klinefelter's.

While Miguel already had most of the necessary papers, Aurelio informed him that he would need a sponsor, an American business owner who would hire Miguel and vouch for him. This was the first Miguel had ever heard of the need for a sponsor.

As was typical of Aurelio, he spoke both very slowly but also with somewhat sharp words, telling Miguel, "Even with a sponsor, it's going to take about three or four months for you to immigrate legally—unless you are a daring man and want to cross illegally. If that's the case, you don't need me. Only one time have I suggested to someone that they cross illegally, and I regretted it. The outcome wasn't good. Let's not go there.

"I know a couple of jewelry stores in Tucson, and I'll see if any of those owners would be willing to sponsor you. Meanwhile let's go get you an application and get everything ready. Who knows, maybe a miracle will happen? But I doubt it, miracles are few and far between, and we humans don't see much of them often . . ."

Miguel asked, "Aurelio, do you know anything about the jewelry store down the street from the bus station?"

"Now you're making sense. I thought there was hope for you, Miguel. A job here in Nogales is a good start. You could meet people. Lots of Americans come here daily to do their shopping. Also, it's possible this jeweler can help you. Maybe he knows someone. Yes, let's see if we can give you a little leverage. Let's visit him."

Among Miguel's papers were two letters of reference from jewelry store owners he'd previously worked for, one in Uruapan and a second in Morelia. In these letters, both owners cited Miguel's experience, inventiveness, and dependability—all of which greatly influenced the marvelous pieces of jewelry he produced. "Miguel Hernández has great inner talent that he applies whole-heartedly to the pieces he creates," one wrote.

When Aurelio read the letters, he told Miguel, "These letters are great. Now we just need a miracle."

Upon meeting Armando, the owner of the very jewelry store that our father had pointed out to Miguel, Miguel showed him these letters. The letters certainly caught Armando's attention. Because Armando came from a family of jewelers, his great-grandfather,

father, brothers, and even his sister were jewelers, he knew the techniques, skills, and creativity required. Armando wouldn't simply take on Miguel based on the letters, he wanted to see what Miguel could do. He asked Miguel to make five angel-figure pendants with fine details, so the angels appeared to be floating rather than simply hanging off a chain.

Miguel started early on a Saturday morning, and by the day's end, he'd crafted the five pendants with hovering angels. He embroidered the wings with fine radiant details. He embossed each figure with intricate, zigzagging oblique lines that suggested a supernatural floating movement. To add additional accent and charm, Miguel incorporated silver and gold.

Aurelio had already warned Miguel, "Your work better be beyond good—amazing—or Armando won't take you on."

And, indeed, it was. Miguel won Armando over and soon began work there. In just a few weeks, clients were inquiring after Miguel's distinct styles. A small following started. Miguel became busy and was able to start saving money.

———

While in Nogales Miguel received a letter from our father, addressed to him at Aurelio's business address. This letter had traveled overland and had taken around six weeks to arrive.

Our father wrote to tell Miguel that Señor Contreras and his wife were doing well. The couple had even visited him in La Mira several times for follow-up treatments after Papá had visited them that second time on his return trip to La Mira. Señor Contreras even seemed a changed man, God willing, and his family much more at peace and more united. Miguel's young siblings were doing well, but Nena had been caught off guard, even a bit frightened, when Miguel had stormed back into the house the day they'd left La Mira. Papá ended by saying that he hoped to hear from Miguel once he was in the USA.

Miguel thought to himself, "Señor Contreras, a changed man—*que milagro*! What a miracle! Maybe I too will experience a miracle and soon get to write Papá that I've made it to *los Estados Unidos de América*."

Three-and-a-half months from the day Miguel arrived in Nogales, Miguel was laying jewelry out on the shop's counter to show to a nice American couple interested in some pieces he had crafted featuring both silver and gold.

While in Nogales, Miguel had been taking English classes for three months. Though still in its infancy, his English was sufficient to communicate with the couple.

"What is your name?" the lady inquired.

"Miguel Hernández. What is your name?"

"I am Margaret Lambert. This is Bernard Lambert. We own a jewelry store in Phoenix."

Margaret and Bernard explained to Miguel that they owned a jewelry wholesale business, and their jewelry was all silver and gems—turquoise, red coral, and sometimes other stones. They employed seventeen Navajo Indian silversmiths and thought Miguel's jewelry style would make a great fit and complement the pieces their shop offered.

"We think you'd make a great addition to our team. Would you consider working for us?"

Miguel's response: he was speechless.

After taking a deep breath, he explained to Margaret and Bernard that he had all his papers ready to get his green card, but he simply didn't have a sponsor. He needed a sponsor to go to the USA.

"Miguel, you are looking at your sponsors," Bernard told him.

From there, they set up an appointment with Aurelio to, once again, set in motion Miguel's application.

The Lamberts returned to Phoenix, Arizona, to retrieve the papers they needed to submit as sponsors—letters from their accountant and copies of their business license to provide proof of solvency.

Miguel also learned that both Margaret and Bernard spoke some Spanish because in the past Bernard had practiced dentistry in a rural area where many people spoke Spanish. He stopped dentistry when he developed a tremor, and that's when he and Margaret got into the jewelry business. It's also why people called him "Doc." Margaret and Doc's business, Silver by Lambert—Indian Jewelry, was actually the largest Indian jewelry wholesale company in Phoenix. Miguel found out that not only would he have employment with them, but also that they would provide him with living quarters in the small apartment above their workshop.

When Miguel presented his paperwork at the American Consulate, accompanied by Margaret and Doc, he moved smoothly from officer to officer. It appeared his papers were in order, and all was going well—thanks to Aurelio's great guidance and Margaret and Doc, the miracle sponsors.

The final signature needed was that of the American Consul himself. Miguel, Margaret, and Doc walked into a room, and there, behind a big desk, sat the Consul. He was looking down, reading Miguel's papers. He looked up for a moment and said, "Take a seat, all of you."

Miguel sat with Margaret and Doc on either side of him. They looked at each other as the Consul proceeded to review the papers. When he looked up again, he had a serious look on his face. He took off his glasses and leaned back in his chair. He appeared to be very professional. A no-nonsense kind of guy.

The interview was conducted in Spanish.

The Consul looked at Miguel and asked, "You are Miguel

Hernández?"

"Yes, sir, I am."

"And these two are Margaret and Bernard Lambert, correct?"

"Yes, sir," Miguel confirmed.

Then the Consul asked, "Why do you want to come to the United States of America? It appears to me that you have been a successful man with all you have done in Mexico. Why do you want to leave?"

At this question, Miguel seemed puzzled.

"You are a successful man, don't you think?" the man asked.

Miguel replied, "Yes, sir, I have been working hard since I was a child. And I hope to do more in life by living and working in America. I have no children, and, someday, God willing, I would like to better my family by bringing them to America, so they too can enjoy a better future."

"We do have a better future here in America, don't we?"

"Yes," Miguel agreed, "It's a great country with unlimited re-sources and opportunities. Mexico has many limited resources, and opportunities are somewhat less."

The Consul asked, "You do understand that there are great re-sponsibilities you must take on when you enter the United States of America, don't you?

Miguel answered, "Yes, sir." Then he elaborated further,, "You see, sir, I felt I was at the end of what I could do here in Mexico. I want to do more. I am hungry for the many opportunities America has to offer, like working for the Lamberts. Years ago, when I was fourteen, I met an American gentleman that planted a seed in my mind about your great country and ever since I've been fascinated about what he said."

"What did he say?"

"He said in America you can achieve anything. If you work hard, anything is possible. There is no limit to what you can do.

He also said it's a rich country. Rich in industry, education, and opportunities for everyone. I have never forgotten his words. And I will learn to speak, read, and write the English language. I will seize the opportunities America has to offer and create prosperity, not just for myself but for America as well."

The Consul looked at Miguel and stated, "I am going to approve your application."

———

In saying goodbye, Aurelio told Miguel, "You are very lucky." And to the Lamberts he said, "You both are also lucky. Miguel will be an exceptional employee."

Miguel told him, "It won't be the last you see of me, Aurelio. I made a promise to immigrate my younger brothers and sisters. It might be in a few years. It might be in a decade, but I'll be seeking your services and advice again. *Gracias* and *hasta luego.*"

———

Miguel sat in the back of the car, and the Lamberts in front. The car made its way through the streets of Phoenix, finally reaching an alley and parking lot behind a building. To Miguel, the whole area, even the alley, was gorgeous. This was the building where the shop was located. It was painted white and stood two stories tall.

They entered the building from the back, stepping directly into the workshop space. The receiving area for customers was located at the front of the building. From the outside Miguel heard the humming and calling of loud motors. It was as if multiple generators were blasting away. He'd never heard such noise coming from a jewelry workshop. The noise only increased in volume when they entered.

Once inside, a large area stretched out before Miguel. There were two rows of ten benches each. Seventeen of those benches served as the personal workstations of the shop's seventeen jewelers. Each station had its own set of tools as well as gas torches. There were additional shared locations for the deep cleaning of pieces or for very rough work. Motorized buffers hummed away, and men wearing thick glasses and masks touched jewelry pieces onto rough grinding and buffing disks, depending on the task at hand. Some used rough sanding machines to smooth out sharp edges. Miguel noticed too that a number of the craftsmen had long hair that they wore in neat, low-hanging ponytails or braids.

There was an air of intense concentration as well as orderliness, with the silversmiths making and designing jewelry pieces per specification. The jewelry pieces got boiled and steamed to clean them before gemstones were added. The last step: a final polish. Such an organized and productive jewelry factory Miguel had never seen the likes of before.

A young lady entered the workshop from another door and stood next to Margaret. Next, Margaret announced to the craftsmen, "Please turn off the machines and take a break!" Then the young lady started speaking in a foreign tongue. It was obvious to Miguel that the young lady—who was Nellie Begay—was translating Margaret's words to the silversmiths. In this way Miguel learned that the other craftsmen, like him at the time, spoke little to no English.

Nellie wasn't translating Margaret's words into Spanish. Instead, it was another language—Navajo. A language that, to Miguel, sounded like a soothing musical whisper. It was the language he'd soon master and speak to a standard second only to his native Spanish.

Once the machines were off, these were the next words that Nellie translated, "This is Miguel Hernández, our new employee. We hope all of you will help make him feel at home here. He brings a different, yet interesting, addition to our traditional Navajo jewelry. He is from Mexico and really only speaks Spanish, so we all must be prepared to help him."

Everyone smiled. Some stood to shake hands with Miguel. Others nodded their heads or waved to acknowledge and welcome him.

Miguel felt as if he'd won *la lotería*, and he was so grateful to the many people who'd helped him achieve this win.

Chapter 3

Hijo de La Mira

By the time Miguel had finished telling his story to the group—
those who'd stayed on at Sampson's baptismal celebration—
the candles had burned out. A soft glow from the waxing moon
provided some light inside the cabin. Some listeners had pensive
faces. Some wiped tears from their eyes. Others were smiling with
a faraway look in their eyes. A serene calm shone from Phil as he
looked at Miguel in wonder.

Miguel, himself, had a face wet with tears. He'd silently wept
when speaking about his family back in La Mira. However, the
room's darkness had kept these tears hidden, for the most part.

The first to breach the silence was Benjamin Begay. "Miguel,
your story humbles me. We feel even more blessed that you are
Sampson's godfather and forever friend to our family."

At these words, the room echoed with others saying, "Amen"
and "Yes."

Nellie volunteered, "You spoke with such feeling about your
family in Mexico. We always knew you worked a lot in order to
help them, but from how you tell it, it seems like your heart is still
with them."

"It's true, Nellie. I love them so much," Miguel acknowledged.

At this point, Phil piped in, "Miguel, tell everybody about the letter."

"Phil, everybody's tired. We should go to bed," Miguel replied. "We can talk about it another day."

Phil firmly countered, saying, "Here, we're your family, Miguel, and I think it'll help you to talk about it with us."

As matriarch of the gathering, Grace said, "Miguel, you are going to tell us about the letter. All night long we've noticed that letter peeking out of your shirt pocket, and we have all noticed you're worried about something. We want to know what's going on. I'm going to light some more candles and get everybody some hot tea."

While Grace was making tea, Nellie and her sister Grace got out more candles, set them up on the table, and lit them, one by one. Others stood up to stretch and look out the window to admire the night sky through the pine trees.

Miguel stayed sitting, obviously preoccupied.

Phil approached and crouched down next to him. "I hope you don't mind, brother, me saying that to you in front of everyone."

After a moment of pause, Miguel turned to Phil and assured him, "I know you are worried about me and only trying to help. And you are correct—this is my American family, and I do need support and advice from everyone here. As you know, I feel conflicted."

When everyone resettled onto the thick carpets with mugs of hot tea in their hands, Grace gave Miguel a nod. He took the letter out of his breast pocket and held it in both hands. He told everyone, "This is a letter from Mexico. It's from Chucho, a good friend of my family in La Mira. He helped my father and me reconcile after a two-year disagreement. He also helped me approach my father to get his blessing to leave La Mira and come to the USA."

Everyone nodded their heads to indicate they remembered Chucho.

Miguel continued, "Nowadays, you can mail letters from Mexico to the US in two ways. There's overland, which is a lot cheaper, but it takes about six weeks. And there's airmail, which is a lot faster. It takes only five days. However, airmail is relatively expensive, especially for a Mexican farmer like Chucho. Chucho, a man of few words, sent me this letter by airmail. So before even reading it, I realized its message was very important.

"In the letter, Chucho wrote that my father is sick. Very sick. Along with Chucho, Nena, my father's current wife, and Andres Maldonado, Nena's father who is like a grandfather to me—they all are extremely worried that Papá might die soon.

"As I already told you all, my father has been drinking and smoking heavily for fifty years now. Not a few cigarettes a day, a few packs a day. Every day. He even gets up in the night to smoke too. Chucho wrote that though Papá tries to hide it, he, Nena and Andres have each come upon Papá when he's having an explosive coughing episode. These attacks can last for thirty seconds to over ten minutes, and it's as if someone is choking Papá and he's fighting an invisible enemy to try to get his breath back. On top of that, he ends up coughing up lots of blood. Once a gruesome attack has ended, Papá's face and hands and shirt and the surfaces around him are covered in a spray of black blood. And people in La Mira are noticing. Patients come to see him, and he has to rush out of the room and out of the house to try to secretly manage the coughing attack.

"Chucho wrote me this news and advised me to return to La Mira. However, it's not just the fact that Papá seems to be dying that is so bad. It is what Chucho didn't write, because he didn't need to, is that if Papá dies, Nena and the children's ability to survive financially isn't certain. You see, though Papá's a brilliant doctor and dentist, he's a lousy businessman. He doesn't ask for payment from patients. If someone pays, then great. If they don't, then maybe they will later; or maybe they'll bring by a sack of corn or a hen or a pail of milk. But if they don't pay or offer something, that's fine too.

"My long-term plan has been to immigrate everyone, including Nena, to the United States to live with me. It's going to take a large chunk of money, and I don't yet have it. Sure, I've saved a lot, but I have to save more and I have to get the house mostly finished so my ten family members, plus myself, can live in it. It's not livable right now. Of course, I'm desperate to see my father and the family in La Mira. Of course, I want to go. But if I wait six months or a year, I'd be that much farther along with the house and with savings, so much so that maybe I could bring back two or three of the children. If I go now, I won't be able to bring anyone back, and I'll miss twenty or twenty-five days of working, which means I'd lose out on some needed income, thus putting off my ability to immigrate family members even longer. I'm telling you all this, so you can see how troubled I am. I don't know what to do. I feel so torn—with my heart saying one thing and my head the other."

When Miguel finished explaining the letter and his situation, a somber silence filled the cabin. It was apparent that everyone was preoccupied with his troubling situation. Their faces showed concern and sympathy. Still, no one spoke. They were waiting for Benjamin and Grace to commence the conversation.

Benjamin finally offered, "If you want me to tell you what I think, Miguel, I could do that. But I believe you already know the right thing to do."

Grace picked up, gently saying, "I agree with Benjamin. You already know. Let us help you listen to your knowing. Miguel, close your eyes and take a deep breath . . . Feel your body sitting on the carpet beneath you."

Miguel followed her instructions.

Grace stood to open the window, all the while instructing, "Breathe in slowly . . . Breathe out slowly."

She moved to sit back down on the carpet, this time next to

Miguel. She took one of his hands and held it, saying, "Feel the whispering wind move in this space. Let the wind talk to you. Open your inner thoughts and let them float with the wind. Float with us here."

Miguel allowed Grace to guide him. The room stayed silent except for the sound of Miguel's inhales and exhales.

"Now open your eyes, Miguel, and look to the moon. The moon holds the wisdom of the saints and the ancestors. Listen to that wisdom. Bask in that wisdom and the comfort this circle of friends offers you."

After a minute, or maybe it was two, Grace softly stated, "When you are ready, tell us what you hear."

Fives seconds passed.

Ten seconds.

With his hand still grasping Grace's and tears in his eyes, Miguel quietly stated, "I must go . . . It's the right thing to do. I will go."

The following day, Miguel and Phil made the five-hour drive back to Phoenix. Upon arriving at their little apartment above the jewelry shop, Miguel contacted Margaret and Doc to get their permission and blessing for the journey to La Mira to see his father and the family.

Margaret told him, "Doc and I—and everybody at the shop— we're going to miss you. But we think you're doing the right thing. You should know, we just got an order for ten belt buckles "à la Miguel"—silver, turquoise, and gold. The client said that even if he had to wait half a year or longer, you were his artisan of choice. So rest assured, Miguel, you've got plenty of work on the docket when you return and a lot of fans who support you."

He called Pedro and Olivia, and told them what he was doing and why. He assured them not to worry and that he'd return in about three weeks. They gave him their blessing.

In the meantime, Phil and Nellie let the other silversmiths know what was going on with Miguel. Everyone put together a small pot of money for him. Margaret and Doc too, so the next day when Miguel left for La Mira, he had a little cushion of money as well as their warm wishes to carry with him.

Because he didn't have time to get the Ford Fairlane serviced and he didn't trust its tires to hold up on that final fifty-mile stretch of unpaved road from Los Coyotes to La Mira, Miguel took public transportation. Miguel took that same series of buses, vans, and pickups from Phoenix to Nogales and then along the same route he'd taken in 1951 to reach America, but this time in reverse. When he finally made it to Los Coyotes, he saw Benjamín Contreras selling gas to someone, but Miguel didn't have time to chat.

That final stretch of road from Los Coyotes to La Mira was the most difficult to endure. For one thing, few buses did that route. Mostly, it was pickups. So Miguel and the other passengers sat on wooden benches set up in an old pickup truck, one bench on each side of the bed. An old tarp acted as a canopy over the back of the pickup, an only somewhat successful attempt to protect the passengers from the overwhelming dust. The dirt- and rock-covered road was littered with potholes, so it was slow going. But at least the road was passable. In rainy season, mud prevented vehicles from traversing it.

Four-and-a-half days after setting out from Phoenix, five buses and one pickup transfer later, Miguel finally arrived in La Mira on a Saturday in the early afternoon.

Miguel grabbed his suitcase, a handsome leather bag that Margaret and Doc had given him, and stepped out of the bed of the pickup. Like his fellow passengers, once on the ground Miguel spent a moment slapping his pant legs and brushing off his shirtsleeves and shirtfront to try to remove some of the dust. Despite the tremendous journey, Miguel looked smart in his teal shirt, khaki pants, leather lace-up shoes, and belt with an exquisitely ornamented buckle of silver, turquoise, and gold that Miguel had designed and crafted himself.

A man at a nearby *tienda* called out, "*Señor, tu eres Miguel Hernández, el hijo del médico?*"

"*Sí, soy yo,* Miguel. You are Señor Morales, yes?" Miguel responded.

The man emerged from his little shop to continue the conversation, "*Sí, soy* Isidro Morales. It's been a few years since you were in La Mira. I remember when you left for *los Estados Unidos de América.*"

Miguel told him, "*Es verdad.* I left in 1951, and I've been in *los Estados Unidos de América.* I've come back—"

"To see your Papá," Señor Morales answered for him. "Yes, I've witnessed your father coughing. He coughed up blood. I was worried. We all are. Your father saved my son from a very bad infection. He helps everybody in this village and in other villages too. Sometimes your father comes here for a few drinks, and he loves playing dominos. He sits there in that corner chair with the red table. Yes, we are all worried about him, but no one dares to talk to him about his health. When I told him that I was worried about him, he just walked away."

"*Muchas gracias* for your candor about my father's health, Señor Morales. It is true, my father is a great healer, but he can be reluctant to address his own needs."

As the two were speaking, others began approaching. Other vendors, women, children, and even some dogs.

Miguel turned and smiled at the circling crowd. Then he looked over towards Señor Morales's little shop and commented, "That used to be my popsicle shop. I owned it with Gilberto Cruz. When I left, it was still Gilberto's popsicle shop, his *paletaría.*"

"Gilberto moved to Morelia. I bought the shop from him before the move and made it into a *tienda*," explained Señor Morales.

"Oh, interesting. That's news to me. What about Chucho—have

you seen him?"

Señor Morales answered, "Yes, he was here last night with his daughters—"

Someone from the crowd interrupted, explaining, "Right now, he's working in his fields."

"*Claro está.* Thank you," Miguel called out in response and then to Senor Morales, "It's been good talking to you. I'm going to walk to my family's home, but I look forward to visiting with you more later."

"The pleasure is mine," replied Señor Morales, "And it would be an honor for me to walk with you."

"But it is about a mile away—please don't think you have to," answered Miguel.

"I want to," Señor Morales said, and pointing to the crowd that had gathered, he added, "I believe we all want to. We are very proud of you, Miguel. It's not easy to go to a new country and to find honest work. And you did it. And you are taking care of your family. You remember La Mira too. We are proud of you."

At that, another vendor relieved Miguel of his suitcase, and Miguel, with tears in his eyes, started walking. Señor Morales and the others walked with him, the dogs trotting alongside the group.

Other than the *paletaría* that had become a small shop, or *tienda*, little else had changed since Miguel had left La Mira. Perhaps, there were a few more dirt roads. Maybe the school, once a faded white, had been painted a sky blue. As Miguel moved past more homes, members of his entourage would call out, "It's Miguel, Miguel Hernández, *el hijo del medico*, he's returned to La Mira from *los Estados Unidos de América!*"

Women doing housework—tending young children, sweeping floors, hanging laundry, rolling and pressing *masa* into flat, round tortilla discs—came to the front of their homes, their young children clinging to their dresses. Big smiles erupting on their faces.

Miguel would call out greetings, "*Hola, Señora Sánchez!* . . .

Buenas tardes, Señora Gómez! . . . *Hola, Señora Flores,* it's been a while! . . . *Cómo estás, Señora García?* . . . *Hace mucho tiempo, Señora Reyes!*" They would return words of welcome, hug Miguel, or exchange a hearty handshake, and many decided to join the entourage.

Everyone was talking—to each other, to Miguel, remembering Miguel from his years in La Mira.

"Miguel, remember when you organized the wedding party for my son's marriage? The goat, *el cabrito enterrado,* you cooked was so tender! The music was loud and clear. An unforgettable fiesta!"

"Miguel, do you see Mario? He's seven now. You arranged the most beautiful baptism for him."

"And for my Julieta too."

"And my Josefina."

"I remember when Gael was ill. Very sick. He must have been two-and-a-half years old. We didn't know if he was going to make it, it happened so suddenly. Overnight. Miguel insisted Gael see Señor Hernández. Miguel even carried Gael himself. And Señor Hernández saved him. *Gracias a Dios.*"

"Yes, he did that for my *tío's* little girl too. Miguel actually brought his father to come to her bedside. They saved her."

People remembered the once-a-year vaccination campaigns when nurses from the big city would come to La Mira to do immunizations. When Miguel had the popsicle shop, he made it the center of the vaccinations. He gave popsicles to each child too as a way to entice families to get their children vaccinated and to reward the children who'd just gotten pricked by needles. In each and every year he had owned the *paletería,* it had been used as the vaccination station, and he also allowed the town to use his premises for important town meetings.

People remembered Miguel's silos—something they continued to depend on. Corn was a major source of food in La Mira, as it was throughout all of Mexico. Practically every meal involved corn in some way. Corn *tortillas*, corn *tortas*, *tamales*, *atole*, *tostadas*, *gorditas*, *quesadillas*, *chilaquiles*, *enchiladas*, *chalupas*, *tacos*, corn soup, and *tortilla* chips—all depended on corn.

It seemed at least once a decade, sometimes even more frequently, La Mira's corn harvests failed due to insect infestations, in particular, plagues of locusts. When a whole year's harvest failed, people everywhere suffered. Not only did farmers' families themselves not have corn to eat, but corn prices skyrocketed, and it became very expensive to buy. Everyone was affected. Everyone struggled when a plague hit the corn crop.

In the mid-1940s, Miguel was browsing a magazine when he happened upon a photograph of a farm in Iowa. The photo featured a massive cornfield and, most significantly, silos for holding dried corn. That photo gave him the idea that our community should invest in shared silos to store corn during good times so that in lean times we'd all have corn to draw on. With the entire community's agreement and support—in the form of labor, building materials, and money—Miguel organized the construction of community silos. Our silos didn't look like the Iowa ones in the photograph. Ours were rectangular storage sheds built to keep the corn dry and aerated, but also protected from insect destruction.

Miguel and the farmers worked it out that all farmers would contribute some of their corn crop to the silos in proportion to the amount of corn each farmer harvested. In the good years, everyone would contribute more corn to the silos than in years when yields were average or below average. Farmers would fill cloth sacks with the decided amounts of dried corn, and these sacks were stored in the silos. La Mira families declared tremendous love and appreciation for Miguel when these silos saved everyone from the plagues of 1945 and 1949. In the following plagues of 1962 and 1963, though Miguel was living in the US, everyone's gratitude and love went out to him again.

Miguel and his parade moved slowly through the village. They made many stops as hugs, handshakes, and greetings were exchanged. The enthusiasm over Miguel's return was palpable. Some of the dogs escorting the entourage would sit during these stops while others circled the expanding group, excitedly trying to wrangle everyone and get them moving again.

At one point in the promenade, a man complimented Miguel on his fine ring made of silver, gold, and turquoise. Miguel gently told him that it was crafted based on a traditional Navajo design.

When Miguel noticed the man's face was scrunched in puzzlement, he explained, "Navajo Native Americans are one of the indigenous people in the US. Just like we have indigenous people in Michoacán, like the Purépecha and the Tarascans, so does the US. I work with Navajo Native Americans. They've taught me how to craft their traditional jewelry. Like this belt buckle too."

"*Qué hermoso!* It's lovely!" the man remarked.

A couple of kids hugged Miguel. Alejandro and Miguel Ángel, both about six years old, told Miguel their names, and immediately Miguel realized they were his godsons whom he'd baptized in the months before he'd departed from La Mira in 1951. Miguel hugged the boys and gave each one an American dollar. Everyone was smiling and laughing.

This exchange was soon interrupted when a woman dashed from the threshold of a small adobe home, shouting ecstatic hellos to Miguel and then embracing him and showering him with blessings. This woman was Valentina Villaremo.

In the late 1940s, one of Señora Villaremo's children, a boy named Josué, fell and broke his leg and ankle. My father recommended that Josué get special care from a physician friend in Uruapan. Because the fracture involved the joint, without a specialist's oversight Josué could end up crippled for life. The problem was that Señora Villaremo had five children, and her husband was almost blind. She simply couldn't be away from home the days it would take for Josué to get to Uruapan and see the specialist.

When our father lamented the situation to Miguel and Nena, my mother, remarking, "I can splint and stabilize the joint, but I am worried about the boy's future," Miguel and Nena decide to intervene. They determined that they could make it work. Miguel would escort Señora Villaremo and Josué to Uruapan, and Nena would care for the other children and their father.

Miguel and Nena worked together frequently when a crisis occurred. When someone lost a family member or a family member became gravely ill or injured, they would arrange a collection to help the affected family. They made it their mission to figure out and organize ways to improve the town and people's lives.

So, they worked together to help Josué and his family, and ultimately Josué's fracture healed seamlessly. Miguel and Josué had been close ever since.

So, when the parade made it to the Villaremo's home, Señora Villaremo was ecstatic to see Miguel. She moved quickly to his side and wrapped him in an adoring embrace, all the while declaring, "Bless you, *mijo*! Bless you! Josué is now seventeen. He is strong. He is responsible. He's working in the fields right now, but he'll be home later. We'd be honored if you could visit us during your time in La Mira."

Miguel hugged her back and promised he would visit in the coming days.

The continuously expanding entourage having witnessed this warm reunion began chattering once again, the sitting dogs got to their feet, and everyone became even more animated, saying that the son of La Mira had returned, *"El hijo de La Mira ha regresado!"* Señora Villaremo joined the retinue, and the procession's slow march continued.

Soon after, the procession halted again to admire a similar scene of astonishment and warm-hearted embraces between a townsperson and Miguel. In 1950, a child named Bautista ended up developing a seizure disorder. However, the medication was only available in the city. Miguel and my mother worked out a system using the pickup and bus drivers—an informal sort of courier system—to get the medication from the city to our village. Because it was a medication in powder form, my mother taught Bautista's mother how to mix it. In this way Bautista's seizures became controlled, and he was able to live a normal life.

When Bautista's mother noticed the procession, she'd stepped out of her door and into her small dirt yard to see what was going on. When she realized it was Miguel at the head, she ran to him, gave him a big hug, and welcomed him home.

Upon witnessing this tender scene, more calls of "The son of La Mira has returned!" sounded out. The excitement became so contagious that some of the dogs began yapping and the children started to sing. A spontaneous celebration.

After Miguel promised that he'd soon have dinner with the family, Bautista's mother joined everyone, and the parade began moving again—only to stall again in front of the Widow Tapia's home, where an even more emotional scene ensued.

Years earlier there was a terrible fire that burned down the Tapia's home. Miguel was the first on the scene and the first to begin retrieving family members from the burning home. Along with assistance from some other villagers, all five children and the two parents were rescued. Sadly, the father and three of the children ended up dying later on from thermal and inhalation burns. Miguel went on to arrange a collection of money, clothes, food, and other items to aid the widow and her two surviving children. The Widow Tapia had been particularly upset when Miguel left La Mira in 1951, pleading with him to stay because he helped so many people and meant so much to the village.

I should also add that Miguel's hands got badly burned in the rescue, but Nena was well experienced with treating burns by that time, so she was able to treat them. However, the scarring from those burns remained over the course of his lifetime, a testament to his courage and determination.

When the Widow Tapia spotted the parade and then Miguel at its head, she burst into sobs and darted out of her house to embrace Miguel. She was weeping so much that she couldn't speak. Half the crowd started crying too, remembering the horrific fire, the lost lives, but also the good fortune that Miguel had arrived on the scene and was able to save two of the children.

The crowd roared out more declarations of "*El hijo de La Mira ha regresado. Aleluya! Gracias a Dios*! Thank God!" accompanied by the baying and barking of the dogs that were feeding on everyone's joyful, infectious energy.

Before the large group could get moving again, two young farmers approached. It was Genaro and Felipe. When they were kids, Miguel had encouraged them to meet at his popsicle shop for a couple of hours on Saturdays to savor hot *ponche de limón*—a sweet punch flavored with lemon juice, lemon peel, and sugar—and read Miguel's Mexican *revistas*, or comic books After warmly hugging Miguel, Genaro and Felipe reminded Miguel of these great times.

After the jubilant exchange of greetings, Genaro and Felipe joined the parade, and it moved on once again.

To get to our house from the village center, you had to walk up a long hill. Once at its top, just on the other side, as the hill descended into a basin-like area, you'd come upon our home and those of our neighbors. The top of the hill offered a panoramic view of the cluster of homes on either side. Looking to the west, you could see the tall trees tracing one of La Mira's two rivers, and above them on the horizon, you saw the vast Pacific Ocean. When facing east, you could see Las Fincas, the name we gave to the area in the mountains where the mines were located.

Miguel's spontaneous welcoming committee gleefully ascended the hill. When they were over halfway up, a man on horseback appeared at the top of the hill. It was Chucho.

Chucho and my grandfather, Andres Maldonado, had been hoping that Miguel would return to the village, but they had no idea when (or even if) Miguel would return. So when Miguel had stepped off the pickup truck two hours earlier, they were unaware of his arrival. Thoughtfully, Isidro Morales, the *tienda* owner, had dispatched a young runner to find Chucho and my grandfather in their fields and inform them of Miguel's return.

When Chucho made his appearance on horseback, he was wearing the traditional garb of the La Mira farmers—a straw hat, a red handkerchief around the neck, pants and a shirt made of white sackcloth, and a machete strapped to his side with a worn-out leather belt. Chucho also sported a little Charlie Chaplin-like mustache. It covered a bad scar on his lower nose and lip. Years earlier he'd been bitten by a spider while sleeping, and the bite resulted in an infection that caused a half-inch loss of his upper central lip. My father treated him, so the loss of flesh was much less than it could've been. Ever since, Chucho wore a mustache to cover the scarred area.

When Miguel spotted Chucho, he picked up his pace, which resulted in a growing gap between him and his congregants. On his trot up to meet Chucho, Miguel became aware of another figure in white sackcloth also sporting a red handkerchief around his neck—it was Santos Ortiz. He was sitting on a large rock with his legs dangling off its side. Santos Ortiz was our village hermit, mystic, and to some—bogeyman. The children, and even many adults, made up stories about Santos Ortiz and his supernatural powers. We were both intrigued and afraid of him. However, Miguel and my mother always respected Santos Ortiz and showed him kindness and concern.

As Miguel charged up the hill to greet Chucho, he realized

Santos Ortiz was keenly watching him from the distant boulder. Though when Miguel glanced over again at the boulder, strangely Santo Ortiz had disappeared. He was nowhere to be seen. Miguel had no time to contemplate this, for he'd reached the hill's summit and met his longtime friend, brother, and counselor. By then Chucho was off his horse, so they immediately gripped one another in a heartfelt hug.

When the parade of Miguel's supporters reached the hill's top, everyone kept their distance, admiring the meeting of the two men, for everyone already knew about the closeness the two men shared.

Miguel, Chucho, and the retinue were on the verge of recommencing the march when Andres Maldonado, my grandfather, appeared. Like Chucho, he'd come from the fields and was wearing the garb of the *campesinos*. Unlike Chucho, he was on foot. Miguel and my grandfather, who was like a grandfather to Miguel too, embraced warmly and exchanged sincere words of greeting. Finally, the procession started its march again, making its way down the other side of the hill and to our house. Chucho walked, holding the reins of his horse, gently and loosely pulling it along.

Descending the other side of the hill, the entourage made for a remarkable spectacle. At this point, it numbered almost one hundred, including men, women, children, dogs, a few donkeys, and, of course, Chucho's horse. Miguel remained at the head, smiling and waving. It was as if a member of royalty, a celebrity, or the President had arrived.

My family—my parents, my siblings, and I—had no idea Miguel was coming. We had no idea he'd arrived. So when my little brother tugged on our mother's dress and pulled her to the doorway, shouting, "*Mira, Mamá!* Look, Mamá! A party!" everyone, even our father at my mother's prompting, came outside to witness the curious celebratory parade descending from the hilltop.

"*Qué crees que está pasando?* What do you think is going on,

Nena?" our father asked.

"Husband, I believe someone important is visiting the village . . ." and upon further inspection, our mother stated, "I believe it's your son. It's Miguel. *Sí, es Miguel*. He's returned from *los Estados Unidos de América*."

With Mamá and Papá in the lead, my family ran to greet Miguel. That is, everyone but me. I held back. Though I was never a shy boy—a bit too talkative according to Mamá—for the first time in my life I was struck mute and immobile. As if frozen. Paralyzed. I was seven years old, and for the first time I was meeting my thirty-eight-year-old half-brother (I was only one when he left La Mira).

When I saw him—like a marshal at the head of a parade of a hundred people—he was smiling, waving, and beaming with incredible charisma and compassion, it was as if I were encountering not just a superstar or celebrity, but rather a being that was beyond human. A super man. A mystic.

It just didn't seem right to me, or even possible, to casually approach, greet, and even touch such a pristine and blessed super man. I didn't feel worthy. I was locked in a state of awe and anxiety.

Miguel embraced each member of the family. My grandfather, noticing I wasn't with everyone, found me, took my hand, and led me over. In introducing me, my grandfather said, "Miguel, you must meet Edgar, my right-hand man and helper. Edgar is the love of my life, and you won't find anybody in La Mira like him."

Miguel, moving nearer to me, responded, "*Mijo*. My son, come close to me," and then he put an arm around me.

Just as suddenly and unexpectedly as the anxiety had enveloped and transfixed my whole being, it vanished once Miguel put an arm on my shoulder. Total composure set in my body and spirit. I moved close to Miguel and found myself smiling with pride. I felt special. He made me feel like I belonged with him. And it seemed that I'd known him forever.

During Miguel's two weeks in La Mira, I was with him almost the whole time. I should also add that my naturally verbose nature quickly returned to full throttle—meaning I was a real chatterbox with Miguel. No holding back!

The La Mira townspeople in Miguel's entourage, understanding that it had been a long and hard journey and that he needed to wind down with the family, dispersed, returning to their homes, their work, and their chores. Children trailed their mothers and fathers, with the dogs trailing the children. Chucho and Miguel made plans to meet the following day, and Miguel headed into the family home to clean up, rest, and relax. All the while, he was keeping a careful watch over our father, noticing how Papá moved, how his clothing hung off his body, how much he was smoking, how much he was drinking, the rhythm and sound of his breathing, and whether or not he ate, talked, or coughed. Miguel was trying to notice all he could, comparing our father's current condition to how he remembered it six years and some months earlier, in order to assess his overall state of health.

Chapter 4

CONVERSATION

The next morning Miguel and I visited Chucho. They had a plan to have a long conversation over breakfast. Chucho prepared a delicious traditional breakfast called *aporreadillo*, which is fried jerky mixed with eggs, simmered in a red hot sauce, and then served over white rice. And, of course, the meal was accompanied by corn tortillas on the side and sweet, hot coffee to drink.

Miguel and Chucho talked about everything, including Papá's precarious health. Everyone knew how ill our father was and how his condition was worsening on a daily basis. He truly was a sick man. Unlike some people that would say my father had "just a little cough" or that he was "sick but not that bad," Chucho refused to play down our father's health.

Like the shop owner Isidro Morales, Chucho told Miguel the truth about what he'd observed. Chucho admitted that our father's coughing fits scared everyone who'd witnessed them, including him. Chucho argued that Papá was likely a lot sicker than we even realized because he was good at hiding things. However, Chucho determined, "I believe he's reached the point where he can no longer hide it because the gruesome coughing is happening more frequently."

Chucho described an incident two months earlier, when he'd brought a man to Papá for treatment. The man had fallen off a carriage, and his leg was cut severely during the fall. Papá would need to clean and close the leg wound. In treating the wound, Papá started coughing severely. His color changed first to blue then to dark gray, purple, and finally to ash. He was experiencing an attack.

"Miguel, that man became so frightened. I didn't know what to think myself—I couldn't tell if it was the man or your father who needed the most help. I didn't know what to do. And ever since, when I've approached your father about the episode, he brushes me off. He either tells me he's fine or he walks away."

They both agreed that the most likely culprit for our father's attacks was his chain-smoking habit. They figured the excessive drinking didn't help, but because he was experiencing coughing attacks, the smoking was likely the cause. They pondered on what they could do to, at best, get Papá to stop smoking, or at the very least to lessen his smoking. They couldn't come up with any remotely likely possibilities.

Miguel lamented, "Even if we had something to offer him to get him to smoke less or stop, I don't think he'd do it. It kinda seems that for a long time now he's been on a mission to die."

Even still, they were going to try. So, similar to how years earlier Chucho had helped Miguel talk to Papá about Miguel's hope to go to America with our father's blessing, the two made a plan to have a serious talk with Papá. They'd include my grandfather in the important conversation too. Because it wasn't just Papá's life at risk—Nena, my siblings, and I all needed our father to lead our household and do work that provided for our family's survival. Sure, he rarely received or collected any fees for his services, but many people brought him food or goods as forms of payment, which our family relied upon.

On the day of the big talk Chucho borrowed a mule and a wagon from a neighbor. First we loaded the wagon with tortillas, tomatoes, chilies, and limes from our trees, and then we got in ourselves. On the journey there, we stopped alongside the river to drink some cool water and so that my grandfather could fish. He caught some amazing river bass.

Once at the beach we fried up the bass and ate it with the other food we had brought. We gathered coconuts to drink their water. And we went swimming. It was magical for me to spend time with these incredible men: Papá, my grandfather, Chucho, and, of course, Miguel. I had never felt so happy.

When it was time for a pause in the activities, we sat ourselves down in the shade of some coconut trees. I sat between Miguel and my grandfather.

Chucho took it upon himself to begin the important conversation. To our father, he stated, "Miguel, you know why Miguel, Jr., is here. I told you I was sending him a letter."

Papá quickly asserted, "And I advised you not to send it. I said you were making a mountain out of a molehill. A tempest in a teapot. I am getting older, but I'm working as hard as always and overall, I'm fine. Just a bit older, and sometimes I have a cough. There's nothing to worry about, and no reason for Miguel to have made the long journey here. Though, of course, we are all very happy to see him."

No one spoke for a moment.

Then Chucho tried again, this time speaking to everyone in the small group, "You aren't like my family. You are my family, both for me and my twin daughters. As such, I felt it an obligation to inform Miguel of my concerns."

Papá's face showed he was uncomfortable but resigned to having this long-avoided discussion. While he was listening, he made no comment. Instead, he continued smoking and drinking a beer. Yes, he brought beers. Of course, he was the only one drinking them because no one else in the small group drank. Not ever.

My grandfather spoke up, "I supported Chucho in writing Miguel, for both Nena and I are very worried about you too."

As I was listening, I noticed that Papá was looking at me. His frowning look indicated that he wanted me to move away and not hear the conversation. However, my father also knew I was very aware of his condition. Suddenly his face softened, and he commented, "Edgar, you are a little man now, and I want you to stay, for we are now five men talking."

"Yes, Papá. I want to stay," I responded.

My grandfather spoke again, saying to Papá, "Miguel, I have never leaned on you in any way or form about your habits. However, now the time is ripe for me to let you know the great agony occurring within the family. Nena is a true angel, always smiling, even about the most minimal things in life. She does all she can, so the children will be happy, even in this time of stress over your apparent illness. Nena is running out of excuses when the violent coughing episodes happen. We so desperately want you to try hard to control your habits, in particular the smoking. I hear you lecturing patients about how they should care for themselves, outlining the things they need to do to better their health and how their families depend on their good health as well. Yet you don't heed the same advice. How can that be?"

The four of us turned our heads to look at Papá, who hesitated for a moment, sipping the beer he was holding to his lips and taking another drag on the cigarette. When he'd completed these actions, he calmly replied, "You're asking me to stop doing something that I've been doing for longer than Chucho and Miguel have even been alive. Andres, from the time you first met me, you knew full well that I was a drinker and smoker. I never hid that, and you consented to my marriage to Nena."

"Yes, you are correct," my grandfather agreed. "I had an opportunity to speak out at that time, but my desire was to have Nena marry a man like you—a good man, a great doctor, a fair and kind husband and father. And as nothing is perfect in life, I accepted you even with your addictions. But now your addictions are wreaking havoc on your body and on your medical practice and within your family. So now it's time to get it together and ease up. Start lessening and lessening, and slowly, after a year or so, you'll have stopped completely. It's a matter of easing this deliberate destruction of both yourself and our family."

My father looked at me several times when my grandfather was speaking. I noticed he had started to tear up. Unexpectedly he crushed out his cigarette and turned over the bottle of beer, so it seeped out, leaking into the sand.

Miguel, who'd been sitting with worry etched in his face, finally spoke to our father. "I made the trip here, which, as you know, is long, so I could see you firsthand. Papá, what I see is a man thinner and weaker, but surrounded by a family and community that deeply love him and that is incredibly worried about him. I too am very distressed. I see you are short of breath after walking only a small distance. Not only do you stop because of your breath, but also because your legs aren't strong anymore.

"Papá, you are the core of our family. You are the mighty pillar of our strength—and it's a strength that is fading. Your strength is what supplies the rest of us with the strength to keep going in life. The children need you. Nena needs you. The people of La Mira need you. The people in the surrounding villages and towns need you. We are scared for you, worried for you, and desperate to help you to decrease your smoking and drinking. Please, Papá, tell me—how we can help you to change your habits? How can we help you to free yourself from these addictions? How can we help you to smoke just a little less each day and drink just a little less as well? I beg you, Papá, talk to us."

Papá closed his eyes and bowed his head. He took in a slow

breath and then released it. After that, he looked up, his eyes wide open and peering at Miguel. He answered, "Yes, *mijo*, it is true. My life will end soon, and I have no one to blame but myself. However, telling me to stop or even decrease these two things that I absolutely enjoy will kill me even sooner. I beg you, all of you, leave me be since stopping my habits will certainly kill me, just in another way. Let me be, and allow nature to take its course."

No one spoke. The only sounds were that of the waves crashing onto the beach, the ocean birds, and the light wind in the trees.

All the while, Papá continued looking at Miguel.

Papá spoke again, this time looking around at each of us in the group, "In my practice I see death all the time from causes more fatal than my habits. Death due to ignorance and neglect. I see death in young people. There's death due to our town's lack of resources. I might know the medicine or procedure necessary to save someone—yet if we don't have that specialty molding or type of clamp that's key to making it work, then the result is death. I'm talking about good people dying from simple medical conditions. Recently, a man died of a thyroid problem. I knew what was needed to save him, but we didn't have access to it. Think of what happened to Chucho's lovely wife and handsome sons—pointless deaths. Real tragedies. Also, children dying from scorpion bites because families use dangerous home remedies and don't consult me until it is too late. I'm saying all this to emphasize that my death is nothing compared to how people so frequently die in our area. Know that I agonize over the fact that there are too many times when there is nothing I can do to save someone—even when I know what is required to do so. It's just the means aren't there."

As Papá was speaking, I looked at the faces of the men surrounding me—Miguel's, my grandfather's, and Chucho's. Not one showed anger in regard to Papá's response. Instead, I saw love, compassion, sadness, and concern.

"Let me tell you about something that happened to me in 1924 when I was thirty-three years old," Papa said, "Miguel, you must have been about five years old, and your mother was still alive. At that point I'd been a steady drinker and smoker for more than a decade, but I decided I was going to quit. I was going to ease off and over time get down to nothing, no alcohol or cigarettes.

"As you all know, in those days, though I was experienced and had apprenticed many doctors and dentists, when I started work with a doctor, even if he was newer to medicine than me, I started as his assistant—this is because I don't have my medical degree. So, there I was, starting to work with a young surgeon. He was performing a thyroidectomy operation on a somewhat influential person outside of Uruapan.

"While he did the operation well, once it was complete, I noticed he hadn't placed a drain onto the wound. So I asked him about it, and he told me there was no need for it. In response I explained how the many other surgeons I'd worked with always did one, that way if the patient bled internally, the drain would buy time, so the patient wouldn't choke. But the young surgeon insisted it wasn't necessary.

"In the middle of the night, the patient's neck became very swollen. He was bleeding internally. And then he choked to death.

"Two days later, I was arrested and locked up in jail. Apparently, the young surgeon had told the accuser that he'd instructed me to place a drain on the patient's neck but that I'd failed to do it, and as a consequence, the patient died when he started bleeding internally. He bled, but there was no place for the blood to escape, so his neck became very swollen, which closed off his windpipe and resulted in death by asphyxiation.

"The nurse who'd been in the operating room knew the truth. She'd heard the conversation between me and the surgeon about the drain, but she did not say anything after I was arrested. She had told her husband, who was a new young lawyer and aspiring politician. But he too did not speak up for fear of losing his status in the community and of damaging the possibility of a great legal future before him.

"While I was in jail, I appreciated all the goodness of life. Inside a jail is a lonely place where desperate thoughts linger. I'd been accused of murder, which meant life in prison. It's the end of life. My children thought that I was away from home for a while, sent out to do some kind of extra studies or something—but that wouldn't last long.

"When I was in jail, I abandoned all the progress I made in easing off the cigarettes and alcohol. As a matter of fact, other than freedom—all I wanted was cigarettes and alcohol. I wanted the comfort and oblivion they could provide. Because there was a practically endless supply of cigarettes available to prisoners, I picked up smoking again at a rate greater than ever before. But alcohol—there was hardly any available. A real disappointment to me.

"I ended up befriending a guard who had some medical conditions. I helped him out, and in return he rewarded me with the occasional drink—so that was something at least.

"The young lawyer ended up talking to an elderly lawyer whom I had treated once or twice before. He shared the story of my innocence that his wife, the nurse, had told him. The elderly lawyer encouraged the young lawyer and his wife to tell the truth. He explained that the best part of being a good lawyer was confronting the truth. And so they did. Once the nurse testified, I was cleared of everything.

"The reason I'm telling you this story is to talk about how that time in jail changed me. In the weeks beforehand, I had started curbing my drinking and smoking just a bit with the long-term goal of stopping completely. However, while incarcerated I felt such acute anxiety that I clung on to smoking more than ever. And once I was released and had access to alcohol, I started drinking more than ever. My addictions, which had already been serious, grew while I was in jail, and here I am before you with a very terrible illness."

"Illness?" questioned Miguel.

"Yes," answered Papá. "Four months ago, I went to Uruapan for supplies. While there, I stopped to visit a friend of mine who is a very good doctor. I told him I was feeling tired and short of breath from even minimal physical exertion. He examined me and took a chest X-ray and blood studies. He asked if I knew what was going on in my body, and I told him, 'Yes, I do. I would like to have you confirm it, so I can make plans for my exit from this world.' And he confirmed it. It's the same diagnosis I'd arrived at."

We sat, absorbing this information and not speaking.

And though Papá didn't then and never would reveal the diagnosis, I know how I would diagnose him. I'm saying this in retrospect after a forty-year career in medicine. I believe my father had lung cancer, which would explain the terrible bleeding when he coughed. Another possibility is tuberculosis.

Finally, Miguel asked, "Does Nena know this?"

"Somewhat. She knows I got a chest X-ray. I told her that I analyzed it myself and it showed that my heart is in good condition, but that I've got tired lungs. She doesn't know that I consulted a doctor while in the city."

Next, Papá turned to me and said, "Edgar, you are sitting here with these honorable men that have shaped, and will continue to shape, your life. The same is true for your brothers and sisters. Don't feel sad. I have had an outstanding life with many rewards. Ups and downs have been part of my life. None of my children drink or smoke, and that is a good thing.

"Today when we started this serious discussion, I wasn't sure that I wanted you here to hear this, but somehow I know it is good for you to know. You are young, way too young to hear what I said, but on the other hand, I feel better about having you know what the future holds.

Miguel is a good son, actually, more than good—he is generous, kind, loving, and never will he abandon you or the family."

We took in these words.

My brother Miguel then turned to Chucho and stated, "My good friend, thank you for bringing me back to La Mira. This visit was essential."

Miguel then got to his feet.

The conversation had ended.

As Miguel was brushing off his pants, he turned to me and suggested, "Let's take a walk, Edgar."

As my older brother and I walked along the shore, both of us barefooted, the ends of waves tickled our ankles and feet. The sun had begun its evening descent in the sky.

Miguel told me, "The United States is a wonderful country. I'm making it my home. I've even bought a house. It's not suitable for living in right now. It needs a lot of work, but slowly and steadily I will get the repairs done. I have a car as well."

"A car?" I asked, especially intrigued because I didn't know anyone who owned their own car. Sure, there was the chubby guy who owned a pickup truck, but he used it to carry people between La Mira and Los Coyotes, so it wasn't the same as having your own car.

Miguel explained, "Yes, a car. Like the house, it too needs repairs. New tires. That's why I didn't drive it here."

I revealed to Miguel, "I want to go to *los Estados Unidos de América* someday . . . And when I see Papá do surgery, I'm amazed at his work and how he changes people's lives. That's something I want to do someday. I want to be a surgeon in the USA."

Without skipping a beat, Miguel responded, "You will, Edgar. I promise you that," and then added, "However, it will take some time."

"I know. But it's okay," I explained, "because my grandfather tells me that I'm young and time is on my side."

He smiled and hugged me, saying, "Edgar, I'm proud of you."

I asked, "Miguel when can I go live with you in the United States?"

"Soon, very soon, I promise."

As we made our way back to the coconut trees to start packing up the wagon, from a distance we noticed our father lighting a cigarette. It was getting dark, and we could see his thinning face silhouetted by the lit match as he moved it to light his cigarette. I looked up at Miguel. His face was gripped anew with anguish. His eyes shone with tears. I tightened my hold on his hand.

Feeling my hand, he looked down at me, and the tears slid from his eyes. I too began to weep, yet at that instant I also felt that my brother and I belonged together. I knew it was not the time for me to leave with him when he departed in a week or so, but I realized in the near future I would be with him in the United States.

Miguel went to dinner almost every night at different families' homes. Each time a different meal was served alongside a different conversation that was influenced by the unique history he had with each of these families. I didn't like it that he was doing all this visiting with all these people. I felt possessive of my brother, and it was evident. My mother had to give me one of those mild motherly scoldings that ended in a hug.

Mamá explained to me, "Edgar, though Miguel wasn't born here, he is a son of La Mira, *un hijo de La Mira*. Like us, the people of La Mira love him. They say, 'We owe much to Miguel,' and you know how Miguel responds to that? He says, 'No, it's I who owes much to you, for you have shaped me. I am indebted to you. I am blessed to know you. You will always be part of my life.' Miguel's visits to these families are a great example for you, Edgar, for Miguel is an honorable man. It is important to show appreciation for people around you, and that's what Miguel is doing."

While I understood with my brain what my mother was saying and I knew in my heart she was correct, there was still a part of me that didn't want to share him. For the most part, I accompanied him on the many visits. I would sit next to him or on his lap, and I became so attached that I knew I would be broken-hearted when he departed. But I also knew that in the near future—perhaps a year, two years, maybe three—I would be with him in the United States. Though I was mature for my age, a year was still a long time to wait for a seven-year-old. Really, it's a long time for anyone of any age.

The following day after our father finished up with two patients, he was going to get cleaned up when he started to violently cough. He coughed and coughed and coughed, all the while his whole body turned blue. He seemed to be choking. With every racking hack, thick blood rained out of him. It was a scene of utter horror, and it seemed endless.

And Miguel was there to behold it.

Miguel attempted to aid our father, grabbing him from behind and bracing him. Doing all he could to help. In response, Papá fought him off—it was like Papá was in combat against two assailants, one invisible who was choking him and the other his own son, trying to assist him. By the skirmish's end, Papá and Miguel were both on the floor, panting and bathed in dark blood. Papá had his eyes closed and was focusing solely on inhaling and exhaling strong, steady breaths. Miguel's eyes were open, staring into nothingness, as if frozen in fear. Finally Miguel had witnessed what Chucho had described in the letter.

Miguel regained function and stood up. Still filthy from the blood, he went outside. My mother followed. She was going to fill up buckets with water, so Miguel and Papá could get cleaned up. Once Miguel had cleaned up, he and Mamá had a talk. She revealed all the concerns she'd been holding back, her worries about the children, the family, their livelihood, and my father's likely fast-approaching death.

The following morning Miguel asked me, "Does our father cough like that frequently?"

"Yes," I admitted. "Every few days. Sometimes at night too."

I wish Miguel hadn't seen it because it changed him in the last days of his stay with us. His worry heightened. His spark gone. That illumination that he'd had around him faded.

———

Two days prior to Miguel's departure, he sat down to review the family's finances, an inventory of sorts. My brother, who had expected the situation to be bad, was surprised at how dire it was, for there was even less money than he'd predicted. As already mentioned, most of our father's services were paid in the form of goods, so at the time we had plenty to eat: five pigs, twenty chickens, four goats, four ducks, plenty of shrimp and fish from the ocean and rivers, as well as beans, potatoes, rice, and flour. Plus, a bottle of brandy specially brought from the city. Though Papá was delighted when his patient gave him the brandy, Mamá wasn't pleased about that form of payment.

Papá noted, "We don't need much money. We do okay with what we have."

Miguel retorted, "And when you aren't able to work, what will happen?"

"Nena and I own the thirty-acre grove of tropical fruit trees and plants—mangoes, coconuts, guavas, and pineapples—and the sale of the produce gives us a fair amount each year."

The reality was that Papá and Mamá had little clue as to how much money the produce from the grove brought in yearly. Because Chucho made all the arrangements regarding the grove, Miguel realized he needed to consult Chucho for a true understanding.

Chucho told Miguel that the yields were variable, "Sometimes it's good and sometimes not so good. When there's a plague, it's definitely bad. And when the rains come, they make the roads impassable. That can mean that any produce that's been gathered to be sold in the markets of other towns—well, it ends up rotten in the trucks."

Miguel's two major concerns were our father's rapidly deteriorating health and our shrunken coffers. However, he had a bit of hope about his Papá's expectancy. While our father had lost a lot of weight and appeared thin to the point of gaunt, he seemed to have a normal appetite. Miguel even witnessed him place four crowns on a patient and remove a mass from another patient's neck. Papá showed not one sign of shaking; he held a steady hand. And, as long as he had a cigarette in his mouth, his energy level seemed normal. That gave my brother some hope as to his longevity.

Miguel was hoping to buy time. He simply needed more time. Time to earn the money to get his Phoenix house renovated. Time to earn the money to get the car repaired. Time to earn the money to increase his savings in order to have the cash needed to move Nena, my siblings, and me from La Mira to Nogales, and to pay for all the needed papers, medical tests, other fees, etc., to get us all green cards, so we could enter the US. It was an extremely ambitious end goal, and Miguel was in a race against time.

The night before his departure Miguel met with Chucho and asked him to sell his thirty-acre coconut grove for a reasonable amount and give the money to my mother. Miguel predicted the money from this sale would also buy him more time because it would allow him to take a break from sending money to the family in La Mira, something he'd been doing on a monthly basis since he'd left in 1951. As long as Mamá had that money from the sale of his coconut grove to live on, Miguel could keep the money he was earning in the US and use it to further the house renovations, fix his car, and increase his savings.

Additionally, Miguel instructed Chucho to take the required money from the sale of the coconut grove and purchase chairs for the school, for he'd discovered that the school had no seating. We students had to carry chairs from home to school each day (and back again), a practice that Miguel wanted to end.

When Miguel spoke to Olivia and Pedro prior to leaving Phoenix, he discussed these financial concerns. They told him they would increase the hours they worked in order to earn and save more money. They were all in agreement. There was total unity within our family.

Miguel had already determined that when he returned to Phoenix, he would work even more hours. Prior to coming to La Mira, Miguel took Sunday afternoons off. This was his only rest each week. He decided he would work sixteen hours a day every day for a while, and if he needed to lighten this load, maybe he would take off only one Sunday afternoon per month. Yes, it was an aggressive plan. That's because he knew he was in a race against the clock.

Leaving La Mira was difficult for both Miguel and the entire family. Miguel was torn apart. He had no choice but to return to Phoenix, yet he didn't want to leave us behind in such a precarious situation.

For my part, I didn't want him to leave at all. Of course, I knew he had to, but I couldn't help myself. I'd grown so attached to him. The night before he left, I pleaded with him to stay.

On the day of his departure I was an utter wreck. Utterly upset. I hated to see him go and despised even watching his departure.

Similar to his arrival, there were about a hundred people at Miguel's departure, wishing him a safe journey, more success, and happiness:

"*Adios. Qué te vaya bien*, Miguel! Goodbye, Miguel, may all go well for you!"

"Until next time, son of La Mira! *Hasta la proxima, hijo de La Mira!*"

"Have a good journey, *hijo de La Mira*! *Qué tenga un buen viaje*, Miguel!"

Even Santos Ortiz, La Mira's mystical hermit who'd briefly surveyed Miguel during his arrival, stood distant from the large crowd of townspeople seeing Miguel off.

After many hugs, kisses, and handshakes with the family and his admirers, Miguel approached me. He gave me a tight hug and promised, "Edgar, do not despair. We will be together soon. You will come to the United States to live with me. And I promise to bring all the family too."

I wept as I watched him step onto the bed of the pickup truck. He sat on one of the benches under the oil-stained tarp. Shortly after, the pickup started to slowly drive away.

From his bench seat in the back of the pickup, Miguel looked at his family and supporters, all waving goodbye. He even noticed Santos Ortiz standing on the edge of the group.

Miguel looked once more in the direction of Santos Ortiz, hoping to take in Santos Ortiz's mysterious, mystical nature, but the hermit had disappeared. He was no longer visible anywhere near the crowd of well-wishers.

Before Miguel had time to search further for Santos Ortiz, the dust curtain descended, blocking his view and preventing him from taking one last look at all of us—his La Mira family, friends, and fans. La Mira and its people were replaced by a smog of swirling dust and the loud humming of the pickup truck's motor.

Chapter 5

MIND, BODY, AND HEART

Two years passed, and it was now 1959.

Miguel hugged Olivia and Pedro. Next he embraced several of his coworkers, including Phil. Then he boarded the bus. He chose a window seat, sat down, and closed his eyes. His head was throbbing, but overall it wasn't as bad as he'd anticipated. He slept the two hours it took to reach Tucson, where he changed to another bus.

On the ride to Tucson his mind had relaxed and he'd fallen into a much-needed sleep, but on this next ride, Miguel's mind and body were the polar opposites—overly alert and anxious. He couldn't wait to arrive in La Mira. His apprehension and impatience were almost beyond his mental control. His mind was racing through disturbing scenarios. While normally Miguel would strike up a conversation with people around him, this time he was too preoccupied, grappling with a deep and hollow sorrow.

At one point Miguel was convinced that his heart was overexerting itself, and soon he'd go into cardiac arrest; but after a few minutes he became equally certain that he had no pulse at all. He felt at times like he was floating. All the while, a sense of helplessness and guilt engulfed him.

He even thought he could hear a ringing noise and then the sound of a violin being played caustically. Tragically. The way he remembered the La Mira mystical, hermetic bogeyman Santos Ortiz playing the violin at children's funerals. Peering out the bus window, Miguel thought he caught site of Santos Ortiz, himself, in the distant scrublands along the Arizona highway. So now he was seeing things, seeing visions—thus, Miguel became afraid of his own faculties, afraid that his mental framework had become too sad and too upset to maintain a firm grip on reality.

Once the bus crossed the border and arrived in Nogales, Mexico, it was time for another bus change. As the passengers gathered their belongings and made for the exit, a young man, about twenty years old, asked Miguel, "Excuse me, *Señor*, could you help me remove my bag from the upper bin? I believe it's caught on something."

In the millisecond before he moved to assist the young man, Miguel glanced at him. He had black hair, worn in a flat-top, dark eyes, and brown skin. He was smiling. His shoulders were broad and his arms strong. There were crutches tucked under his shoulders. Because the young man's pants were pulled up at his ankles, Miguel noticed one of his legs was a wooden prosthetic, and on his full leg he wore a sizeable brace.

After two tries, Miguel was able to disengage the bag and remove it from the upper bin. He placed it on the floor.

"Thanks for your help," the young man told Miguel. Then he removed a crutch, grabbed the bag, shook his arm to scoot the bag up and onto a shoulder, repositioned the crutch, and slowly started to move towards the exit. It was an apparent struggle.

"Let me carry the bag. It's not a problem," Miguel suggested.

The young man called back a thank you but declined the help. Haltingly, he maneuvered down the aisle and off the bus.

Once outside, Miguel asked him, "*Como se llama?* What's your name?"

"I'm Fernando. And you?"

"I'm Miguel Hernández. Nice to meet you. Where are you going?"

Fernando answered, "I was in Phoenix, and I'm going to visit some friends in Hermosillo. What about you?"

Miguel explained, "I'm taking that bus too. But I'm not staying in Hermosillo, I'm continuing on to Michoacán. Tell me—what were you doing in Phoenix?"

As they moved slowly to find the Hermosillo bus, Fernando told Miguel, "I was in Phoenix for three weeks to be with my mother at the hospital. She had cancer"—he paused—"And we just lost her . . . Now I hope to settle my thoughts and prepare myself to go to college again in Tucson."

"I'm sorry to hear your news," Miguel replied, "I offer you my condolences. You seem a good young man and a loving son." Miguel went on to ask, "Tell me more about your mother and her cancer. What happened?"

"About two-and-a-half years ago she was diagnosed with brain and bone cancer. We didn't know how long she had left to live, but we knew it would only be months or a year or two at most. During that time, she was in a lot of agony. I dropped out of school to be with her fulltime. I have a sister in Texas, but she has four kids and could only visit a few times. I felt it was my duty to be with Mamá. I actually see it as a blessing that I got to be with her for the last part of her life."

"You've shown tremendous love and dedication," Miguel noted, "Like a good son."

"She was in constant agony and wanted to die, but I didn't want to let her go. Finally, she passed . . . But I don't like people to feel sorry for me—that's why I refused your help on the bus. As I see it, I need to do things for myself to succeed in this uphill life of mine—I'm referring to my leg—I mean my lack of a leg. It's a fake. I have to wear a brace on the right side to keep myself upright. I want to go back to college and be something. I don't know what right now—a doctor, a teacher, or even a school bus driver, driving children to and from school."

"That's wonderful. You're an amazing young man," Miguel voiced. "Tell me something about your uphill life. Tell me about your leg."

"When I was seven years old, I developed a bone cancer in my left leg. They had to amputate it. Because I came to overuse my right leg—compensating for the missing left—over time, I developed poor alignment at the knee. That's why, for now at least, I have to wear this brace, but soon I can have knee surgery. I actually think I'm managing pretty well."

"Yes, I agree," Miguel confirmed, adding, "but not just that. You're providing me with much-needed inspiration as well. You have true will and a deep belief in yourself, Fernando. You have exemplary determination. So many people, myself included, can learn from you. You are inspiring me and teaching me as we speak."

Fernando replied, "Miguel, I've learned that it's all in the power of the mind to find the strength to do what's right."

"Yes, Fernando, that's exactly what I believe too. I agree with you, and I thank God for putting you in my path because I needed to be reminded of that today."

Once they located the bus to Hermosillo, they proceeded to board it, Fernando in front, moving carefully and slowly. Once they settled into their seats, Fernando asked, "It's a long trip to Michoacán. What takes you there?"

Upon hearing his question, Miguel noticed that the extreme agitation and anxiety that had been plaguing his mind and body on the previous bus ride, and for the last week, had vanished. Instead, he felt grounded. Calm. And he knew it was due to Fernando. Hearing about Fernando's loss, his struggles, and his resilient mind and spirit, had restored in Miguel that same strength and resiliency.

Miguel answered, "You are correct. It's a long trip. It can take four or five days, one-way, by bus and pickup to get to the little village in Michoacán that I'm going to. It's called La Mira, and it's just a few miles from the Pacific Ocean. I lived there for almost twenty years before I moved to the United States eight years go." Miguel paused, taking in a slow breath and then continued, "I'm going to La Mira because I got word that my father died. At this point, it's been several days since his death, but I couldn't leave immediately upon receiving the news, so I've been feeling distressed. I really want to be present for his funeral and be with the rest of our family, so I'm anxious about whether I'll arrive in time."

Fernando quietly stated, "Miguel, I am sorry to hear of the passing of your father. I offer you my condolences. I feel like I can honestly say I understand how devastating it is, the passing of a beloved parent. And how important it is to be there at the funeral. I get it. Miguel, tell me about your father. Do you know why he died?"

And so Miguel told Fernando what happened, starting with his visit to La Mira two years earlier when Chucho had sent him that worrying letter and then all that had happened since.

In 1957, upon returning to Phoenix after the trip to La Mira to assess the state of our father's health, Miguel felt like he was in a race against the clock. He knew that once Papá died, Nena and the children would need help. So, he had to work as much as possible to earn as much money as possible in order to have a sizeable amount of money to help everyone—and maybe even bring some or all of us to the United States at the time of our father's death.

Miguel didn't know how much time he had—a few months, a year, a few years—he didn't know when exactly Papá would die. As a result, he had to apply himself as diligently as he could for as long as he could. And that was what he'd been doing for the past two years, working twelve- to sixteen-hour days crafting jewelry and usually only taking off the one afternoon per month. Also, he had commissioned workers to restore the dilapidated house and garage at 206 N. 9th Street to make it livable for when the family came to Phoenix. More or less, that was what Miguel's previous twenty-four months had looked like.

Ray Fasio, one of Miguel's good friends, never saw anyone as determined and hardworking as Miguel. Miguel and Ray met in Phoenix in 1952 after Miguel had been in the USA for only a few months. Ray had been a mechanic in the Korean War. He was well spoken, with a smile a mile wide, tan-colored skin, and slightly wavy hair. After the war, Ray and a friend started a business selling, installing, and repairing swamp coolers. Their business became successful. Because Ray worked in a lot of neighborhoods, he had a lot of knowledge about the Phoenix-area real estate market. In 1952 when Miguel was looking to buy a home, he ended up talking with Ray. The two hit it off and had been friends ever since.

As one of Miguel's good friends, just like Phil Stone, Ray came to know of Miguel's large family back in Mexico. Also Miguel shared with Ray his big future goal of bringing everyone in the family to the United States, a goal that intrigued and impressed Ray. As a business owner in Phoenix, Ray was often looking for hardworking and trustworthy employees. That meant that Ray sometimes would hire Mexican workers living in Phoenix, legal and illegal. When possible, Ray would act as a sponsor, so they could get their green cards and live and work legally. While Ray didn't know the intricacies of the immigration process, Ray learned over the years that it was lengthy and expensive, and that for some individuals, documentation complications could pop up that were not solvable (or it took an even greater amount of time, effort, and money to solve them). Ray sometimes would think, "The immigration process can take a long time and be expensive as well, so how in the world is Miguel going to bring all his brothers and sisters to the USA?"

Currently, at the writing of this book, Ray is eighty-five years old, and when my brother Jorge and I visit him, he stills tells us that he's never seen anyone work straight for thirty days in a row, starting from early morning to very late, every day, like Miguel did. For as long as Ray can remember, he's never seen anyone work like Miguel. He remembers that for about fifteen or so years, he would see Miguel socially only one day a month when they gathered for an afternoon barbeque.

Ray told us that sometimes he would visit Miguel at the workshop late at night, sitting at one of the nearby silversmith workbenches as Miguel sat at his own, working away. Ray would chat with Miguel, talking about business, family, and life while Miguel worked. Ray commented that it was apparent that Miguel was on a mission to earn and succeed with his plan to have a house, a car, and the entire family together in Phoenix. Miguel even talked about how the Hernández and Fasio families would become great friends, celebrating life's happy events together and supporting one another through life's trials.

Ray describes Miguel as brilliant, a fast learner, and a man who was magnetic and charismatic. He recalls how Miguel could make a friend like a spark.

In those two years from 1957 to 1959, even with the ongoing hard work, Miguel made time to enjoy his role as godfather to Nellie's son Sampson. It was customary for a godfather to visit and celebrate a godchild's birthday, and Miguel carefully planned a trip to Window Rock to celebrate Sampson's first birthday and also visit Benjamin and Grace Begay and the rest of the family. However, on the day before the celebration, Sampson was taken ill. Miguel, who had made him a tiny silver cross with a row of fine turquoise stones embedded in it, ending up placing the cross on Sampson's neck just before Nellie took him to see the doctor. It turned out Sampson had an intestinal infection. He recovered, but there was no one-year birthday celebration.

In 1959, when Sampson was turning two, there was a party at Benjamin and Grace's in Window Rock. Similar to Sampson's baptismal celebration, Miguel drove there in his Ford Fairlane with Phil riding shotgun. Ray Fasio joined them as well, sitting in the backseat. The three admired the stunning scenery along the highway and had substantive conversations.

Phil told them, "You all know how I've been having headaches and feeling nauseous for the past few weeks? I finally made it to the doctor's yesterday, and they told me it's because my blood pressure is high. I'm supposed to change my diet, be careful to avoid salty foods, and in a few weeks, I should feel better. Otherwise, I might have to take some pills for it. I've noticed how I've had to slow down on how much I can work. I hope I can pick back up soon."

Ray explained, "Phil, I know how troubling it is to have persistent headaches. I have an almost constant ringing in my ears, and I get really bad headaches a lot. It's been happening for years now, ever since my time in the war."

"Yes, I remember you telling me that before," Phil confirmed.

Ray continued, "I've found that when I hang out with Miguel, he is such a good listener, that I can talk and tell him about the nightmares and those scary memories—and that makes my nightmares go away. And when I can sleep soundly, the headaches disappear, and the ringing reduces too. I'm no doctor, but the medicine I recommend is our friend, Miguel."

Before Miguel could respond, Phil quickly replied, "I know that's right!"

Miguel told them, "You all are too much. You all are the ones that act as my medicine—really, my energy. I get to tell you about my goal of bringing my family to the United States, and because you encourage me, I'm able to keep up the long hours of work."

Ray observed, "I, for one, find it incredible that you are able to give us so much of your time when you've got so much on your plate to take care of."

"Speaking of seeing a doctor," Miguel said, "When I was at the tortilla shop last week, I met this lady and her husband, and they asked me about a doctor. Apparently they're living in a shack that's behind the Miller-Bryant apartment complex. The lady told me that her husband's boss told him he'd have to let him go if he kept having seizures."

Phil interjected, "I think I know the lady you're talking about. She was crying when I met her. She needed to find a doctor for her husband. I told her about my doctor at the Indian Hospital, but I knew she wouldn't qualify because she wasn't a Native American."

"Yes, I imagine it's the same lady," Miguel agreed, "And I figured it was possible that Dr. Schwartz could help the husband."

Ray interjected, "Remind me who Dr. Schwartz is."

"He's the man Olivia has been dating for a year, maybe two, now. He's a nice guy, and he's helped, free of charge, other people that Olivia, Pedro, and I have asked him about. I talked to Olivia and she spoke to Dr. Schwartz, and he did it. The husband came to his office and got a thorough physical as well as a prescription for the medication he needs to keep the seizures under control."

"That's the thing about you, Miguel—you provide people with solutions," Phil asserted.

"It's true, Miguel," Ray added, "You aren't just a great listener. When it's time for action, you act and get things done."

Miguel countered, "I wouldn't say I got things done. In this case, Olivia and her boyfriend got it done. Dr. Schwartz even had a month's worth of the medication on hand for the husband to begin taking, free of charge. That's pretty great."

Phil spoke up again, "Ray, I don't know if you realize it, but Nellie's parents, Benjamin and Grace Begay—they don't speak much English. Benjamin is Navajo, and Grace is Apache. Last time we were here at Sampson's baptism, it was a fun celebration. Everybody was talking, exchanging stories—but we were primarily speaking Navajo with some Apache and Spanish in the mix. We must've said only ten words of English."

"Yes, Miguel already told me that. But he promised that you all would be my translators when I needed it," Ray responded.

"You better believe it," Phil confirmed, " I was just about to say that Miguel and I would translate everything for you. And you're going to love little Sampson. He's eating, walking, and talking. He seems like a little athlete too. Super strong and fearless. It's going to be a great party. Fine Christian people. I can't wait to see them again."

As Phil was talking, Miguel was slowly moving his head up and down, and then turning it back and forth. He'd been doing it off and on since he'd woken that day.

"Phil, do you think you could drive for a while?" Miguel asked, explaining, "I woke up with a crook in my neck, and usually it gets better as the day goes on, but this time it's feeling worse. And as we were just talking about headaches, I notice that I'm starting to get one."

"Of course, I'll drive. We should stop at the next gas station too and get you some aspirin," Phil answered.

"No, I should be fine. I think you driving will make it better," Miguel replied.

Once they stopped and switched seats, Phil started driving, and Ray continued the conversation, asking Miguel, "Have you heard from your father lately?"

"I've sent three letters since my visit two years ago. The last letter I received was two months ago. They seem to be doing well. There's been little mention of my father's health, so that seems good. But it's hard to tell because my father's the one who has been writing me. However, I think if things were really bad, Chucho would write me like he did before."

Around this time, the car made the turn down the pine tree-lined drive, and the reception committee of hounds began baying notice of their arrival. Benjamin and Grace exited the cabin with the robust-looking Sampson in Grace's arms. Everyone started hugging and shaking hands and admiring Sampson.

Phil didn't want to dampen the jolly mood, but he was worried, so he asked Miguel, "Tell me how you're feeling because you don't look like you're feeling very good."

Grace and Benjamin were nodding their heads in agreement. Benjamin spoke up, "I agree with Phil. What's going on with you, Miguel?"

"It's a headache," Miguel explained to them, "but I will be okay."

At this point, though everyone was speaking Navajo, Ray could tell they were discussing Miguel. Ray touched the back of Miguel's head, noting, "Miguel, you have a red spot on your head back here."

Miguel explained, first in English to Ray and then in Navajo to everyone else, "It's because two days ago, I hit my head pretty hard on an old wooden doorframe. It's fine. I'm not worried."

To convince everyone he was okay, Miguel took Sampson from Grace's arms and lifted him up in the air, and the boy laughed and looked around to see everyone. Sampson's smile was wide and showed off his newly sprouted front teeth. He grabbed Miguel's cheeks and hugged him.

Miguel observed, "Sampson, you are very friendly. Not shy at all."

Grace told the little boy, "Sampson, this is your godfather, Miguel."

Sampson smiled and then indicated he wanted to be back in Grace's arms. As she was taking him, Miguel asked, "Where's Nellie and Grace? What about Roger?"

Benjamin replied, "They're coming," and then he added, "Plus, we have a surprise—Sampson's father is arriving today. It will be his first time seeing Sampson."

All the while, Phil was translating to Ray, and he also explained to Ray that Sampson's father was in the military, and that's why he was only just meeting Sampson. Ray nodded his head, for he understood the sacrifices of military service.

As everyone was making their way inside the cabin, Grace quietly asked Miguel, "Are you okay? Tell me."

"I would love a glass of cold water and an aspirin, Grace," he answered.

"Let me feel your head too," Grace requested. And upon feeling his head, she told him, "Miguel, you have a fever."

"Grace, I'll be fine. The water and aspirin will help."

Once the rest of the family had arrived, including Sampson's long-awaited father, there was a jovial celebration. Turkey, mashed potatoes, gravy, and cranberry sauce for dinner with apple pie for dessert, and apple pie was a favorite of Miguel. After hearty eating and warm conversation, everyone went to bed.

In the morning, Phil discovered Miguel awake and sitting at the kitchen table. The left side of his scalp was red and very swollen. When Phil touched his forehead, he could tell that Miguel was dangerously hot with fever.

Phil told Miguel, "We must take you to the hospital."

Ray helped Miguel make it to the car while Phil woke Grace to explain what was happening. Grace could hear the car driving away as she said a prayer, asking God to watch over Miguel.

Miguel was very ill by that time. He was in agony and felt confused. They arrived at Phoenix's downtown hospital around midday. The staff discovered a large abscess under Miguel's scalp. He was in the operating room, during which time surgical staff drained the abscess under the scalp.

Phil and Ray never left the hospital during that time. They contacted the Lamberts, Olivia, and Pedro, all of whom arrived early the next morning to be present when Miguel woke.

Upon opening his eyes and seeing everyone around him, Miguel was surprised and confused. Everyone had looks of great concern drawn on their faces. Olivia and Margaret were crying.

"*Que pasa*? What's going on? Why are you crying?" Miguel asked.

No one spoke. Then Doc Lambert handed Miguel a telegram. Miguel took it and read that our father had died, and the family was summoning him back to La Mira.

Miguel didn't speak. He closed his eyes, as if trying to fall asleep. Everyone was watching him. Phil and Ray didn't know what was going on, for they hadn't known about the telegram. They'd thought everyone's concern and sadness were due to Miguel's illness.

Phil turned to Olivia to quietly ask, "Is it your father?"

"Yes," Olivia confirmed, explaining, "Margaret drove over last night to let us know that a telegram arrived at the jewelry shop for Miguel. I was the first one to read it. *Qué terrible*! We need to go to La Mira. We need to be with the family."

As she was speaking, a doctor entered the room. Noticing the sadness and worry on everyone's faces, he reassured them, saying, "Do not worry. Miguel is going to be okay. He simply needs to recover, but he will be fine."

That's when Doc spoke up to explain to the doctor, "We just got news that his father died in Mexico."

Realizing the doctor was in the room, Miguel opened his eyes and looked at the man, asking, "Sir, when can I leave?"

The doctor informed him, "While you will be fine, at present you are still sick. You have blood poisoning from an aggressive infection. You had an abscess that likely came from a dirty nail. I've given you a tetanus injection, and you will need antibiotics by vein for a few days."

Miguel waited for the doctor to finish speaking only to repeat his question, "Sir, when can I leave?"

"You must stay here for two days, possibly three. You'll need antibiotics by mouth for three weeks."

Miguel pleaded, "I have to go to Mexico to be with the children and their mother. I need to be at the funeral, which is likely in three days. I'd like to leave this evening, tomorrow at the latest. Please!" Then he burst into tears, lamenting, "I should have paid more attention to my father. All these years of smoking and drinking right in front of me, and I didn't do anything about it!"

"*Hermano, no. No es tu culpa*. Don't torture yourself," Olivia countered. "Pedro and I will go—"

"No, that's not possible. You can't go because the family you work for is so strict. If you go, you might lose your immigration status. Just you two being here now puts you in jeopardy. No—it's better I go," Miguel retorted, "You need to stay here and work. I'm in a better position to go."

"Yes, Miguel should go," Margaret stated, "but only after the doctor discharges him."

Phil stated solemnly, "I will go with you, Miguel."

"Me too," Ray added.

Miguel ended up spending two days in the hospital, receiving intravenous drugs to help with the blood infection. When he was discharged, he was prescribed three antibiotics that he would have to take for the next twenty days. This was necessary because, as the doctor explained, "The operation isn't the issue. It's the type of infection you have in your blood. That's why your recovery will be slow—good but slow."

When it was time for Miguel to board the bus in Phoenix, the first of many buses to finally reach La Mira, no one else was accompanying him. Olivia asked her employer if she and Pedro could take two weeks' unpaid leave, but they were told they'd lose their jobs and that there were three other people inquiring after their jobs as well.

The day before, Phil had had a mild stroke due to high blood pressure. His doctor warned him against doing the journey because he needed to recovery. Phil was broken-hearted.

Ray also had a crisis on his hands that unfolded while Miguel was in the hospital. Three of his best workers ended up getting deported, so Ray was having to sort out their situation and at the same time rearrange the next few weeks' worth of jobs, which were now in disarray due to the absence of those key workers.

The Lamberts—as was typical—were stellar. They told Miguel he would always have a job with them. They fronted him five hundred dollars, which in 1959 was about a month's worth of wages. They knew he'd need the extra cash and told him not to worry about paying them back quickly. It was a loan of honor based on a handshake.

Miguel's fellow silversmiths gave him two hundred dollars. Phil, separately, gave Miguel two hundred fifty dollars. These weren't loans. They were gifts. From brother to brother. From compassionate human beings Miguel considered family rather than coworkers.

Though supported by his Phoenix family, Miguel was tremendously agitated, anxious, and sad when he boarded that bus in Phoenix. He desperately wanted to be with our family and present at our father's funeral. He felt incredibly guilty and upset that he hadn't done more, done something, to have gotten our father to change his habits. He was overcome by this grief.

Miguel went on to explain to Fernando, "Yes, it will be a long ride to La Mira. My father just died, and I need to be there for his funeral if I can make it in time. I need to be there for my father's wife and my many siblings who are suffering and afraid for their futures. And, as you can see, I have a scar on my scalp from that awful abscess. But now, because of you, Fernando, I am better prepared mentally and spiritually. As you said, it all rests in the power of the mind. I totally agree and lean on your sense of bravery in this time of sorrow."

At Hermosillo, Miguel and Fernando said goodbye. Fernando wished Miguel continued strength on his journey.

In turn, Miguel told him, "I wish you all the best of luck in school. I am most certain you will achieve your goals."

They shook hands, hugged, and Fernando left, slowly moving away in one direction while Miguel searched among the buses for the one traveling to Guaymas. At Guaymas he would change buses again as he would need to once again in Culiacan and then Guadalajara.

With his heart and mind more at ease, Miguel engaged in conversations with the many people he met in his travel—business people, locals, students, etc., all with specific destinations. Some traveling to close a deal, some to visit loved ones, others starting new jobs or looking for work, others going to school in Guadalajara, a city with several universities.

Upon arriving in Guadalajara, Miguel changed to another bus that would take him to Uruapan, then onwards down to Los Coyotes, and finally to La Mira. He felt total tranquility. He again had lengthy and deep conversations with people about their families, their occupations, and their goals for their children and grandchildren.

Miguel had no children, but in reality, he had us, so he talked about Pedro, Olivia, Surama, Jorge, me, and the rest of us. He talked about how he was returning to La Mira due to the death of our father. He shared his big plan of bringing my mother and the rest of us to the United States. He would smile when he thought of all these plans, and he felt good because he had a great job and coworkers who were brothers, pulling for him and awaiting his return. He knew as long as there was work, then there was no limit to how much he could earn.

He was smiling and talking to people with enthusiasm and optimism.

He arrived at Los Coyotes to change to the familiar pickup with benches in its bed and a tarp on top. He didn't see Benjamín Contreras, his wife, or daughter. It had been eight years since he'd first met them when leaving La Mira with our father to go to the USA. Even still, as he had two years earlier when passing through Los Coyotes, he looked for them, hoping to say hello.

When Miguel finally arrived in La Mira, there was no celebratory arrival parade. The villagers were in mourning over our father's death, and they knew how grief-stricken Miguel would be as well. A small group of people met Miguel. Isidro Morales again sent a fast-running child to fetch my grandfather and Chucho. They both met Miguel when he was halfway into the walk to our house.

Solemnly Miguel embraced each man.

Chucho gently explained to him, "The funeral and burial couldn't wait."

Miguel wasn't surprised. He had expected it. He understood but obviously wasn't happy about missing it.

Miguel found us at our small adobe home. He hugged each of us in turn. I could tell he'd been crying. I noticed the bandage on his scalp. Later, when he was changing it, I'd see that it was covering a two-inch sized slit on his scalp that was well on its way to healing.

While Mamá wanted Miguel to rest, he insisted upon visiting Papá's grave immediately. He asked my grandfather and me to accompany him.

When we arrived at the cemetery, Miguel approached the fresh plot and fell to his knees.

"Papá," Miguel began, "I beg you for forgiveness because I wasn't here for you at your funeral." When he paused to take in a breath, he heard the wind whispering in the leaves and what sounded like the bellowing cries of a violin.

"I'm so sorry about my absence. And years ago, when we had an argument and I moved out of the house and lived with Chucho for awhile—I'm so sorry. Please forgive me.

"It was Chucho who talked me into going back home, and I thank Chucho for his patience, kindness, and advice.

"Papá, I will miss you greatly, and although I have been away for many years, I always thought of you. You were always on my mind."

At this point my grandfather and I began to walk away to give Miguel some private time at the graveside, but he turned to us, saying, "Don't leave. Stay here by my side."

Miguel then told our father, again as if conversing with him, "I will be taking Edgar with me back to the United States, and I want your blessing."

I looked at my grandfather, smiled, and hugged him. Then I went to my brother and hugged him. I cried for a moment.

My grandfather placed his right arm around my shoulder and asked, "You see the moon coming through the large leaves?"

"Yes," I confirmed, looking at the moon.

"It's a moon with a great future for you, Edgar. It's the right time for you to begin a new journey, a journey that will prove to be great for all of us, especially for you. I will miss you terribly, but your future is with your brother. It is the right time for you to go."

The following day we held a remembrance feast for our father. It was a large gathering with many families doing the cooking. The townspeople stood in long lines to embrace Nena and Miguel, offering condolences. There were many offers to help my mother and my siblings and me as best as our fellow villagers could. Many had no real economic means to do so, but my mother and the family greatly appreciated their love and genuine desire to help.

I spent most of the afternoon and night with my grandfather, excited about going to the United States with my brother. My mother was busy trying to visit with all our guests. She tried to listen to everyone's conversation as she appreciated their sincere condolences.

Before our departure Miguel, Chucho, and my mother had a serious talk about finances and the future. Miguel shared, "I promised Papá that I would bring you, Nena, and the children to the United States, and that's a sacred promise that I shall keep. However, I need at least four, maybe five, years to earn and save enough to get the house I'm renovating ready and to pay for everyone's immigration requirements."

Chucho had already sold Miguel's thirty acres of coconut palms two years prior. Miguel instructed Chucho to now sell our mother and father's orchard, which was also around thirty acres and consisted mostly of coconut palms, but also mango and guava trees, as well as pineapple plants. Nena would receive that money.

Finally, the day of our departure arrived. I was leaving La Mira to go to America with my beloved older brother, Miguel. *Qué fabuloso!* At the same time, I was leaving my grandfather, my mother, Lupe, Asunción, Reyna, and Manuel. I didn't know if I'd ever see my grandfather again. And I didn't know how many years it would be until Miguel and I would reunite with the rest of the family in the USA. *Qué triste! Qué trágico!* Even at nine years old, I recognized that I was in a bittersweet situation.

After tearful goodbyes, Miguel and I boarded the pickup truck and sat down on one of the wooden benches in its bed. An oil-stained tarp offered us some shade and protection from the dust. Once the truck drove away, my whole family, who stood waving and crying, soon disappeared behind a curtain of dust.

It was my first time making the several-day journey from La Mira to Nogales. Over those days, Miguel and I had many long conversations. We talked about telephones, televisions, cars, movie theaters, bicycles, roller skates, vanilla milkshakes, and shopping centers, all of which were totally new to me. I was fascinated, curious, and at times frightened.

Miguel also had long conversations with fellow travelers. He seemed a magnet for attracting people and making new friends. At times, however, he would go off in a mental sleep-rest-trance state with his eyes shut. I was very protective about people talking to him during these quiet moments.

A frequent topic people wanted to discuss was how to immigrate to the USA. People of all kinds—professionals and non-professionals, laborers, young parents, elderly people, and students—wanted to learn how it worked. Some professionals were hoping to find a sponsor but had no ability to contact anyone. Other people wanted to come in as a family unit but also needed a sponsor. Some talked about work visas or seasonal temporary visas for farming work of any type.

I noticed that Miguel was a good listener. He commented only when it seemed the speaker wanted to know particular facts. Miguel, at that time, had already begun to understand many of the intricacies of the immigration process, so he had solid facts to offer if people asked.

Some people talked about entering illegally by way of a *pollero*, a term that in recent decades changed to *coyote*. The terms refer to human smugglers. *Polleros* and *coyotes* smuggle people into the USA for a fee. Because Miguel knew a bit about the rogue work of *polleros*, he discouraged people from entertaining the method, explaining, "It's crude, unpredictable, and dangerous. Instead, make the effort to get all of your papers together and get a proper green card. Sure, snags can come up in the immigration process even with proper planning, but snags can be worked out."

Sometimes Miguel would use me as an example to explain the immigration process: "Take Edgar here, he's going to immigrate with ease. He's only nine-and-a-half years old, and he'll be with me to provide for him and act as his sponsor. He could immigrate either with a student visa or a green card. A student visa is easier and requires less time to process. For adults it's different. You are required to have a job waiting in the USA, and your sponsor would be the American business owner providing that job. Another option is marrying an American citizen."

While I was unfamiliar with the immigration process, green cards, visas, and much that Miguel was discussing, I was impressed with the information he provided.

⎯⎯•••⎯⎯

Aurelio was the notary who'd assisted Miguel in getting his green card in 1951. Miguel wanted to consult with Aurelio about getting my green card as well. Consequently, soon after we arrived in Nogales, we went to his office.

At the office, we found a young couple with a four-year-old child waiting to meet with Aurelio as well. They were from the Mexican state of Nayarit and had been pursuing legal immigration for two-and-a-half years already. The husband was a water engineer, and after some searching, Aurelio was able to locate a contact in an engineering firm in Tucson that needed an agricultural engineer. The man's Spanish was considered an asset with the farming community in that area of Arizona. The couple was relieved that after years of trying, they had a sponsor and would get to move to the United States where their young son could learn English and become educated.

"That's wonderful," Miguel told them, adding, "That's what I want for Edgar too."

When Aurelio opened the door of his office to greet us, it seemed the doorway was about a foot too short for him. Peering at us from the doorway, he reminded me of a turtle sticking its head out of its shell. He was tall and skinny, a praying mantis, palm tree figure, with a small head and long arms, and hunched over because his height didn't match the contours of the room. Miguel had already told me about Aurelio's unusual appearance. He'd also let me know how intelligent and dedicated Aurelio was in helping people get their green cards.

When it was our turn, Miguel and Aurelio did the talking, and I listened. I was impressed with how much Aurelio knew about our family. He asked Miguel about our father. He knew that I was among Miguel's many siblings that Miguel was immigrating to the USA. He was well informed and compassionate.

After examining all the papers Miguel had gathered for my immigration, Aurelio was optimistic that everything was in order. He did point out, "While your papers appear complete, expect the Consulate to take twenty-four to forty-eight hours to review them."

Aurelio walked us to the Consulate, and because he wouldn't be allowed into our interviews, he wished us well and told us to check in with him afterwards.

Inside the Consulate, after an expected wait, our number was called, and we proceeded to meet with an immigration officer, the first of several interviews.

The officer arranged all the papers on the desk in front of her and began examining each one.

In perfect Spanish, she told my brother, "You have very nice letters, sir, and you should be proud of all the things your friends and your employer said about you."

Then she asked about our father. After Miguel explained that he recently died, she kindly replied, "I'm sorry about your loss."

Next, she asked about a death certificate. Basically an official certificate of death had to be filed, first in the government offices of La Mira, and then transferred over to Uruapan for proper recording, and then a copy gathered to show the Consulate.

Surprised and confused, Miguel pointed out, "I didn't think a certificate of our father's death was necessary considering we have an official letter from Edgar's mother granting me power of attorney over him. This grants me total responsibility for him."

"I'm sorry, but we have to have a copy of the officially filed death certificate. This certificate has to be signed by the filer in the city of Uruapan, Mexico. Without it, it suggests that Edgar's father may be alive and not in support of that letter from Edgar's mother granting you power of attorney over him."

Miguel was stunned. I didn't know what to say.

We left the Consulate and headed immediately back to Aurelio's office. When we told him the news, he too was shocked, for he hadn't foreseen this.

Because the bureaucratic machine of most any government typically moves at a mind-numbingly slow pace, and perhaps even more so in Mexico, Aurelio and Miguel knew it could take a few months, or perhaps even a year, for the death certificate to be properly filed and recorded in Uruapan.

The result—a big problem. As I've already mentioned and can't emphasize enough, Miguel had responsibilities in Phoenix. Plus, he had responsibilities in Mexico, meaning my mother and siblings. He was desperate to continue working the long hours to meet his promise of bringing my siblings and mother to the USA and also to complete the renovation of the 206 N. 9th Street property. He'd already expected that to take five to six years of concentrated effort. So, waiting with me in Nogales, Mexico—for a few months, a half-year, or a year—would add even more time before the ultimate goal would be accomplished. Sure, he could probably find work again at a Nogales jewelry shop, but it wouldn't pay as much and it could mean that the Lamberts would replace him as well.

Because of this incredibly difficult situation, at Aurelio's suggestion and with my consent, Miguel agreed that I should cross the border and live with him in the USA illegally while we waited for the death certificate to get filed. Illegal entry was not something either Aurelio or Miguel condoned at all. We all hated it. But, we did it anyway.

At the age of nine, I was living and going to elementary school in the United States without papers. I was an illegal.

Chapter 6

MAN AND GOD

Several months before Sampson's second birthday and our father's death, Miguel and Phil were enjoying *carne asada* at a Mexican restaurant in Phoenix when a stampede occurred. Servers, cooks, dishwashers, fellow patrons—suddenly and without warning—were dashing for the door. There was an almost violent intensity about it, like they were fleeing a tidal wave or a ticking time bomb.

With fear in his eyes, Phil asked Miguel, "What's happening? Are we in danger?"

As Phil was moving to get to his feet, Miguel replied, "We're okay, Phil. You can stay seated. This is an immigration raid."

Phil sat back down at the table, his face showing that he was confused but that he trusted Miguel. They sat silently watching as two officers in green uniforms marched the seven people that they had corralled out the door.

"An immigration raid? I don't get it," Phil murmured.

Miguel explained, "Many of the people working and eating here apparently had no papers, so when they saw the men in green uniforms, they knew it was La Migra, or immigration officers, so they fled. But those seven got trapped, and the officers were able to snare them."

Before Phil could ask more questions, the restaurant owner came to their table to tell them, "We're sorry, but we're closing for now. I'm going to have to ask you all to leave. We should be open again tomorrow or the day after, and I hope you'll come back. Sorry for the inconvenience."

Once outside, one of the officers in green approached Miguel and Phil, and demanded, "*Papeles*? Can I see your papers?"

Phil's face showed he was puzzled. When he saw Miguel moving for his wallet, he got out his as well. Miguel handed the officer his driver's license and green card, and the officer inspected both carefully and then returned them. Next Phil handed over his driver's license. The officer gave it a quick glance and then returned it.

The officer asked Miguel, "Do you frequent this place?"

Miguel answered, "I was here about two months ago."

"Do you know anyone here?" he asked.

Though it was apparent the officer was questioning only Miguel, Phil piped in, answering, "No, sir, we do not."

Still looking at Miguel, he inquired, "Do you have friends here?"

When Phil began to answer, the officer cut him off indicating he wanted to hear from Miguel only.

"No, sir, we don't," Miguel answered.

The officer then stopped the interrogating, and Miguel and Phil got in the Ford Fairlane and departed.

Once in the car, Phil observed, "That was weird. It was like he assumed you were a criminal."

Miguel didn't say anything.

Phil asked, "You've got your green card, and you're working hard to get your brothers and sisters green cards too. Why didn't those other people have theirs?"

Miguel replied, "Phil, even though I had all my papers in order, I had to wait in Nogales for a few months before I was able to complete the process and get my green card."

"You mean it's not just getting papers together and paying some fees?" Phil asked.

"No. You also have to have a sponsor, in my case, the Lamberts. They own their own business, and they have the paperwork to prove it's a real business and that they can pay my wages. Plus, they were willing to vouch for me as one of their employees. Without a business owner sponsor—or an American spouse, which is the other way, marrying an American citizen—you can't get a green card. It doesn't matter if you have all your papers in order and the money to pay the fees. And it's not easy—especially for people coming from Mexico who don't know any Americans at all. No connections in the USA and they don't speak any English either—to find a business owner who will sponsor them is all but impossible. The Lamberts are honest-to-God miracles for me."

Phil observed, "But those people came here anyway. You didn't have to wait in Nogales. You could've come over anyway. Seems to me once you're over here and working, then it would be easier to find a sponsor than just waiting in Mexico."

"A lot of Mexicans come to that same conclusion. They cross the border illegally, often hiring a *pollero* to help them cross. But, once they are here, they are working and living in fear of La Migra. Just think, those folks that we saw get rounded up—they might have friends, families, homes, savings, whole lives over here in America, but now they are going to get deported, taken back to Mexico, and released somewhere over there—and none of their friends and family in America will have any clue what happened to them. It could take weeks or months for them to receive word. For those deported folks, some will give up and stay in Mexico. Others will cross back in illegally. They'll have to find new work, new housing, new everything only to live in fear of another raid and once again getting deported and losing everything. It's no way to live."

"Is that why you waited it out in Nogales?" Phil asked.

"Two reasons—one, I had a good job at a jewelry store in Nogales that allowed me to earn money. Secondly, I had great guidance from Aurelio. I feel lucky to know him. He works helping people navigate the immigration system to get green cards and enter and work in the United States legally. He built up a lot of contacts in the US to help people like me find sponsors. He found my situation a little more difficult, as finding a sponsor for a jeweler is more difficult than for a good plumber, electrician, mason, architect, or nurse."

"How about those people who don't have schooling or a real trade?" asked Phil.

"I remember Aurelio telling me that sometimes it's nearly impossible to find a sponsor in some cases, but sometimes he's found sponsors for general laborers. Some American farmers will take on people. While sometimes it can be quite challenging for Aurelio to find sponsors, his fee is less than what a *pollero* charges, and his way might be slower but it's safe because you won't get deported when you have a sponsor! But if you cross illegally, now that's a terrible gamble. Something I wouldn't do. Plus, it's dishonest and plain wrong."

Phil responded, "Yes, it sure seems risky. A real gamble with destiny."

Witnessing this raid and then talking to Phil about it acted as the catalyst for Miguel to turn an idea that had long been developing inside him into fruition. Five years earlier, back in 1954, Miguel first beheld the terror and sadness of an immigration raid. And since that time he had been wondering what he could do to aid his Mexican brethren in getting their green cards, so they could live with honor and without fear in the United States.

Because of the close work he'd done with Aurelio to get his green card and the research he was doing to gather the necessary papers for immigrating the rest of the family, Miguel felt fairly confident in his ability to help other people navigate most of the immigration process. Primarily these would be people already in the US illegally, who couldn't access Aurelio in Nogales, Mexico. Miguel decided he could be their informal point person.

However, he never imagined that just a few months later, at the same time he was helping illegal Mexicans in the United States, he would be harboring me as an illegal in the US as well. It was a bitter pill to swallow.

———

While I was thrilled to arrive in Phoenix, eager to start school, meet new friends and teachers, and excited to learn English, I could tell Miguel was deeply troubled. He'd already warned me about the possibility of deportation raids and how I could get captured in a raid. He explained that he'd witnessed several and that they were chaotic, intense, and frightening—and that was just how it felt to simply witness them. He couldn't imagine how upsetting it was for those who were fleeing or those that got caught and deported.

I knew he felt guilty about disregarding the law and about putting me in such a risky situation. When he explained the whole situation to Margaret Lambert, he voiced the guilt, pain, and displeasure he felt.

Margaret told him, "Miguel, you found yourself in a very tough spot, and you did the best you could do. I don't like it either, but I know you're doing the best you can do for Edgar given the circumstances. And Doc and I are going to do all we can to help you keep Edgar safe and occupied in the shop when he's not at school. It's going to be okay, and before any of us know it, his paperwork will get in order and he'll have his green card. Don't you worry."

I, personally, wasn't worried. I was mesmerized by the novelty of American life—the apartment above the shop, the sleek cars and trucks, the rich milkshakes and juicy hamburgers, the wide and clean streets, the always-available electricity and electric lights, the super tall buildings, the refrigerator, the television, and the radio! Miguel's American family was so kind and generous—Margaret, Doc, Phil, Nellie, Grace, and Ray Fasio. I deeply missed my mother, grandfather, and siblings in La Mira, but I quickly immersed myself in my new American life. As I was hungry to learn and to succeed in this new world of vast opportunities, once I started school, I became even happier.

Miguel was a man on a mission to earn, earn, earn. Each day he left the apartment and started work around 5 am. I would see him each day after I returned from school to do chores in the shop. After an hour or two I had completed my shop duties, though Miguel continued to work, only stopping for the day after dark. Of course, he'd take a break to eat dinner with me, but he knew that I was responsible and focused on completing my homework and shop chores, so I didn't need his supervision. Plus, Margaret and I would spend time together. She was particularly excited about having me around. We grew close, and she became a second mother to me.

Though preoccupied with earning money, Miguel continued to feel guilt about my illegal status. When he and I were out and about in Phoenix, he would furtively scan our locale, near and far, searching for "officers in green." It was like we were on the run the way he'd survey parking lots, entrances and exits, and far up and down the sidewalks and streets. When Ray warned us that immigration inspectors were making the rounds in southwest Phoenix, this unwelcoming information added to Miguel's already considerable level of anxiety.

However, something that delighted Miguel was seeing me working and helping Margaret.

In fact, I did little to no socializing outside of school unless I was with Miguel, Margaret, or Phil. Phil taught me how to make leather braids for bolo ties, each of which earned me twenty-five cents. I would get the leather strips and braid them. I got so good at making them I could almost do them in my sleep.

Gangs around our neighborhood were still in their infancy, but assaults on students walking to school and also on school grounds were on the rise. This possibility of violence combined with the deportation raids gave me even more reason to keep a low profile and to stick to school or the shop, for the most part at least.

———◆———

Soon after Miguel returned to Phoenix with me, Ray Fasio met with him. He told Miguel the whole story on what happened to those three key employees that got deported about three-and-a-half weeks earlier. The three were at a laundromat that had been raided and that was how they got caught. Ray knew that Miguel had been advising Mexicans working illegally in the Phoenix area on how to get their green cards, even going to the Consulate himself to get applications for them, so Ray asked if Miguel could help the three workers as well. Apparently, they'd made their way back to Nogales but needed help with the immigration process.

Miguel told Ray, "I'm more than happy to help."

Miguel was already planning to return to Nogales in the next few days because just the day before, he'd promised a man named Alfonso that he would help him get his green card. As he was going to the Consulate in Nogales to get an application for Alfonso, he explained to Ray that he could easily meet with the three workers there and start them on the application process as well.

Miguel cautioned Ray, "It could take them a few months to receive all the needed certificates, letters of recommendation, and such, from their hometowns in Mexico. I'm telling you this, Ray, so you don't get your hopes up that they'll be back next week and working with your swamp coolers. It's possible, depending on what papers they have on hand, but if they don't have any papers at all—then it could take months. Even a year."

"Miguel, I figured that already, but I thank you for telling it to me straight. I knew I could count on you for assistance and frankness."

"Lucky for them that they used fake names when they were deported, so they can apply for green cards using their real names," Miguel commented.

———

About Alfonso—the day before, Miguel was evaluating the house on 206 N. 9th Street, surveying the remodeling that had been done and planning out what to do next. As he stood on the front porch contemplating, he noticed a man walking by on the sidewalk in front of the house. As was his custom, Miguel hollered out a greeting, in English and Spanish, "Good afternoon, friend. *Buenas tardes, amigo. Espero que estés bien.* I hope you are doing well."

With that opening, the man approached and the two began talking. The man let Miguel know his name was Alfonso, that he didn't speak English, and that he was in the US illegally and looking for work.

Miguel was still spinning emotionally from all that had happened to him—the hospital stay due to the abscess, our father's death, going to La Mira, bringing me back, and having me cross illegally. Because he felt overwhelmed by his own life's issues, he was unsure he could help Alfonso. He knew he didn't want to approach the Lamberts, seeing as they'd done so much for him as of late.

Finally, this is what he told Alfonso, "I'm going to help you find work, but there's some promises I'm going to need from you."

"*Sí, por supuesto. Dime.* Yes, of course. Tell me," Alfonso responded.

"I want you to not only find work, but also get your green card. I'll help you with the process, but I want you to agree to see it through."

Alfonso agreed, and Miguel went on to clarify to him that it wasn't just a matter of gathering the papers, but also Alfonso must keep his nose clean the months it would take until the green card came through. "To prove your dedication to a life in the USA, you're going to have to start taking English lessons too. You can't get in trouble with the police or get caught up in a raid, so you'll have to stay away from *cantinas*—and abstain from all liquor. It's about maintaining a low profile and focusing on working—that should be your top priority. Do you think you can do all this?"

Alfonso consented heartily and pledged to Miguel that he would do everything that Miguel advised.

Next, Miguel asked Alfonso to come with him, and they walked to a house on the opposite side of the street. This is the house where Miguel's good friends, the Davises, lived. Glen and Evelyn Davis were from Mississippi. Mr. Davis's father worked for an aerial pesticide company, and after he died, Mr. and Mrs. Davis decided to move to Phoenix where they'd inherited a small home. Once in Phoenix, Mr. Davis started his own termite and pesticide company, and it was successful.

Because they lived in a neighborhood in which Spanish was the prevalent language and because Mr. Davis's company worked with the Arizona farming community in which Spanish was also a commonplace language, the Davises learned to speak Spanish. And it was the Davises that Miguel decided to approach first about work for Alfonso.

After Miguel knocked on the door, Mr. Davis opened it and greeted him with enthusiasm. Mrs. Davis came to the door too. Both noted, "Miguel, we haven't seen you at your property for a while. We hope you're doing well. Please come in and talk to us."

Miguel pointed to Alfonso and introduced him, requesting that they speak in Spanish so Alfonso could follow the conversation. The Davises agreed, and everyone entered the house.

Mrs. Davis hurried to get everyone glasses of milk and slices of her famous chocolate cake while Mr. Davis sat down with Miguel and Alfonso. Once everyone had servings of milk and cake, Miguel related to the Davises his unexpected stay at the hospital and trip to Mexico following our father's death.

Both the Davises gave Miguel their sincere condolences. Then the conversation turned to Alfonso, who had been sitting and listening attentively the whole time.

Alfonso explained his situation—that he was in the USA illegally and looking for work. He also iterated the promises he'd made Miguel and his appreciation that Miguel would help him find work and get a green card.

Without Miguel or Alfonso's prompting, Mr. Davis said, "Alfonso, it just so happens that we need another employee at my pesticide business." He went on to explain the type of work the position entailed and that if Alfonso proved a dedicated employee, Mr. Davis would be happy to act as his sponsor for a green card.

Alfonso accepted the job offer and promised again that he would prove himself dedicated, responsible, and honest.

Mr. Davis next asked Alfonso, "Where are you living now?"

Alfonso admitted that he'd been wandering, staying in abandoned buildings while he was looking for work.

Miguel already knew the Davises didn't have accommodations for Alfonso—asking that of them would be too much—but he had an idea. While the house he was refurbishing was far from complete, its back area was surrounded by a secure wooden fence and also contained a large seven-bay garage that had stored the previous owner's collection of antique cars.

"Sure, it's a bit rustic, but the conditions are better than an abandoned building. It's certainly much safer. And there's running water from a spigot as well as electric lights. Alfonso, if you like, you could stay there. You can stay as long as you need to get back on your feet, save some money, and get a place of your own."

Alfonso eagerly took Miguel up on the offer. Not only that, he regularly dedicated his free time to making needed repairs on the run-down house.

And so, Alfonso became the first of many guests that Miguel would welcome into his 206 N. 9th Street property. Some stayed for a few weeks, some a few months, some around a half-year. I want to point out too that Miguel referred to these people as "guests," "brothers," or "sisters"—never as "strangers"— because that's how he saw them and how he saw everyone: all people are brothers and sisters. We are all related, and as such we should treat one another with love, kindness, and respect.

Mr. and Mrs. Davis ended up treasuring Alfonso as a trusted employee. They sponsored him, and he attained his green card about a year later. As the years continued, Mr. and Mrs. Davis became part of the informal network of business owners that Miguel would connect hardworking individuals with. Most of the hardworking individuals, not all but most, were in the US illegally and needed sponsors. These trusted business owners frequently needed new employees, and they agreed to act as sponsors if necessary. Later, the network would flow the other direction as well, with business owners contacting Miguel to see whether he could locate a trustworthy person to work for them. This wasn't a side business for Miguel. It was an informal and unpaid assistance he gave to people in need.

In addition to the Davises with their pesticide company, other business owners in Miguel's informal network included Ray Fasio and his swamp cooler company, Stanley and his painting business,

Monte Sage and his excavating and concrete company, Jorge and his framing business, the Smith family electricians, the Campos brothers and their roofing company, the owners of a plumbing company, restaurant owners, hotel owners, and, of course, Doc and Margaret Lambert with their jewelry business. These business owners hired many individuals recommended by Miguel. The majority of these individuals were illegal aliens. The business owners trusted Miguel's recommendations, and, in turn, they agreed to sponsor the people they hired with the understanding that Miguel would guide the people through the long and complicated process of gathering the needed papers in order to get their green cards.

Take this family of three: Samuel, Pancha, and Ernie. Samuel and Pancha both had their green cards, but it was seventeen-year-old Ernie, Pancha's son from a previous marriage, who was in the US without papers. After Ernie narrowly escaped getting caught in a raid and deported, Pancha—incredibly upset and shaken—asked around, and people directed her to Miguel as someone who could potentially help.

While the meeting was presumably about Ernie, another issue emerged: Samuel's job status. Like Miguel, Samuel was a jeweler, but because of his deteriorating eyesight, he was frequently injuring himself and had problems with fine, detailed work when crafting jewelry. As a result, his jewelry pieces no longer looked good.

Therefore, their discussion encompassed two issues: one, looking to find a jewelry-making position for Samuel that did not require fine, detailed work, and, two, Ernie's vulnerability to deportation. Miguel sympathized with Pancha because I was in the same vulnerable position as Ernie.

Miguel asked around his network of business owners and found Samuel a great job with a jeweler friend. The job wasn't about detailed work. Instead, it focused on cleaning particular jewelry pieces, which was an important part of the new and emerging art of jewelry casting (jewelry casting involves filling a wax mold with molten metal, so the resulting piece is not hand-shaped and hand-crafted). Relatively quickly Samuel became situated and adept in the new role.

Unlike Samuel, Ernie's dilemma was much more complex. Actually, it was quite similar to the problem I faced getting my green card.

Pancha had already pursued the green card process for Ernie, but due to discrepancies in his documents (discrepancies that were similar to mine), Ernie never got his green card and entered the United Sates illegally via *pollero*. Because Ernie's father was in prison in Los Angeles for armed robbery, and he had documented mental problems, the Consulate didn't deem the letter of consent the father had signed authorizing Pancha as Ernie's sole guardian to be valid. The Consulate considered the father's consent equivocal. On top of this, Pancha's divorce with the father wasn't finalized.

To help Ernie, Miguel went to see a friend, Lee Kussard, a retired lawyer. Miguel originally met Mr. Kussard and his wife through the jewelry shop, for the couple adored Navajo Native American jewelry and, in particular, Miguel's pieces. Over the years, they developed a friendship. Mr. Kussard homed in on a letter Pancha's husband had signed prior to going to prison—a time when his mental state had been deemed sound—agreeing to a divorce. Apparently, the father and Pancha had met with a social worker on three different occasions to get assistance with their divorce. The social worker's official notes from these meetings also stated that the father had verbally agreed that he wanted Ernie to seek a green card.

Mr. Kussard felt that with these documents Pancha could petition a judge to agree that, by letter of the law, she should have all rights over Ernie, and nothing from her imprisoned husband's current situation should prohibit her from making decisions for the future of her son.

Pancha pursued Mr. Kussard's advice, and four months later, a judge signed such an order. About a year after their initial discussion with Miguel, Ernie got his green card. Let me add too that Mr. Kussard ended up helping Miguel many times over the years to resolve technical legal issues like this.

Perhaps you are wondering, as I was at nine-and-a-half years old, why Miguel would devote so much time and effort helping people navigate the extensive, expensive, and sometimes very complex immigration process, particularly when he had his own immigration goals for me and the rest of the family he was working on. And for individuals like Alfonso, why would he expose himself to the great risk that comes when you aid and harbor illegal aliens? Miguel himself at this time was only in the US on a green card, which, unlike citizenship, isn't permanent. Green card status entails yearly check-ins at the immigration office in which, among other things, they check police records. Green cards can be revoked and are revoked when their holders are prosecuted for breaking the law.

La Migra didn't solely raid business establishments like restaurants, grocery stores, and laundromats—they raided private residences as well. If the house Miguel was refurbishing got raided, officers would discover that Miguel was assisting illegal individuals, not one, but typically several. This would not only put him in jeopardy but make it practically impossible for me, my mother, and my siblings to get green cards. If Miguel was arrested for harboring individuals who were illegally living and working in the USA, then he could lose his green card. If this happened, then he'd certainly lose his status as a responsible and law-abiding person, a status required for him to serve as a sponsor for me and the rest of our family in our quest for green cards. It would also certainly negatively impact his own future citizenship application.

I'm sharing this not to emphasize that Miguel was a law-breaker but rather to emphasize Miguel's deep-seated belief in carrying out God's law, no matter the personal consequences. Matthew 7:12— the Golden Rule—states, "Therefore all things whatsoever ye would that men should do to you: do ye even so to them: for this is the law and the prophets." Miguel's belief in aiding his brothers and sisters was incredibly strong, stronger than simply pursuing his own goals with blinders on and ignoring good people who needed help. Also Miguel saw his assistance to these brothers and sisters in need as another way of furthering his ambitious goal of getting green cards for me and the rest of the family. I know this sounds contradictory—but let me explain.

At nine-and-a-half years old, I was perplexed not just by the risk Miguel was exposing himself, me, and our dreams of bringing the rest of the family to the USA to—but I also saw something else going on. Daily, practically seven days a week, Miguel was devoting twelve to sixteen hours working at the jewelry shop. On top of this, I noticed him at times spending whole days at the Consulate in Nogales, Mexico, helping people who weren't related to us by blood. From my part, as a child, I worried that Miguel was wearing himself down and spreading himself too thin. To me, the area to back off from was putting so much effort into helping these other people.

When I spoke to Miguel about this, he gently explained to me that while I was in the US illegally, we had the Lamberts, everyone at the shop, and many friends helping us. Plus, we had a fairly good understanding of the immigration process and our pursuit of my green card was in action. We simply had to wait the several months it would take for our father's death certificate to be recorded and then registered at the Consulate. So, sure, we were waiting, but our plan was in action already.

"But, Edgar, our brothers and sisters, like Alfonso and Pancha's Ernie, they have no one to help them. It's like they are lost and living in hiding. Just like I don't want anything happening to you—no raids, no deportation—I don't want anything happening to them. Yes, it's wrong to break the law as they did—and as we are—but helping them find work and sponsors, offering them a place to stay, and guiding them through the complex immigration process—that's a way for them to become honest and legal, both on paper and in their hearts. That's how they can live here without fear and with pride. That's the very same thing I want for you too—and eventually for your mother and siblings. Helping them is the right thing to do. We are pursuing a mighty dream, and we need God's grace to see it come true. Helping these brothers and sisters is a way to honor God because we're honoring His law."

So even though it might seem contradictory, Miguel saw the possibility of achieving green cards for me and the rest of the family as intrinsically connected to the assistance he devoted to these folks who came to him in need. Helping these people might demonstrate to God our devotion to His word. In turn, God might be moved to grant us a bit of grace in the pursuit of green cards for our family.

It was mesmerizing for me to listen to Miguel's perspectives on life and God. He thought beyond what most humans ever consider. He believed that we are being watched by a Super Being who is untouchable but strong in spirit and might. Even more than Miguel's awe-inspiring thoughts and beliefs was the fact that Miguel acted on his beliefs. Miguel walked his talk—and for me, our guests, our Phoenix-area business owner friends, our fellow silversmith friends and brothers, my family, really almost everyone Miguel met—he demonstrated to all of us what it meant to pursue human kindness, compassion, and honesty, no matter how perilous it could be at times. Miguel demonstrated how to manifest the optimal version of yourself and what it meant to live as a single extended family of human beings.

An interesting post script: in 1964, a few years after we finally managed to get my green card—a harrowing set of challenges I relate in the next chapter—Miguel requested I watch an old movie with him: *Border Incident* from 1949, starring the Mexican actor Ricardo Montalban and the American actor George Murphy. While fictional, its story was based on facts about the atrocities Mexican migrant workers commonly experienced in reaching the US, oftentimes at the hands of *polleros*, as well as their horrific experiences when working on the farms in California.

By 1964, I'd already personally witnessed the barbarity smugglers were capable of, as well as heard tales from our guests and others in the community about the horrors they endured at the hands of smugglers; about the slave-like conditions American employers put them through, taking advantage of a worker's illegal status; or about how some sponsors wielded the power to take away a green card if the worker didn't essentially work for free or "reimburse" the employer for acting as a sponsor.

I appreciated that Miguel had us watch *Border Incident* together because it supplied visceral, evocative imagery and stories that only served to further strengthen my own understanding, empathy, and commitment to help these vulnerable people and to better understand Miguel's drive to help them too.

Chapter 7

THREE TIMES

The first time—Miguel and I were visiting some friends of his, fellow Mexicans in the Phoenix area. We were gathered on the patio at the rear of the house, enjoying a meal together, talking and laughing.

When I heard the patio gate open, I scooted my chair over to allow the newly arriving guests—two well-dressed men—space to walk past me.

Before I could settle back into the chair, mayhem erupted. Fellow guests—men, women, and kids—shot up from their seats and began running for it, over the fence, out the patio gate, through the house.

Miguel had warned me about this very situation. I knew what to do even before he shouted, "Get out of here and hide! It's La Migra!"

I took off.

Behind me, I could hear one of the men, yelling, "Hold back! Hold back!"

I dashed down the street, searching for a place to hide. I decided on a parked car, hoping its owner wouldn't be using it anytime soon. Lying flat, I scooted myself under it.

My body was trembling. I put all my energy and concentration towards not crying, not making a sound, not moving.

For at least three hours I lay hidden, waiting and afraid, underneath the car.

Once it became dark, I made my way back to the jewelry shop, sticking to the most obscure of routes, skirting in the shadows and alleyways.

I'd known what to do in case of a raid because Miguel had warned me. He'd prepared me many times already, explaining that it was practically inevitable it would happen. And likely to happen more than once. He warned me that La Migra's surprise raids could happen at restaurants, homes, on the street, at church, the movie theater, even while I was riding in a car or on a bus—anywhere. He told me that I had to be prepared to escape from wherever I found myself. And if we were together, I'd be fleeing on my own. Without him. I'd have to run and hide and stay hidden for hours—and then make my way back to the jewelry shop once it was nighttime or once I felt safe.

So, finally, it had happened. While I was certain Miguel's preparation helped me flee successfully, I also wondered if God had intervened and let us off the hook because of Miguel's great effort to assist fellow Mexicans in need, like Alfonso, Samuel, Pancha, and Ernie.

During the months after that first raid, there were days and even weeks when I didn't think about raids and deportation. I was able to be on the ready, but not overly worry about it. I immersed myself in school and chores. But at other times, when I was out with Margaret or my brother, or when I was at school or the jewelry shop, I'd look around and plan my getaway in case a raid suddenly occurred. Moments of paranoia would descend upon me. It was a burden and a horror knowing that in the span of a few minutes my life could be turned around completely. Miguel had been experiencing that burden and horror from the moment I'd entered the US illegally, but it took me experiencing that first raid to take it on as well.

The second time—Miguel and I were at Rosita's, a popular Mexican restaurant in Phoenix. We'd just taken our seats when we heard crashing, rattling, breaking, and stampeding sounds. Both staff and fellow patrons were bounding for the restaurant's front door.

Again, I was on my feet. I joined the storm of prey, assaulting the only exit to escape the predators in green.

This time an officer in green chased me.

I jumped fences. I sprinted through one alleyway, then across a street, and down another smaller street. I made my way behind a house, found an alcove, and slid myself into a thin crevice between a wall and a water heater. Standing straight up, I could just fit in the small, shadowy slip of space.

It was agony, standing and waiting. But I didn't make a sound. I closed my eyes and pretended I was at the ocean with my grandfather. I waited and waited—ten, fifteen, twenty minutes passed.

Then I heard soft padding. Footsteps. They were getting closer.

I dared to open my eyes, just a slit. A crack.

Right next to me stood a predator in green. Staring at me.

I turned my head and opened my eyes fully. We locked eyes.

Without a word, he turned and walked away.

I stumbled out of the space and fell to my knees. I stayed there on the ground. I couldn't move. I could hardly breathe. I felt ill.

After many minutes, an hour, I don't know, I made my way to standing and carefully trekked back to the jewelry shop, where I found Miguel standing outside the rear entrance, pacing, his face contorted in worry and fear.

Miguel and I had no doubt that it was God who had saved me this time. There was no other accounting for the man in green—who'd spent so long hunting me—only to leave me be. But how many chances would God grant us?

————◆————

Third time—Miguel and I were at Pitman Foods, a specialty grocery store that was very popular with customers from all different
backgrounds because it offered a selection of food items from all
over the world. We were searching for a certain *chilé* when boxes
and bags went flying. Customers and employees dropped what they
were doing and tore out the door.

Another raid.

I joined the melee and managed to push my way out the front
door even though a number of people had gotten trapped there.

Over fences, under shrubs, down alleyways, I sprinted. When I
located a house, elevated on cement blocks a few feet off the earth,
I decided to crawl under it. I slithered around and located a hiding
space to the rear of that damp, dark confining space.

I could hear sounds from outside. I couldn't tell if it was pass-
ers-by, traffic, or the predators in green. I pulled myself into an even
tighter ball in the shadowed, earthy-smelling crawlspace.

To see if I could make out anything in my surroundings, I lifted my face a little, off my knees, and cracked open my eyes. As
I turned my head, my gaze locked on to a beam of light. There
before me, I made out a face staring straight at me. A man, also
on his hands and knees, with his eyes looking directly at me, was
positioned a few yards from me in the crawlspace. He was wearing
the distinctive green uniform.

As we looked at each other, our gazes didn't waver. Without
warning, I felt the fear and horror inside me melt away. I was exhausted. I no longer cared. "Three strikes, you're out, and I give up,"
I remember thinking.

However, before I could make a move or voice my resignation—
the man reversed his crawl and exited from underneath the house.
He walked away.

I burst out crying. I cried hard for only a minute and then I made my exit too. I left the backyard, jumped another fence, and made my way to the jewelry shop.

Miguel's compassion and dedicated hard work helping fellow Mexicans without papers, as well as others in need, likely encouraged God to protect me in those three raids.

However, Miguel and I decided that we should stop relying on God's good will. God had granted us more than our fair share of grace. It was time to return to Nogales and try for my green card again. Our father's death certificate had been properly registered just a week prior, so I should be able to get my green card relatively quickly.

Miguel informed Margaret and Doc of the plan to return to Nogales. In the meantime, I let my teacher, Mrs. Tudor, know that I'd be missing school. I was upfront with her and revealed that the seven-plus months that I'd been her student, I hadn't had the papers to be in America legally. I told her about the three raids and how finally the necessary paper had been registered, so Miguel and I should be able to get my green card and return to Phoenix relatively shortly.

Mrs. Tudor was supportive and kind. She gave me a warm hug and wished me a speedy return.

The second attempt for my green card—Miguel and I said farewell to Phil, the silversmiths, and the Lamberts, and we headed south to Nogales. On the drive there, Miguel let me know that Aurelio, the notary who had provided us with dedicated assistance, had died in the seven-plus months that I'd been in Phoenix, so we would be meeting with Juan Robles, the notary who had taken over Aurelio's business.

While Aurelio may have had a peculiar appearance and excruciatingly slow manner, he had been persistent in supporting Miguel as well as all the folks that came to him seeking help to obtain their green cards. Juan Robles was the polar opposite. His repeated looks in the mirror and touch-ups to his hair during our meeting with him showed his vanity. Plus, he scoffed at Miguel and me, and let us know he found it disgraceful that any Mexican would "desert" Mexico for the United States or anywhere else. Finally, he was preoccupied about getting paid. As I said—the polar opposite of Aurelio.

He eventually conceded that with our father's registered death certificate, my papers looked complete, and we should go to the Consulate.

At the Consulate, as we sat waiting for our number to be called, we found ourselves again amidst a large room full of fellow Mexicans, all of us nervous and hopeful about the state of our papers and eager to start new lives in the USA.

When it was my turn, an officer carefully checked my papers, found them all satisfactory, and recommended that I prepare for round two. I'd need to get a TB test and four photographs and return with those for another review. Miguel and I departed feeling good.

Because it takes forty-eight hours for the skin reaction to the TB test to be completed and read, we returned to the Consulate two days later. As we waited our turn, Miguel had a lengthy conversation with a man named Omar who was a painter. His cuticles and fingernails were crusted with different colored paints. It seemed that over the years, paint had pretty much penetrated the thick keratin of his nails and nail beds.

Omar was explaining to Miguel that it was his fourth attempt at getting his green card. "I've got a lot of doubt about the American who agreed to sponsor me," he confessed, "because he's offering me seasonal work. It's not fulltime, so I don't believe that will count."

Miguel agreed with Omar that the chances were slim. At the same time, I could see Miguel's mind churning, pondering, "How can I help this man? Who do I know that could sponsor him?"

Miguel gave Omar the name of the hotel where we were staying in Nogales as well as Juan Robles's address and phone number as ways to contact Miguel if Omar's green card didn't work out. He also gave him his contact information in Phoenix.

When it was our turn to meet with a more senior-level official, the gray-haired immigration officer was already examining my twenty-five papers when we took our seats in his office. Without looking up, he informed us, "Edgar passed the TB test. The photos are acceptable too."

"Yes, excellent," Miguel replied.

"However," he continued, still staring down at the papers before him on the desk, "there appears to be a major discrepancy in Edgar's papers. On the birth certificate Edgar's last name reads 'Hernández- Hernández.' But on his father's papers, we see the last name 'Hernández-Cabrera.' It doesn't make any sense."

Miguel was equally perplexed but for different reasons. He pointed out, "We saw an officer several months ago and another two days ago, and neither made any mention of this."

"Well, sir, that's why there are several rounds of interviews and paper checks. They are neither as experienced nor as senior as I am. Here's the problem: how to differentiate this Edgar Hernández from another Edgar Hernández. If Edgar's last name was aligned across all the papers, it could prevent potential fraud and confusion. It would be most clear and easy for the Mexican and American governments if his last name were listed the same across all his papers. So, you are going to need to get his birth certificate corrected for him to get a visa."

Miguel listened carefully. Without hiding his desperation, he asked, "It could take months—even a year—for that correction to come through. Can we just go ahead and process the application? I'll file to get the birth certificate corrected at a later time, and that way we won't have to wait so long?" Then he added, "The priest who wrote the birth certificate was in his eighties when Edgar was born, and it is likely he made an error."

The officer then informed us of a second problem. "But that's not all that's missing. We also need documents from Edgar's school. The papers you've given don't account for what Edgar has been doing this current school year."

Needless to say, Miguel and I were devastated. Once again, we faced a real problem—and a new problem. Miguel mustered the energy to try to clear his mind and get into problem-solving mode. After a moment, he asked, "Would an addendum to the birth certificate be appropriate?"

"Yes, an addendum signed by the city president and by the boy's mother—I think that will suffice. We must have an official letter explaining the error and giving the correction. Also we need to have a letter from the principal where he's been going to school this school year. It's essential that we have that. We'll go ahead and keep the application on file until you produce the required papers. We'll leave some of these segments blank until you produce the requested items."

We exited feeling defeated. Shocked. I didn't say anything. Both of us were speechless and utterly disappointed.

By the time we reached the hotel, Miguel made me a promise, "We will not give up on this. Edgar, I promise you that we'll find a solution. How many of those hundred-plus people in the waiting room at the Consulate do you think will be successful? How many are facing obstacles greater than ours? Maybe some of them will never even have a chance. But we have a good chance. Let's go ahead and sleep on it. In the morning, we can see Mr. Robles to get his advice."

The next morning we met Juan Robles again. He had neither sympathy nor new ideas for us on how to resolve the matter in a timely fashion.

"That's the law and you have to live with it," he declared, "Other than the illegal way—which you've already done—you are going to have to do exactly what everyone else does: wait it out until your papers come through."

With heavy hearts we left his office and went to get lunch. As we walked to a restaurant, Miguel explained to me, "Because this will take several months, in all likelihood, Edgar, you are going to have to stay here in Nogales while I return to Phoenix and work. I'll visit you regularly. I'm not abandoning you. We are going to have to find a good person or family for you to stay with. Does this make sense?"

"Miguel, I understand, and I'm not afraid," I told him in all sincerity, for I believed in Miguel's ability to make the impossible possible. He'd done it for so many others already. Plus, I knew that God was on our side. In the meantime, though, we'd have to find a good person or family in Nogales that would take me in.

Within the hour we found the right person—or rather, couple. We just needed a few days to show them that they could trust us.

We were having lunch at a restaurant and, of course, Miguel ended up talking to our waitress. In explaining my green card troubles to her, Miguel got the idea that perhaps she would be able to take me in during the months I'd have to spend in Nogales, waiting for the papers.

Her name was Elvira. She phoned her husband, Javier, so he could meet us and together they could discuss the possibility. The four of us spent an hour talking. While they were both open to the idea—though they hadn't let on yet—understandably, they wanted more time to think it over.

Miguel suggested, "Can we have breakfast, lunch, and dinner together for the next two days so that we can become acquainted and more comfortable with this possibility?"

Javier and Elvira agreed.

After two days, we were all in agreement. Miguel and I were thrilled to have found Javier and Elvira, whom I would live with for the next half- to full year They trusted us and trusted our sincerity and good intentions. Miguel made arrangements to compensate them regularly for their help, and we set it up so that he'd visit me twice monthly.

After Miguel departed and Elvira was situating me in their tiny apartment, she assured me, "You have no reason to worry. Javier and I both work, we don't have any children, and I think it will be great to have you here."

Elvira was right—it was great. I kept very busy, running errands for patrons and assisting management at the hotel where Javier worked. Because the hotel was a hub for Mexican and American businessmen, I was constantly mingling with professionals and often got to practice my English.

Because my own English had improved during my seven-and-a-half months in Phoenix, Gloria, an English tutor in Nogales, gave me a job where twice weekly I led some of her young pupils in brief conversations in English. It was a way for them to practice.

Inspired by Miguel, I also started helping people coming to Nogales who were trying to get their green cards. I was in a great position to help because I knew all the general requirements. I could locate all the departments, agencies, and health centers. I knew where to go to get professional photos as well as blood tests, skin tests, and vaccinations. I knew the most efficient and economical notaries. I also knew the reliable lawyers.

Through word of mouth, individuals and families sought me out. People would tell them, "Go over to the hotel, and you'll find a kid named Edgar. He knows the process and the people. He's trustworthy too. He can show you around. He speaks really good English too."

In this way, I helped many people get their green cards. It gave me great joy to help people, who, like me, were seeking better lives for themselves and their families in the USA. And it was Miguel who inspired me to see everyone as my brothers and sisters, and to assist them as much as I could and for no reason other than to be of help.

The third time—after ten months, the proper papers, both for my last name and the school records, were ready. Miguel and I were returning to the Consulate. I was looking forward to the appointment, but at the same time I felt an acute anxiety. I worried about the meeting somehow failing, but also I thought about everyone in Nogales that I'd be leaving behind if we were successful. I'd grown close to Elvira and Javier in our months together.

I could tell Miguel felt anxious too. The way he sat so quietly, not engaging in conversations with those around him as he typically did. Lines of stress were carved in his forehead.

Because my papers were in order, we were meeting with the Consul, himself, for he was the one that would make the final decision. It was a tense meeting. It wasn't easy. The Consul felt uneasy about me leaving my mother and going to live in the US with an older half-brother that I hadn't grown up with. Miguel had me leave the room, so I don't know the exact conversation that ensued. All I know is that Miguel convinced the Consul of his sincerity and good intentions. It ended with our success. I got my green card.

After tearful goodbyes to Javier and Elvira—and promises to visit and write, promises which we kept—Miguel and I headed to Phoenix in his Ford Fairlane.

Something Miguel would always say to me was: "We are here for a reason. Don't waste it. Make it count. Edgar, you can be as great and unique as you want to be."

While Miguel never took credit for the help he gave to so many people, including all the help he provided me, I saw Miguel's super-sized work ethic, bottomless compassion and desire to assist our brothers and sisters in need—whether related by blood or not—as his greatness. His uniqueness. He had an enormous human kindness that he imparted constantly in all the time I knew him.

This brings to mind another great and mystical incident. First, let's go back to 1959 when Miguel was hospitalized due to the abscess in his scalp and the resulting blood poisoning. In those few days he was in the hospital, he met a young couple, Paulo and Dorotea, and their five-year-old son, Joselito. They were in the hospital because Paulo was recovering from brain tumor surgery. Miguel ended up becoming good friends with the three of them, a friendship that continued for years afterwards.

In 1964, after battling brain cancer for five years, Paulo died. When Miguel was at Paulo's funeral, he saw Dorotea and Joselito, who was now ten. He recalled that several months earlier, Paulo had planned on getting Joselito a bicycle. Miguel realized that Paulo was never able to fulfill his plan.

After I returned to Phoenix in 1961 and started my life in America as a legal immigrant, in addition to attending school and doing odd jobs at the jewelry shop, I worked a newspaper delivery route. In 1964, the *Phoenix Gazette* ran a contest that I ended up winning because I got over four hundred new people to subscribe to the newspaper. My prize: a trip to Disneyland and a new Schwinn Stingray bicycle.

When I returned from Disneyland, Miguel sat me down to talk. "Edgar, do you remember that Joselito was promised a bicycle?"

"Yes," I confirmed.

"And you know that his father died about a week ago, and he's very sad?"

"Yes, Miguel. I know that."

"I want to ask you a big favor . . . You know what I'm going to ask of you?"

I braced myself and then acknowledged, "I believe so. You're going to ask me to give the bicycle that I won to Joselito."

This was a difficult thing Miguel was asking of me. I had worked really hard for a very long time to win that bicycle.

Miguel spoke, saying, "Edgar, you worked for over two years to win that bicycle. You used focus, discipline, and intelligence— and I am so proud of you. Now, I'm giving you another challenge, perhaps one that's even more difficult than all you did to win the bicycle. I'm challenging you to give up this most precious gift to someone else. Joselito is heart-broken over the loss of his father. A new bicycle would mean so much to him. You are in a unique position to provide him with some much-needed happiness at this awful time in his life."

Miguel stopped speaking and simply looked at me—looked at me pointedly, right into my eyes. It was Miguel's soul-penetrating gaze that seemed to infiltrate right to the heart of whomever he was looking at—in this case, me. All his love, kindness, and sincerity shined through to me in his gaze, so that my initial resistance and reluctance started to melt away.

Yes, Miguel was asking something big of me. I'd worked so long and hard for that bicycle. No, I didn't want to give it up. I'd never want to, but Joselito was suffering a lot. I could see Miguel's point that a new bicycle would provide him with a happy distraction during this time of great sadness. I didn't *want* to, but I knew I *could* give it up. I could rise to the challenge because it was the right thing to do. I wanted to do the right thing, especially when Miguel asked it of me. He was teaching me a bigger life lesson about the rewards of generosity, sympathy, and self-sacrifice.

While maintaining the intense eye contact, Miguel said, "Edgar, I am only suggesting this to you. It's not a requirement. In the end, it is your decision." Then he hugged me.

While we were hugging, I told him, "Miguel, you are right that I worked so hard for the bicycle. I love the bicycle. It isn't easy to give it away, but Joselito will be so happy. I know how awful it is to lose a father. After Papá died, I got you—and that's more precious than anything. Let's visit Dorotea and Joselito today because I want him to have some happiness. I want to give him the bicycle. He will love it."

"Edgar, it's a golden opportunity for us to do this. Trust me."

In his looks, actions, and words, Miguel inspired, challenged, and showed me what it meant for his often-repeated words to manifest: "We are here for a reason. Don't waste it. Make it count. You can be as great and unique as you want to be." Great, unique, and utterly mystical—that's Miguel Hernández.

Chapter 8

THE FOUR AGREEMENTS

A few months prior to our return to Nogales for our second try for my green card—Miguel and I visited the 206 N. 9th Street property where the house and garage were under renovation. On this visit there was a meeting of the construction team—the electrician, plumber, concrete person, roofer, carpenter, and Ray Fasio. They gathered to discuss the next stage of the renovation. All of these skilled workers were Miguel's friends as well. Because they knew Miguel and understood the importance of the rebuilding project, they gave him a discount on their services.

Their plan was not to start work on the house itself, but to focus on the garage at the rear of the house. They were going to redo it to be like a hostel. The original owner had built the garage to house his collection of Model N and T cars in its seven bays, so those seven bays would serve as the personal space for each person staying at the "hostel"-garage. Because Model Ns and Ts were notably smaller (both shorter and thinner) than the cars of the 1950s, '60s, and certainly the cars of today, each guest would have very limited personal space. A cot that folded up in the middle and a tiny table were really all that would fit in each space. Plus, each stall had no door—so each space was more like a cubicle than a room.

Other than the roll-up door you'd lift to enter and exit the garage, the only other door, this one hinged, was the door to a tight space where the toilet resided. To provide privacy when showering, a curtain hung from some pipes near the ceiling, pipes that were set up in a U shape. Not only would guests staying have to trust Miguel and his good intentions to help them by offering them accommodation in this hostel-like garage, but they'd also have to trust one another because this guesthouse-hostel was very much "open-plan," so to speak.

While the toilet was connected to the city sewage system, the grey water from the shower actually flowed into a drain and travelled down a pipe that emptied into the outside garden space, thus providing water to the plants there—this was Miguel's smart idea to use water to its max! The shower and toilet room along with a very basic kitchen and eating area lay in a bigger vestibule-type area.

A hallway stemmed off the vestibule area and the seven cubicles were located on one side of that hallway. Obviously, it wasn't by any means luxurious, but Miguel's guesthouse-hostel-garage offered protection and comradery to our guests who were enduring so much in order to launch better lives for themselves and eventually their families.

Ray found an old eight-foot long sink that had once been used in an operating room for surgeons and staff to wash their hands prior to surgery. It was lying around outside a hospital where Ray was doing a swamp cooler-related job, so he picked it up and brought it to the property. The long sink with four faucets would work well in the vestibule area.

Miguel had several contractors working with him, doing concrete work, framing, roofing, plumbing, and flooring. He was even able to barter with some of them who preferred to be paid with jewelry pieces. Miguel would make them particular jewelry pieces, according to their specifications, in exchange for their services.

Alfonso—the man without papers whom Miguel connected with the Davises and their pest-control business—was the first guest to move into a bay in the garage. Admittedly, the garage area wasn't completely ready to take on occupants when Alfonso moved in, but he was appreciative anyway. The garage offered him safe shelter as well as running water from a spigot—which was better than moving from abandoned building to abandoned building as he had been doing.

As with Alfonso, and all the brothers and sisters who became guests at 206 N. 9th Street, it started with these four agreements:

1. Don't drink or smoke.
2. Learn English.
3. Make work your focus.
4. Pursue the green card process.

With every guest, Miguel promised he'd do all he could to help them find work, land a sponsor, have a place to live, and navigate the immigration process, just as long as they were on board with those four agreements.

Agreement #1—don't drink or smoke. Because of our father, all my siblings and I learned at an early age the destruction that alcohol and smoking abuse leads to. Miguel never touched the stuff, nor have I.

Five of Miguel's fellow silversmith coworkers had been heavy drinkers. In Miguel's first year-and-a-half at the Lamberts' jewelry shop, these five went on occasional binges and ended up missing days or a week or two of work. The Lamberts warned each of them that they would lose their job if it happened again.

When Miguel joined the team at the jewelry shop, he typically started work each day before everyone else and finished work each day after everyone else. This meant that he was producing more pieces, thus making more money than his colleagues. Initially these five craftsmen perceived Miguel, with his highly disciplined work habits and abstinence from drinking, with some jealousy. However, because of Miguel's sincere nature and habit of supporting others, soon their jealousy faded. In fact, Miguel actively helped them make it through times when they felt tempted to drink. Miguel shared stories with them about our father and his drinking and smoking addictions. After 1957, everyone at the shop knew all about our father's health problems. In 1959, they knew that his death was due to his addictions.

Overall, Miguel's five colleagues who'd struggled with alcohol addiction cited Miguel's ongoing support as the reason they were able to stop drinking altogether, so that as of 1958 none of the silversmiths at the Lambert's shop drank any longer. Everyone was free of alcohol abuse and the personal, familial, and community problems that came with it.

When Miguel made the decision to become highly involved in helping Mexicans illegally in the Phoenix area, he realized that their abstaining from drinking would be key in their achieving success in America. For one thing, drinking too much could lead to raucous behavior, which could result in getting arrested and triggering a problematic trifecta—deportation, job loss, and a police record— all of which would make it essentially impossible to recover from in terms of obtaining a green card. Even if the drinking never led to an arrest, it increased the likelihood of missing work or having a problem at work—which could mean the person would lose the possibility of their boss sponsoring them, and likewise, no green card.

Because Miguel had helped his five colleagues tackle their drinking temptations—and because Phil had recovered from his alcohol addiction and could offer support and resources—Miguel was confident that he would be able to help any of our guests overcome the desire to drink, providing they were upfront and honest about it.

During the fifteen years Miguel was most active assisting

people, everyone pulled through on their pledge against alcohol, everyone except two people: Israel and Poncho.

Israel and Poncho loved the taste of alcohol more than they wanted a life in the USA. Miguel pleaded with them, saying, "You are here illegally, and that means you are in a precarious situation. You must conduct yourself with the highest discipline and caution, and behave like you are a guest. If your behavior stands out at all, the police will stop you—and then it's over for you. If I find out you are drinking, then you won't be able to stay here at the residence because you could very well jeopardize the rest of our guests too. Also, you'll jeopardize your jobs and the possibility of getting your green cards. It's never worth the risk."

Israel and Poncho both ended up getting arrested due to drinking. Israel was arrested for public intoxication and then deported. Poncho ended up doing prison time because he was driving drunk (and also without a driver's license), and he caused a serious accident.

Agreement #2—learn English. Miguel impressed upon all those whom he was assisting that they must try to learn English. He felt that in order to succeed and compete in the USA, you must try to communicate in English. Also, in the many interviews in the immigration process, it made a noticeable difference when the applicant could speak some words in English and share that they'd been taking lessons. It showed how serious they were about integrating.

In this area, Friendly House in Phoenix, a nonprofit started in 1920, which to this day continues to help refugees and immigrants, was among Miguel's key partners and allies. Friendly House offered night classes for people to learn English. From 1961 until 1972, Miguel connected fifty-two people—forty men and twelve women—with Friendly House. For Miguel the Saturday night classes—an hour of

English plus an hour of bingo—were especially important for guests to attend because it gave them something productive to do on a weekend night. In turn, this decreased the potential to go out drinking.

Friendly House's volunteer English teachers were typically older, around seventy-five to eighty years old. Often, they had been teachers in their careers, and now that they were retired, they were looking to keep busy and active, and stay involved in the community helping folks in the way they were most experienced and talented: as teachers. Miguel saw it as a win-win for the guests and the volunteer teachers. The guests learned English, and the retired former teachers got to pursue their God-given talent and love.

I remember an eighty-one-year-old lady named Norma whom Miguel introduced me to at a Christmas Eve party at Friendly House. Norma had taught the fourth grade for over fifty-five years.

She admitted that she'd become very depressed after she retired. She realized that she would love another chance to teach. "And once I started volunteer teaching here at Friendly House, I felt that depression lift. I don't think a doctor could've prescribed a better treatment."

Norma taught conversational English every Saturday night. She loved to teach, and according to the people living with us, she was very good. She also taught American history for those preparing to take the citizenship exam.

Norma's biggest fan was our guest Rafael. Rafael was in his seventies with bushy eyebrows resembling large, wilted palm branches twisting over his small round eyes. He was balding on the top of his head and had small patches of gray hair on the sides and a skinny ponytail. Spider-web-like wrinkles stretched across his bronze skin. His one gold tooth added extra dazzle to his charming smile.

Once Rafael got older, he lost his teaching job in Mexico to a younger person. At a restaurant in Mexico City, he happened to meet an American architect from New Mexico. This architect told Rafael that in America even the elderly could find work. The architect even promised Rafael that once he (the architect) was better positioned, he would hire Rafael and sponsor him. As a result, Rafael decided to go to the USA. He ended up entering illegally.

After months living outdoors as a vagrant, Rafael happened to meet Miguel. Miguel offered him a place to stay and help finding work and gathering the necessary papers for a green card, so all would be ready to go once, or if, the New Mexican sponsor came through.

Although Rafael's hands were deformed due to crippling arthritis, he ended up doing prep work at a bakery. Because bakers start early in the morning, baking breads, pastries, and cakes, Rafael's prep work started even earlier. He worked a nightshift, starting around 7 pm. However, on Saturday nights he would start work at 9:30 pm, so he could take lessons with Norma at Friendly House.

As a former history professor, Rafael was highly interested in learning American history as well as English, so he studied both with Norma. She was astounded at his knowledge. "Rafael knows more American history than most people born in America," she often told us.

After staying with us for four-and-a-half months, Rafael finally received a letter from his architect contact in New Mexico. It read:

> *Dear Rafael,*
>
> *I hope you are well. I hope your arthritis is holding up. I am back in New Mexico after finishing the yearlong project in New Jersey. As per your writing, you have been going to night school, learning some English, and have assembled all your required papers for immigration. That is good. Once you get here, we can set up a time to go to the immigration office together, so you can get your green card.*

I vividly recall an emotional, tearful Rafael asking me to read the letter out loud to everyone, so we all could share his good fortune and joy. Although he was leaving his newfound community in Phoenix, we were confident that he would be warmly received.

I remember when two brothers at my high school, Jesús and Francisco, were left homeless. The two boys and their parents, José Juan and Paloma, had been eating at a diner when a raid occurred. They were all captured, but Jesús and Francisco got released since they both were born in the US, thus were US citizens. Their parents were deported since they were in the US illegally.

"Let's help them, Miguel," I begged.

"Yes, we will. Let me see what I can do," Miguel responded.

At that time the seven-bay hostel-garage was totally occupied, but the back room in the house we were refurbishing was available. So that's where Jesús and Francisco stayed. Like me, Jesús and Francisco were serious about their studies. They hoped to be engineers someday. Plus, they were both heart-broken that their family had been split up. Miguel wanted to find them better accommodations and also figure out a way to get their parents green cards, so the family could reunite and live in the US without fear and further damage.

That's when Miguel thought of the Ralstons. They were an elderly couple, former teachers, who volunteered as English tutors at Friendly House. They were incredibly kind, and Miguel also knew they had a basement at their home, probably one of the few basements in Phoenix as basements are a rarity there.

Miguel spoke to the Ralstons about taking in the boys temporarily while Miguel considered options on how to get their parents green cards. The Ralstons agreed to take Jesús and Francisco into their home. The four quickly became close. The Ralstons paid for the boys' clothing, school expenses, and trips to Nogales to visit their parents.

When Jesús and Francisco returned from one of the visits to Nogales, they revealed to Miguel that their parents had not used their real names when they'd gotten apprehended. If they had, they would have had to wait for about ten years to apply to enter the US legally. Because they'd used fake names, it meant they could apply for green cards using their real names, and their application wouldn't be automatically denied. This was great news.

And so Miguel got creative. While the Ralstons had told Miguel that they would help with whatever he needed, Miguel did not want to abuse their generosity. However, he did have one additional big favor to ask of them. Miguel had learned that the Ralstons were good friends with the Shumways, a dairy farmer and his wife who lived in East Mesa, Arizona. The wives had taught at the same school together, and they went to church together every Sunday. Miguel asked the Ralstons if they could invite the Shumways for dinner at their home, and Miguel would cook enchiladas for everyone.

At the dinner, Miguel learned that "Slim" Shumway—a skinny man with white hair, a crew cut, and deep blue eyes—was a lifelong dairy farmer. Even Slim's parents and brother were in the dairy business. Bertha Shumway hailed from a long line of teachers.

Eventually, over the course of the dinner, Miguel turned to the subject to José Juan and Paloma's situation—how they'd been in the USA illegally; how Jesús and Francisco, their sons, were legal citizens and conscientious high school students aiming for engineering degrees; how the family had been roughly split up; and how José Juan and Paloma were in the process of gathering the necessary papers from Jalisco, Mexico, their home state—but that the two still needed an American business owner to sponsor them for their green cards; otherwise the family would not be reunited.

Miguel turned to the Shumways, saying, "As longtime American dairy farmers, you are in a great position to employ these two hardworking parents and also act as their sponsors. I was wondering if you'd consider it."

At first, they were taken aback by Miguel's total honesty, relating the facts of the parents' deportation and why the two boys were living with the Ralstons. After that, they were once again taken aback by Miguel's direct appeal to them.

Slim Shumway, tightening and loosening his belt as he spoke, lamented, "Seems to me those folks broke the law, and I worry that hiring them would make us lawbreakers too."

Bertha commented, "They might have broken the law, Slim Sweetie, but they did it to better their lives and they paid for it when they got deported. We could help these folks. I think we ought to consider it."

Still loosening and tightening his belt, Slim muttered, "I don't want to go to jail . . . I don't want to break the law. This whole thing just isn't right."

Bertha would reply, "Slim Sweetie, we need to help Miguel. Miguel is not even related to these kids or their parents, and look how he is helping them. He is not concerned about going to jail, are you Miguel?"

Miguel assured them, "Sir, nothing will happen to you and your wonderful wife, I promise."

The Ralstons made a joke, saying, "Look at it this way—would it make you feel better if we promise to visit you in jail? . . . Slim, we're just pulling your leg. Besides, you'd never look good in striped clothing . . . Now seriously, Slim, we would never lie to you, and Miguel would never lie to you."

Slim eventually asked, "What exactly do you want me to do?"

Miguel then explained to them how sponsorship worked and what exactly they'd have to do to sponsor José Juan and Paloma.

A week later, Miguel accompanied Slim and Bertha to Nogales. They met José Juan and Paloma, became their legal sponsors, and helped them get their green cards. José Juan, Paloma, Francisco, and Jesús stayed with the Ralstons for about three years until they could get their own place. For six years José Juan and Paloma worked on the Shumway's dairy farm, and after six years, José Juan and Paloma became US citizens.

———

Agreement #3—make work your focus. Miguel kept his word to Omar, the painter he met at the Consulate in Nogales when we were trying for the second time for my green card.

After Miguel left me in the care of Elvira and Javier in Nogales and returned to Phoenix, he asked Ray Fasio if he knew of anyone in his construction contacts looking for an experienced painter. Ultimately, Ray, himself, arranged to sponsor Omar in one of his partner companies. Ray and Miguel ended up returning to Nogales together to complete the documentation process and interviews with Omar. Omar ended up entering the USA with his green card within a few weeks of first meeting Miguel, which meant that Omar got his green card many months before I did.

Omar went on to become good friends with Miguel. He ended up living in the garage on our 206 N. 9th Street property, and in his off-time he helped Miguel with some renovation work. Omar was very focused on his painting work for Ray. Similar to Miguel, Omar had a serious work ethic and a bigger goal: once he became self-sufficient, he would immigrate his wife and three children.

By the time I immigrated to the USA with my green card in 1961, Omar had his feet on the ground, had moved to a place of his own, and had started the immigration process for the rest of his family.

Emilio, a man from Mexico who was around forty years old, was also determined to succeed in the USA. He came to live with us for seven months. He attended every English language session on Saturdays and practiced English daily. I remember Emilio's prodigious drawing talent. He could draw a building, a house, a cat crossing a street—in a matter of a few minutes—and what he drew was brought to life with movement, feeling, and a sense of dimension and space.

In the past Miguel had crafted a belt buckle for Mr. Jenkins, an architect, and the two ended up becoming friends. Miguel proceeded to introduce Emilio to Mr. Jenkins, explaining, "Emilio is an expert artist, particularly talented at real-life sketching. Plus, he's a steadfast worker."

Mr. Jenkins hired Emilio soon after. Because Emilio's devotion and talent were evident, within a few months the two were heading to Nogales to complete the green card process with Mr. Jenkins acting as sponsor. Like Rafael, within a year Emilio earned enough money to immigrate his family. Emilio proved to be an ideal case with a perfect sponsor. Due to his hard work and devotion, he was living the dream that all of our guests hoped to achieve as well.

Agreement #4—pursue the green card process. From my own repeated attempts at getting my green card, it was evident that the green card process could get complicated. There could be a lot of waiting and a lot of additional expenses. As opposed to my case, when Pancha and her son Ernie were working with Miguel to figure out how to best help Ernie, they at least could pursue possibilities on the American side. This made it easier simply because American infrastructure, communication (mail and telephone), and bureaucracy, though not speedy, were certainly much faster and more transparent than that of Mexico at the time.

For Miguel to help most guests, it meant a trip to Nogales, Mexico on his own without them to lodge petitions for notarized papers from their Mexican home state's capital. Also he would obtain paper copies of the application at the American Consulate there (this is before application material became available in Phoenix). As the guests were in Phoenix illegally, they couldn't travel back and forth to Nogales with Miguel as they would then have to re-enter the US illegally. It was safest for them to focus on their work, English lessons, and staying out of trouble while Miguel did the footwork for the application process.

Something that many people today may not realize is that back then simply picking up a paper application from the Consulate in Nogales—an application that is for someone else, not you—and returning to the USA with it was considered suspicious. For instance, at one point when I was first living in Phoenix without papers, Margaret went to the Consulate in Nogales to pick up an application for me. It was after I experienced that first close call with the immigration agents. Margaret thought she was being helpful and hadn't consulted with Miguel beforehand. The officer whom she requested the application from started interrogating her, trying to elicit her name, address—anything that would reveal needed info, so they could do a raid on her because they assumed she was harboring an illegal alien, which she was—me. Margaret ended up leaving without answering their questions or getting the application.

It was a huge risk for Miguel to go to Nogales so many times to retrieve applications, and it was also a testament to his magnetism that he was always successful in attaining the paper copies without incident. But as you'll see, and as was customary for my older half-brother, he didn't simply attain paper copies of immigration applications; he converted many of the very people whose job it was to apprehend illegal immigrants and prevent illegal immigration into his devoted friends and allies. Miguel was simply that remarkable. That magnetic. That mystical.

In late 1962, Miguel was again visiting the American Consulate in Nogales. He was accompanying Andres, one of our guests who was undertaking his final interviews to obtain his green card. Miguel also planned on getting an application for another guest.

Miguel had succeeded in getting the application with no problem and was waiting for Andres to conclude his interviews when a higher-up officer (you could tell from his dress) approached Miguel, saying, "I've seen you here before, I believe."

"Yes, sir, I've been here several times. I try to help some people with their immigration papers."

"Are you a lawyer?" the officer asked.

"No."

"A notary?"

Miguel paused a beat and looked the man intently in the eyes. Pointedly. Then he answered, "I'm a silversmith."

"A silversmith. What's that?"

"I make jewelry—traditional Navajo Native American jewelry—like your belt buckle. And, I see that your belt buckle is missing a small turquoise stone."

"It's missing a stone?" the man asked, looking down and inspecting the buckle. "Well, yes, I see you're right. I didn't realize that."

Miguel offered, "If you ever come to Phoenix, stop by Silver by Lambert—Indian Jewelry, and I'll fix it."

"Really?" the man asked.

"Yes, I'll take care of it," Miguel assured him.

"Thank you," he responded.

Miguel then gave the man the shop's address and said, "Please come by and ask for me, Miguel Hernández. What's your name?"

The man answered, "William Thompson, but call me Rex."

"Nice to meet you, Rex," Miguel told him.

"So, tell me, Miguel, you're a silversmith. So what are you doing here?"

"I occasionally help people with their immigration papers and guide them to this office in hopes of obtaining their green card."

"I see. As I recall, you were here two months ago, yes?"

Miguel confirmed, "Yes."

"For the same thing?" Rex asked.

"Yes, that was when I accompanied a very nice man who got married to an American lady. I came with them both to finalize his papers."

Rex commented, "I see. Interesting. Because we usually see lawyers or accountants accompanying people."

Miguel asked him, "Do you remember a Mexican man by the name of Aurelio? He was very tall and very thin? He moved noticeably slowly?"

"Yes," Rex answered, "Yes, I remember seeing that man. He was unique looking."

Miguel explained, "Aurelio died two years ago. He helped me with my papers in 1951 and also helped my younger brother. I learned a lot about the intricacies of the process through him, and he aided me and my family tremendously."

"When I saw you here, I thought for sure you were some type of legal assistant," Rex commented and then asked, "So why are you doing this? Do these folks work for you? Are they related to you?"

"No, they are only close friends," replied Miguel.

"I see . . . But you live in Phoenix or here?"

"In Phoenix."

Mildly puzzled, Rex asked, "How do you know these people then?"

Without hesitation, Miguel answered frankly, "Many of them live with me in Phoenix."

"They live with you in Phoenix?"

"Yes, they are like brothers to me."

"I see—but not related?" he asked again.

"Well . . . somewhat related," Miguel told him, "As I see it, we are all related. You, Rex, you too are related to me. You probably don't look at it that way, but someday when we are no longer here, we will see each other again in the beyond, and you will know what I am saying."

Miguel looked at him with a pointed gaze, not aggressive but pointed. Their eyes locked. As already mentioned, Miguel often looked at people right in the eye as if looking directly into their very soul.

Rex noted contemplatively, "Okay. Alright, next time I'm in Phoenix I'll stop by and see about this turquoise in my belt buckle." He extended his hand, they shook hands, and they both smiled.

When Andres emerged from his interview, smiling with success, Miguel told him congratulations. When the two started moving to the doors of the building to depart, Miguel noticed that Rex had been watching him all the while.

As the two exited the building, Rex continued observing them.

Miguel turned around to see who had tapped him on the shoulder. He found Nellie. He turned off the torch, so he could give her his full attention.

"There's a man at the front asking for you," she said in a loud voice so that he could hear her above the other machines.

"Thanks, Nellie. I'll be there soon."

Nellie left the shop and returned to the store's front reception area. In the meantime, Miguel removed his safety glasses and placed his torch on the hanger to his left. He turned off the goose-necked lamp, straightened it some, and pushed it out of the way. He removed his apron and placed it on his bench. Next, he went to the sink and washed his hands. Only then was he ready to go to the front of the store.

At the front, Miguel found Mr. William "Rex" Thompson, wearing a cowboy hat and a cowboy shirt. His white mustache was curving upwards in perfect harmony with his smile.

"Miguel, how are you?" he called out, "Do you remember me? It's been about three months since we met in Nogales."

"Of course, Rex, I remember you. How are you?"

"Very well, thanks. Nice place and beautiful jewelry."

"Yes, this is a wonderful place to work," Miguel responded and then said, "Oh, I'm sorry. Let me introduce you to Nellie."

"Happy to meet you, sir," Nellie said to him.

"Nice to meet you too. My name is William Thompson, but most people call me Rex."

Turning back to Miguel, Rex said, "I will be here for a week for an interview for a position at the immigration office that's opening in Phoenix, so I figured I should get my buckle fixed."

"Yes, let's see it," Miguel requested.

Rex handed his belt to Miguel, who expertly unlocked the buckle from it and returned the belt to him, saying, "Give me ten minutes, and I will fix it, so it looks like new."

Rex nodded in agreement, and Miguel went back to the workshop area. There was a slit of a window in the store's front reception area where clients could catch a glimpse into the workshop to see the silversmiths at work. Rex could see a row of silversmiths, Miguel's Navajo Native Americans colleagues, sitting and working at their benches. Whispers of flames shone as if from small candles. The sound of sanding and power-buffing machines could be made out, though muffled.

Nellie asked, "Rex, can I help you with anything else?"

"You know what? I think I'm going to get a couple of items, something for my wife and daughter." He went on to ask, "Tell me, which pieces were made by Miguel?"

"Miguel's pieces are the ones featuring gold, silver, and turquoise," she explained, pointing out various pieces.

"Wow. Exquisite."

"Yes, when Miguel started work here in 1951, he introduced elements of gold into the Navajo traditional jewelry. We think he was the first to do it."

"Is that so?" Rex asked, marveling.

"Yes, indeed. Miguel is an amazing silversmith. Really—he's an amazing person. He is the only non-Native American craftsman working here. He has adopted our culture as well as our jewelry traditions."

"Really?" Rex commented.

Nellie went on to share, "Miguel is the hardest worker at the shop. He starts before everyone, and he finishes after everyone. We all know why he's working so hard. You see, he is earning money to bring the rest of his family from Mexico here legally. He's already helped several of his siblings get their green cards—Pedro, Olivia, and Edgar. But he has more siblings as well as his step-mother that he wants to immigrate too. We're all so proud of him."

Rex asked, "How long have you known him?"

"About thirteen years now. I was a young girl when Miguel came to us here. He is the godfather of my son, Sampson, who is now six years old."

Rex was listening intently, nodding his head.

"You should hear him speak Navajo," Nellie said.

"He speaks Navajo?" questioned Rex, incredulous.

Nellie affirmed, "Yes, he does—and perfectly too. And something else is how he helps everybody at the shop—not just with work stuff but also with their life issues. Some of the craftsmen here struggled with drinking problems, and Miguel helped them tap into their strength. Now nobody is drinking, missing work, or in danger of getting let go—"

"Here it is, Rex," Miguel announced as he entered the front of the store, holding out in his hand Rex's buckle. It was now very shiny and had all its turquoise pieces intact.

Miguel starting placing it back onto the belt when Rex observed, "Miguel, you made this look new again as well as replacing the missing stone. This is wonderful. What do I owe you?"

"Nothing. It is my pleasure," Miguel replied with a broad smile.

"You won't mind if I buy something from Nellie to give to my wife and daughter?" Rex inquired.

"That would be wonderful. There are many precious pieces here to select from," Miguel told him.

The two shook hands warmly, and then Rex gave Miguel a card with his contact information on it: "William 'Rex' Thompson, Enforcement Officer, United States Immigration Customs Office," and his phone number and address.

Miguel put the card in his pocket, gave Rex a see-you-later wave, and returned to the workshop area.

In Rex Thompson's first encounter with Miguel at the Consulate in Nogales, he was skeptical. He was suspicious of Miguel and how Miguel had admitted readily that he assisted and even housed illegal aliens. It also was strange to him that Miguel had freely supplied his workplace's name and address, for Rex could use it to easily track down Miguel and find the house where he was harboring people illegally.

But after this second visit, his skepticism and suspicion vanished. In their place came respect and admiration. Rex understood Miguel as a man focused on human kindness. He understood that Miguel was a rarity of a human being. He was the genuine thing.

And so their friendship began, a friendship that lasted for years. Until Miguel's death. The two regularly had meals together and discussed their work and lives. When very difficult situations arose, related to immigration and life in general, Miguel even contacted Rex, seeking his advice or help.

One time, it wasn't Miguel, but my mother and I that Rex ended up helping. This was years later in 1968. By this time Miguel had successfully immigrated my mother and the rest of our siblings into the US (something he accomplished in 1966). In 1968 my mother and I were picking up a green card application in the immigration office that had opened up in Phoenix. We were getting an application to help an illegal guest that wanted to attain legal status. The immigration officer ended up holding and interrogating my mother and me, trying to intimidate us into giving information that would compromise our guests or that would somehow show that we were law-breakers. The officer was relentless.

It just so happened that after an hour of interrogating us, her superior, a tall man with a white mustache, entered the interrogation room to find out what was happening. When I read the name on his badge, "William 'Rex' Thompson," I realized exactly who he was. I introduced myself and my mother to Rex as Miguel Hernández's family and Rex rapidly arranged for us to be released.

To make it clear—retrieving an application at the immigration office was not a criminal offense. The immigration officer was simply overzealous in her interpretation of the law. Rex rapidly, firmly, but not rudely reminded her of proper policy and behavior. My mother and I were very grateful to him. He also directed the officer to give us the requested application.

Chapter 9

INSPECTION CONNECTION

I'll never forget the first time I went to Emily's diner. It was 1959, and Miguel and I were delivering a pendant necklace that Emily had commissioned from Miguel. We also planned on having a meal there. As we walked in, we noticed a sign on the door that read: "No niggers or spics allowed." Even though my English was still in a formative stage, I knew enough to understand the sign, and I was worried that it would be dangerous for us to enter the diner. It puzzled me that Miguel would consider Emily a friend when she'd posted such a sign.

Seeing my worry, Miguel said, "Edgar, don't pay attention to it. Ignore it. Like I said, I've known Emily for years, and she's a wonderful person." Miguel often warned me that if you allowed nonsense to interfere with your relationships with people, it would hold you back from moving through and succeeding in life. "Even in the face of bigotry, assume the best in a person. Treat them with respect. That's how you seize the many opportunities America has to offer and find success and happiness. You'll see." Miguel accompanied these words with his trademark eye contact—a long-held, unflinching gaze into my eyes that seemed to penetrate to my very being—which further emphasized the sincerity and gravity of his message.

When I met Emily and observed her interacting with Miguel and me, I realized he was right. Emily was incredibly warm. She hugged both of us and praised Miguel for his talent. She insisted that our meal be on the house. Even her husband, Ernest, treated us with respect.

Later, in the 1960s, when Reverend Dr. Martin Luther King, Jr., was leading the black civil rights movement, Miguel would point him out to me, saying, "Now there's a true angel. Although Dr. King has been arrested several times and was treated terribly, he's never called for violence. He's all about peace and love. He even thanked the people that arrested him when they released him from jail. That man loves everybody. He's a big inspiration to me."

Years later, when I was working as a surgeon, I remember feeling frustrated and coming to Miguel for advice. I had a patient who didn't want me to work with him because I was Mexican American and had a slight accent when speaking English.

Miguel recommended that I not give up on the man or pass him off to another surgeon. Instead, Miguel encouraged me to continue treating him with compassion and respect. And, again, Miguel's philosophy of human kindness and assuming the best in people worked out. This patient came to value me and even recommended me to his friends and family when they needed medical attention.

Yet another testament to Miguel's mysticism is that he persuaded Emily to become a part of his network of business owners supporting and sponsoring illegal aliens. There was a kind man named Jaime who found his way to Miguel's "hostel" and became our guest. Jaime was a talented cook with an out-of-this-world *albondiga* soup, which is a Mexican meatball soup—think meatballs, vegetables, sometimes rice but not always, and spices. When Miguel approached Emily about Jaime, she agreed to take him on at her diner. Jaime was so talented and hardworking that she made him the main cook, and she would end up sponsoring him as well. He ended up staying as our guest for only four weeks—four weeks of unbelievable food for everyone at the property.

———

Miguel first met the Johnson twins in 1961 at Emily's diner. He was eating alone there, and as was his custom, after taking his seat, placing his order, and then washing his hands, he surveyed the other tables in the restaurant, taking in the three separate parties and then making his way to greet each one in turn.

As described already in this book's introduction, Miguel's practice was to approach people unknown to him (you could call them "strangers," but Miguel never used that term. To him we are all brothers and sisters), give a greeting, and extend his hand for a handshake, all the while he'd be looking into the person's eyes with an open-eyed, pointed gaze that was full of kindness and intensity.

His unsolicited greetings were often met with total surprise and bewilderment, but Miguel usually managed to make a connection anyway through his elegant, unassuming, and cheerful manner—a handshake, a smile, kind but soul-penetrating eye contact, and a comment like, "The wonderful smell of good food has brought us together. I hope you have a wonderful day." Most people could not help but return a comment or a smile or both. Miguel was very charismatic and sincere.

Miguel made a big deal about handshakes. He was skeptical of anyone with a so-called limp and non-grasping handshake, "unenergetic" as he called it. He said that from a person's handshake, you could tell about their honesty and fears. He would shake a person's hand and look pointedly into their eyes. A person's eye contact indicated a sense of their honesty and conscience as well. He would tell me to beware of those who look away as they shake your hand.

Some people would look around as if embarrassed when Miguel greeted them in this manner. For Miguel it was about connecting with his brothers and sisters. Plus, he got telling information from these handshakes and exchanges of eye contact.

When Miguel approached the Johnson twins' table and gave them his name and extended his hand, it was apparent they were bewildered. Even still, they each shook hands with him. On Miguel's part, he thought his hand would be crushed because of the significant difference in size of their hands. The Johnson twins were big guys—about six-feet, four inches tall. They looked to weigh about 270 pounds each and had very muscular frames, large and broad shoulders, and thick forearms. On the contrary, rather than crushing, their handshakes were firm and smooth. Each brother also maintained steady, undisturbed eye contact.

After greeting the three tables of people in the diner, Miguel returned to his table to enjoy his meal. While the Johnson twins had been surprised by the unsolicited greeting, later they turned to Miguel and across the tables gave him a thumbs-up to indicate their enjoyment of their food. Miguel reciprocated with a smile. Because Miguel and the twins finished their meals at the same time, they exited the diner together, and outside they talked for a bit.

"You told us you are Miguel Hernández, yes?" one asked.

"That's correct, and you are Gary and Jerry Johnson—am I remembering your names correctly?" Miguel responded.

"Yes, that's correct. Miguel, tell us, what do you do for a living?"

Miguel answered, "I am a jeweler—a silversmith. I work at a jewelry shop on Washington Street"—although he already knew he asked them—"What do you do for a living?"

One twin answered, "We are Immigration Custom Enforcement Agents."

Miguel already knew this because he had seen them before in the grocery-store raid that I'd managed to escape from. He easily remembered the two almost-identical blond-haired men who were both very tall and muscular.

"Do you know what that means we do?" the other twin asked.

"Yes, I know. Honestly, I already knew before asking that you are both with immigration and that you're related."

"Really?" they said, surprised.

"Yes."

"Miguel, where do you live?"

"Close by here," Miguel answered.

"Do you live with a wife? Family?"

"I have a big family, but it's my younger brother, Edgar, that shares an apartment with me. It's a small apartment located on the second floor of the same building as the jewelry store where I work."

"So just the two of you live there?"

"Also Phil, a Navajo Native American friend of ours. He works at the shop too."

"Is that so?" they asked.

"Yes, it's true," Miguel confirmed.

"Miguel, what type of papers do you have? And your younger brother too?"

"We both have *micas*," Miguel answered. A *mica* is synonymous with a green card. It is how Mexicans refer to green cards.

"Both of you?" they questioned.

"Yes."

"When did you get them?"

"I got mine in 1951. Edgar first came here in 1959 but didn't get his until '61."

"What do you mean about Edgar?" they both asked with piqued curiosity.

Miguel explained, "When Edgar came in 1959, it was quite eventful. He went to school for eight-and-a-half months and his English became excellent. But then we returned to Nogales to immigrate him legally."

"Wait a minute—you mean to tell us he entered illegally in 1959?" one of the twins asked.

"Yes, sir," Miguel confirmed, "He escaped three raids, one at a small outdoor gathering at a friend's home, one in a restaurant like this one, and another in a grocery store."

"Hmm," they both responded. Then one asked, "Do you have your green card with you?"

"Yes, I do. Have a look"—Miguel retrieved the card from his wallet and showed it to them—"See the date, 1951?"

"Yes. It's certainly authentic," they agreed.

Now that they'd been speaking for about ten minutes, Miguel was able to distinguish the slight features between the almost-identical twins, so he could more easily differentiate Jerry from Gary and vice versa.

With his soul-penetrating, sincere, and open-eyed gaze, Miguel asked them, "You two don't look like you are from Arizona. Where did you grow up?"

"We are from Oklahoma," Jerry answered. "Do you know where Oklahoma is?"

Miguel answered, "I've never been there, but I believe it's above Texas."

"Bingo," Gary said.

"But we grew up in Texas with a distant uncle," Jerry explained.

"Is your uncle still alive?" Miguel inquired.

"No, he has long passed. He was an alcoholic and died brutally. He bled to death. You don't drink do you, Miguel?"

"Never. I've never touched any kind of alcohol. I've never smoked. Those are deadly habits," Miguel stated.

"I guess that's true because drinking and smoking killed our not-so-dearly-departed uncle," Jerry observed. "And they are costly habits too."

Gary asked, "Do you know people living here without papers?"

"Oh, yes, many."

"Where?" Gary asked, incredulous that Miguel would admit such a thing to them. Jerry was equally amazed. Both stood with eyes alit, almost as if they'd struck gold.

"All over the place," Miguel replied.

"Around this diner here?" Gary asked.

"Yes, around here and other areas too."

From their faces and body language it was apparent that Miguel perplexed them. "Who is he? Is he for real, or is this a setup, a trap of some sort? Is he telling the truth or maybe he's fabricating tales for an unknown and unsavory reason?" they seemed to be thinking.

"So, what happened after your uncle died?" Miguel asked.

"We were only sixteen at the time of his death."

"What about your parents? What happened to them that you lived with your uncle?" Miguel asked.

"Our mother died when we were born, and our father abandoned us when we were five. We moved from place to place, went to school off and on, but we stuck together. We did everything together. We've never been separated," they explained.

"That's nice to have that closeness. My mother died when I was born as well. But my father soon remarried. Though he wasn't violent, my father had a lifelong addiction to alcohol and cigarettes," shared Miguel.

"We lived in different homes and around the age of ten a distant uncle took us in," Gary said, "We have doubts he was a real uncle. He abused us in many ways, but we had no other way to survive, so we just put up with him until he died. It was miserable living with him."

Miguel had noticed from the time he'd shaken hands with them in the restaurant that their forearms were dotted with scars that looked like they came from cigarette burns. He figured that this so-called uncle had tortured them in that way. He also determined that since these men had managed to emerge from such ferocious abuse with even tempers and quality manners, that they likely had the capacity in their hearts to sympathize with those seeking better lives—even though the twin brothers were immigration officers.

Jerry went on to explain, "From the time we were sixteen years old until we hit nineteen, we lived with an elderly lady who took us in. She was living alone and had no family. It was a doctor who'd helped us over the years that connected us to her. He thought it would be good for all of us to live together. This lady treated us like sons."

"When we were with her, we had the best three years of our lives," Gary added.

Jerry continued explaining, "Gary had a girlfriend who was also a stray, and she came to live with us. When the elderly lady couldn't move around easily, we took care of her. She refused to go to a nursing home and wanted to die at home, so we cared for her, and Gary's girlfriend helped with her personal hygiene."

Miguel looked at them as they talked. For some reason, Miguel felt there was some type of connection between the three of them, despite their apparent differences. The blond-haired twins were tall and big with thick but well-kept beards. Miguel was dark-haired, clean-shaven, slim, and only five feet, seven inches tall to their six-foot, four-inch statures. Miguel no longer found them threatening. He felt at ease with them and confident that they understood the suffering that happens in life and the strong will that people have to escape it. He was confident that they were good people and that he could trust them, even if they were La Migra.

To the Johnson brothers Miguel continued to remain an enigma. Although he was confident in them, they weren't confident in him. Why was he so freely giving them information about illegals in the community? Was he being honest? Was he trustworthy? Maybe he was another immigration agent—a higher-up—whose job it was to test them? Was he setting them up or was he just whacky?

Gary brought the subject back to immigration issues, asking, "Miguel, do you have people without papers living with you?"

"Yes, I do. Seven total. They aren't living with me in the apartment though. They are living at a dilapidated property on 206 N. 9th Street that I bought several years ago," Miguel revealed.

"Seven!" they responded with surprise. They exchanged looks with each other as if to check in about Miguel's truthfulness.

Miguel confirmed, "Yes, seven people. They live in the garage area, and they work all day. Well, everyone except Rafael."

"Rafael?" Jerry asked.

Gary also asked, "Who is Rafael? Does he work?"

Miguel explained, "Yes, sir, he works hard, but he works at night."

"At night you said?" one asked.

"Yes, he does prep work in a bakery, and it's a nightshift. He has very bad arthritis and has deformities in his hands. He rests during the day and drinks aloe vera juice and rubs aloe vera on his hands too. This helps with the arthritis. He also reads during the day. He is a very educated man. He left Mexico two years ago. He was living in a dumpster when I picked him up and brought him to stay at the garage on the property. He has been there for three months. He was a professor in Mexico."

"I am curious about this Rafael," said Gary.

"When can we meet these people?" asked Jerry.

Miguel's reply was to ask, "May I call you Jerry and Gary. Is that okay?"

"Yes, please do so."

Miguel looked at each of them right in the eye with his unmistakable piercing gaze.

Miguel then asked, "You lived with the older woman for three years, and you said she was getting worse. What was wrong with her?"

Jerry explained, "What happened was that we went to see our doctor to get physicals, so we could be on the high school basketball team. Dr. Brown had known us for a few years and was worried about us. He told us that we needed to quit roaming the streets and we should find a steady place to live. He explained to us that one of his patients was an elderly lady with very bad arthritis. She had trouble getting around, and living alone was proving more and more difficult. He was worried about her and predicted she wouldn't survive for long. He recommended we get to know her, and if we were up for it, he would introduce all of us."

Gary then took over. "A few days later, we met her at her house, and Dr. Brown was with us. He was the one that proposed to her that it could be a good fit to have us all live together at her house. Jerry and I could help her around the house and provide her dependable company, and she would provide us a safe and stable place to live. She agreed to take us in. And, as we already said, those were the happiest three years of our lives up to that point."

Gary stopped talking and started to cry. Jerry hugged his brother, all the while saying to Miguel, "That elderly lady and that doctor changed our lives, and we thank God for all they did for us."

Miguel touched them each on the forearms, the forearms dotted with the marks of torture they'd endured, and he said to them, "Thank you for sharing that with me."

As the three men stood outside near their vehicles in front of the diner, Miguel thought to himself, "We are distinctly different people. They deport people who have no papers. I help people get their papers, and I protect them. The Johnson brothers are good Christians, but they must do their job, and they will for certain act upon the law. So, those who have no papers will be deported."

Miguel looked back over at Gary as he wiped his tears away, and then Jerry smiled at Miguel. That's when Miguel was reassured that the Johnson brothers had hearts full of kindness and that no harm would come to Rafael or any of his guests if the twins visited his property.

"What was her name—the elderly lady?" asked Miguel.

Jerry answered, "Geraldine, Geraldine Sutton. We loved her very much. Bonnie, Gary's girlfriend, was incredible to Geraldine. She bathed her and kept her clean. In her will, Geraldine left $3,500 to Gary and the same amount to me, and $2,500 to Bonnie. The house went to Geraldine's church. Gary and I used the money to go to junior college where we earned degrees that opened the way for us to get our current jobs."

Now the man with the tears was Miguel. Wiping the tears away, Miguel asked them, "Would you like to visit Rafael now?"

"Miguel, I don't know that we feel up to visiting. This conversation has drained us. The meal and the conversation were nice, and hopefully we don't have to meet and ever confront your friends, after all, we are Immigration and Customs Enforcement Officers," Jerry stated.

So the men shook hands and told Miguel, "You are a fine man, and those around you are lucky to have you. Let's just leave it at that."

The Johnson twins then got in their 1957 Chevrolet, but they didn't leave right away. Instead, they sat in their car and talked. Jerry looked at his brother and asked, "Gary, do you remember how we felt like prisoners at our supposed uncle's home?"

"Yep," Gary answered.

"Do you remember when we were fourteen and it was summertime and we were up on the roof, hiding from him while he was screaming for us, desperate to find us and give us a beating? And we stayed up on that roof late into the night? We had plenty of lemonade to drink and the moon was almost full?"

Gary quietly answered, "Yes, I remember. I remember looking at the bright moon and below us our uncle was pacing about, hollering. I was frightened, and all I could think of was the way the moon shined upon us. It gave me strength and tranquility. I don't know how we put up with so much torture. He loved burning us with the tips of his cigarettes just to satisfy his sick need to feel dominance. He loved to see us suffer."

"We were prisoners," Jerry said again, "He threatened us about ever talking to anyone. We were watching that moon, following its clear arc of movement across the night sky. Like it was saying, 'Follow me and I will lead the way to freedom.'"

As Miguel got into his car, a lady approached. She wanted to thank him for helping her fiancé, Bartolo, with his immigration papers. She was a US citizen and Bartolo was an illegal alien, and the two were getting married. With Miguel's help, they gathered all of Bartolo's necessary application papers and were heading to Nogales to present their papers. In this case, she would act as Bartolo's sponsor because the two were getting married.

After talking together for about five minutes, Miguel was about to start his car when he noticed the Johnson twins were still sitting in their car. They hadn't left yet. Miguel decided to go make sure everything was okay with them.

When he approached, Jerry rolled down the window, and Miguel asked, "Are you two okay? I ran into a friend and got to talking, but then I noticed you were still here, so I just want to make sure you are okay."

"Yes, we're okay. We were wondering—did you say Rafael has arthritis?"

"Yes, he does," Miguel confirmed.

"We'd like to meet him."

Miguel was surprised. Why had they changed their minds? What happened?

"We'll follow you and you take us to your property, so we can see this Rafael," Jerry told him.

Miguel answered, "Yes, sir, I will take you to him."

Even though the Johnson brothers, for the most part, trusted Miguel and thought he was a decent person, there was still a part of them that doubted him and his intentions. This doubt led them to wonder whether the people whom Miguel was supposedly housing were safe with him or whether it was a human trafficking scheme. They were ambivalent—sure, Miguel seemed like one of the most compassionate people they'd ever met, but their years with their "uncle" also made them wary.

As they trailed behind Miguel, the two brothers pondered the mystery of Miguel Hernández.

Gary wondered aloud, "What does Miguel have to gain having these people with him? He's risking his own green card status by offering them housing. It doesn't make sense. We need to investigate."

Next Jerry asked Gary, "What's this guy Miguel all about? He seems calm, respectable, and serious about these people living with him—but why is he doing it? Why?"

"The uniqueness of this guy Miguel—shaking hands with people he doesn't even know in the restaurant. Is he as sincere as he seems, or is he a con man?"

"Well, think about it—if he already knew those people, he wouldn't shake their hands. He'd simply wave at them. Right? I don't know anymore what to think about this Miguel Hernández."

They were brainstorming about what they had witnessed in the restaurant: a most unusual and unprecedented case of weirdness or else a vision of human kindness? Miguel presented a mystery that had crawled under their skin. They needed to understand.

Jerry declared, "Okay, Gary, let's see what the hell is going on with this whole situation. It's killing me."

"Amen," said Gary.

Then Jerry divulged, "I have to admit, I kind of like Miguel. He's like no one we've ever met."

"Yes, I agree," said Gary, "but I think we still need to investigate.

Following Miguel's car, they turned onto Monroe Street, then took a left on 9th Street, and saw Miguel turn into the narrow driveway of 206 N. 9th Street. The house was almost completely surrounded by tall, mature trees, most probably over fifty years old, with fat trunks and long branches. There was a small front gate surrounded by plants and trees.

As they got closer and followed Miguel's car up the narrow drive, they could see a fairly run-down house with missing windows and a torn-up roof. There at the far end of the driveway, behind the house, was exactly what Miguel had described—a large garage.

As they were stepping out of their car, Miguel, who was already out of his car, told them, "Here is my house. As you can see, it's being worked on, I'm renovating it slowly. I plan to have it finished in three to four years, so I can have it ready for the rest of the family."

"The rest of the family? What family?" Jerry asked.

"My family still in Mexico. Remember, I told you that my younger brother Edgar is here? Well, it's his mother and our siblings," Miguel explained with a smile. Then he said, "Come, come over and meet Rafael."

"You said he works at night at a bakery. Yes?" Gary inquired.

"Yes, his shift is 7 pm to 4 am, I believe. The bakers depend on him to prepare all the ingredients to make about ten types of Mexican pastries."

"Ten?"

"Yes, ten or so. You know how in a Mexican bakery there's many types of bread, cookies, and pastries? And some of them are colorful as well?"

"Yes."

Miguel went on to explain, "Rafael prepares the different colors of sugar and the flour. Then he mixes these into large bowls and pans, so the bakers can shape and bake the various pastries and breads. He also cleans after the bakers are done. If you walked into the work area during the daytime, you wouldn't have any idea about happens there each night because it's so clean. The baked goods have to be ready on the shelves by 7 am. You see now how important Rafael is? The aloe vera juice he drinks and applies to his hands helps him function even with the severe arthritis."

Both Jerry and Gary looked at each other, recalling Geraldine and her debilitating arthritis.

"Who is helping you remodel your home?" they asked.

"I have a very good friend, Ray, who owns a swamp cooler business, and his workers also do duct work and many other things on the property. He will do part of the remodel. Then I have roofers, concrete workers, painters, plumbers, and electricians—I know them, and they will help when needed."

"Are they all legal?" Jerry asked.

"Some are, and some aren't. The ones that don't have papers are good people who work hard so that someday they can bring their families here to have better futures."

"It seems like you know a lot of people without papers, Miguel."

"Yes, and I wish I could help all of them," Miguel responded. "The six people here in addition to Rafael work in various trades, and many of them help when they can with the renovation work. By the way—how did you two manage to care for Geraldine because you said that like Rafael, she had bad arthritis?"

"Yes, and it's too bad we had no aloe vera plants to help her with her arthritis. For two years we had to carry her to her bed and to the dining table. Her wheelchair only helped for a while. She lived on the ground floor, and we lived upstairs," Jerry explained.

Gary added, "Jerry gave her a bell to ring in case she needed us. The biggest challenge was trying to help her with her personal hygiene—bathing and using the toilet."

"Gary and I loved to bowl," Jerry said, "Bowling was a great pastime for us. Two hours every weekend Geraldine wanted us to leave the house and enjoy ourselves, so we would go bowling. At the bowling alley, Gary started making friends with a young lady named Bonnie who was a terrific bowler."

Gary picked up, saying, "It came to me and Jerry that we needed more help with Geraldine. Both of us would put her into a standing shower and close the curtain, but she had difficulty hanging on to the sides while showering. She just could not effectively take a shower, so we thought that Bonnie might be able to help with Geraldine's showering and using the toilet."

Jerry said, "At first when we talked to Bonnie, we didn't present it right. We told her that we were living with an old lady with bad arthritis and that we couldn't bathe her. We asked if she would bathe her. But Bonnie didn't even know Geraldine and didn't know either of us very well. She thought it was strange that the two of us who she really didn't know were asking this of her, so she said no."

"But," Gary said, "Bonnie returned to talk to us more about it. She admitted that she would like a new housing situation because her current roommates smoked and drank too much. When we explained to her that Geraldine was kind and that Bonnie would have a room of her own as well as meals in exchange for helping, Bonnie agreed to go to the house and meet Geraldine. The two of them immediately clicked, and soon she was living with us and we were together like a happy family."

"That's wonderful. Someday I hope to tell you about the lives of the Hernández family," Miguel told them.

Miguel then pointed out the aloe vera plants growing along the fence, explaining, "Rafael uses the aloe vera plants here. He describes his arthritis as universal—meaning all over his body. Every joint hurts, including the joints in his skull. He grinds aloe vera, lets it sit in warm water, and then uses some for bathing and some for drinking. Rafael once told me that even before he met me and moved to this property, he knew he would find a place in the United States with many aloe vera plants."

"How did he know that?"

"I don't know, but Rafael is a philosopher and an educated man. He taught classes at a university in Mexico. He reads a lot in Spanish. He writes beautiful letters for a few of the guys staying here when they need to send money and letters to their families in Mexico."

"I see," said Jerry. "Where is he?"

"He's inside the garage. His cubicle is the last of the seven. Let's go in."

Miguel leaned down to grab the handle. He gave it a sharp pull upwards to raise the garage's slatted roller door. With the slatted door rolled up, the vestibule revealed itself. Miguel began walking down the corridor that stemmed off it to reach the cubicle at the end. The Johnson twins trailed a few feet behind him.

As he walked, Miguel called, "Rafael? *Soy Miguel.*"

"*Si*, Miguel," a voice answered.

Gary commented to Jerry, "Okay, now we are making progress. Let's see this Rafael."

When Miguel reached the final cubicle at the end of the hall, he turned to face its opening. The Johnson twins were right there next to him. Sitting on a folding chair was a small, white-haired elderly man (he'd folded up his cot to allow just enough space for the folding chair). The man wore a white sackcloth-type shirt and brown pants. His skin was smooth and shiny, and his hands were bent into crooked balls. His short legs dangled off the seat of the rickety metal folding chair without reaching the floor. He had a book in his hands.

Rafael looked up at the three men standing in the entranceway and stated, "*Buenas tardes*, Miguel. *Yo te extraño* [I've missed you]."

Miguel replied, "*Si, yo tambien, pero estoy muy ocupado,*" meaning, "Yes, me too, but I've been really busy."

Miguel then drew Rafael's attention to the Johnson twins, "*Mira*, Rafael, *estos señores*, these men are my friends, and I want them to meet you."

Rafael slowly stood up. Probably weighing only 110 pounds, he seemed miniature next to the Johnson brothers who looked down and reached out to shake his hand. Each man in turn gently shook one of Rafael's deformed hands.

The conversation continued in Spanish, which the Johnson twins spoke fluently.

"What is that smell?" asked Gary.

"You are smelling aloe vera," Rafael replied and then asked, "How is it you speak Spanish?"

Gary answered, "When we lived in Texas and went to junior college, we studied Spanish, and we rented a small place where most people around us spoke Spanish. That's also how Jerry learned to cook just about every Mexican dish you can think of."

"Really," Miguel said, "I too enjoy cooking."

Jerry added, "In junior college in El Paso we studied both Spanish and law enforcement. Now here we are—working law enforcement and speaking pretty darn good Spanish."

"College—that reminds me that Rafael was a professor in Mexico," Miguel added.

"Yes, that's true," Rafael confirmed, explaining, "I taught math, history, and agriculture until I was told that I was old and out of touch and I needed to make room for young, vibrant teachers. They told me I was washed out, so they got rid of me. That was about six years ago. I became depressed, my arthritis worsened, and I decided to come to the USA after meeting an American architect at a restaurant in Mexico. The architect invited me to come to New Mexico where he lived."

"You mean to tell me you came to the United States because an American guy in a restaurant told you to?" one of the twins asked him.

"*Si, señor*. And strange enough, I guess my arthritis has come in handy because in my journeying from Mexico up to here, many people have wanted to help me. Look at Miguel—he has been helping me. The American man I met in Mexico even told me, 'Don't worry, you will get to New Mexico, there will be angels guiding you all the way,' and he was right." At that, Rafael winked at Miguel.

"Miguel, tell me, what is the future of Rafael and the other men here?" Jerry asked.

"Each of them is in the process of gathering all the required papers. At the same time they work a lot, and they take English language classes. And in order to stay here at this property, they must promise to stay away from liquor and focus on the other goals, with the main goal being attaining their green card. They know they can't live here forever or live forever in the US illegally. Because I've already helped people get green cards, I know the process and can give assistance to the guests staying with me. They know they can count on me. You see, my big goal is to immigrate the rest of my family in Mexico to the United States. So I figure that the more people I can help out along the way, the more grace God may be inclined to grant me and my family so that we can be reunited in a few years' time in this very house. Once the renovation is completed, of course. Rafael, these men, and others around that I know, and even I, myself—we spend most of our time working. We are working to secure our futures in this great country."

Gary turned to Rafael to ask, "So, you work at a bakery?"

"I work at El Fenix Bakery on Washington Street. I work a night shift, 7 pm to 4 am."

"Yes, Miguel told us what you do," Jerry responded and then asked, "Are there other illegals working there?"

Rafael, afraid to answer the question, looked at Miguel. Miguel looked at the Johnson twins and answered, saying, "I tell you no lies as it's not proper to disrespect you. Yes, there are three good people there without papers—they are also trying very hard to become legal, gathering the required papers and locating sponsors."

Gary looked at Miguel and asked, "Why did you tell us all this? You could have simply said goodbye at the diner and that would have been it, so why?"

"I knew both of you were kind and good Christians. I just knew that you two were kind but that you also had a tough upbringing."

"How did you know that?"

Instead of immediately responding, Miguel looked at each of them in turn. He looked them pointedly in their eyes. It was his special soul-penetrating gaze where he looked right to their very inner essence. Then he asked, "Was I wrong to think that?"

The Johnson twins returned his direct eye contact.

They softened and smiled.

One replied, "I suppose you are correct, Miguel."

The other, looking at the stack of books on the tiny table in the cubicle, asked Rafael, "Do you read all these books?"

"Yes, of course."

"Let's see, you have an American history book, an agriculture book, a biography, a book on math, books with home remedies—"

Rafael interrupted to add, "And soon I will buy a book about nutrition."

"Why nutrition?"

"I have seen stunted growth in children, poor bone development and overall nutritional deficiencies. I figure that if I come back in another life, which I think I will, I want to be a nutritionist."

Miguel explained to the twins, "Trust me, it might sound strange, but I know people who have returned from previous lives."

Rafael said, "*Sí, señores*, I am in agreement with Miguel. Miracles do happen."

Gary turned to his brother to say, "Jerry, I think that Geraldine is our miracle. We lived a fear-filled and violent life for sixteen years without any hope of love and family—beyond each other—and then along came Geraldine. She gave us all a mother could give, and because of her, the course of the rest of our lives changed for the better. She is our miracle and the reason why we are here."

Everyone paused a moment to take in Gary's words.

Finally Miguel commented, "We are all so blessed to have angels guiding us and holding our hands. Indeed, this is a great country. A great and generous country. That's why people all over the world risk their lives to come here."

Rafael stated, "It is great to be here, even for people like me in precarious situations. It's by far better for us here than where we were. It's amazing that people who live here illegally, even in hiding, we still say it's better than where we came from."

Miguel said, "It's what you put your mind and soul to that makes things move in your life . . . Jerry and Gary, no one else is here other than Rafael, but I can show you the rest of the garage area if you like."

"Yes, sure," they agreed.

With Miguel again leading, they traversed the corridor and returned to the vestibule area. As Miguel was showing them the shower, toilet, long sink, and such, he continued conversing with them. "What happened to Bonnie?"

"Do you want to see her?" Gary asked.

"Yes, sure, if that's possible," Miguel replied.

"Here you go then. Here's a picture of her and me. We married three years after Geraldine died . . . And here is another picture of Bonnie and Geraldine together before she died. And here is a photo of Bonnie and our daughter, Geraldine."

Miguel marveled at the photos and then noted, "Your daughter looks like Geraldine."

"Yes, I've been told that many times."

Jerry then spoke, "Like we said before, Gary and I always do things together. We've never been separated, and we make decisions in unity. We'll never discuss what we've seen today, that we guarantee, Miguel. You, however, do understand that defiance of the law is not good. Even still, you haven't actually broken the law because you are not the one bringing these guests into this country illegally. That is a fact.

"Housing and protecting them, though, is a gray area. But, like you, my brother and I live by two laws—the law of legal immigration and the law of good Christians. I think your honesty with us and you helping these people can be interpreted as innocent and well intentioned. You aren't being malicious. Again, this is the Johnson brothers' position, which remains between you, us, and God, our witness.

"Gary and I have discussed it, and we've concluded that this will remain confidential. I think we have enough criminals, traffickers, and smugglers to deport without needing to harm these people here."

Miguel listened intently and then replied, "Our meeting together today and all we have talked about will never be discussed, no matter what happens."

Rafael, who had stepped out into the vestibule, was listening to them. Without saying a word, he extended his arthritic hands to bid them goodbye.

In order to keep in touch, Miguel gave them his address and phone number at the jewelry shop. The men embraced and said goodbye.

Jerry, Gary, and Miguel stayed friends for years. Along with Bonnie, they attended my high school graduation. When they made the plan to move out of the Phoenix area, Miguel and I attended a good-bye supper for them at Emily's diner, to enjoy a final meal together. Even after they moved, we exchanged Christmas cards and the occasional photos. The friendship that developed between the Johnson twins and the Hernández family was a highly unlikely one, but an incredibly unique one. It's another testament to Miguel's uniqueness. His mystical nature.

Chapter 10

WOUNDED

"*Que pasa*? What's going on?" I yelled out to Miguel.

"Stay there! Don't move! Don't come over here!" Miguel yelled back.

I'd been doing homework when I'd heard the screaming. Looking out the window onto the back parking lot, where the jewelry shop employees parked, I saw Phil and Miguel rush out to the alleyway, towards the source of the screams. I decided to go outside to see what was going on.

Though Miguel had warned me not to approach, I walked over anyway. It was dark, but I could make out Miguel and Phil standing over a body lying on the ground. The person was writhing around. From the wailing, it sounded like a woman. Once I was close enough, I could see that, indeed, it was a woman—a white woman, probably in her twenties—and she was covered in blood. Her scalp, face, and mouth were scraped, bleeding, and pasted over with dirt and grit. Her jacket and dress were torn, exposing her chest.

Phil was shaken but managed to say, "I heard a vehicle speeding away. I think we need to call the police."

At the mention of the police, the woman insisted, "No! No police!" all the while trying but failing to make it to her feet.

"What happened to you?" Miguel gently asked her, trying to calm her and assure her that she was no longer in danger.

"What do you think happened?" she spit back. "Can't you see, you dumb shit? I was thrown off a truck by some animals—that's what. Now fuck off and let me be!" she snarled but then began to weep.

I noticed her dress had bunched up around her waist and upper thighs, exposing her legs, which were scraped, scratched, and bleeding.

Miguel turned to see me standing a few feet away. He told me, "Edgar, run and get a blanket."

I quickly returned with a blanket. Miguel and I moved to wrap her up. Phil remained immobile, almost stone-faced, clearly scared and uncertain.

Phil again suggested, "Let's call the police."

Slightly less aggressively, she begged, "Please don't do that. No police—please, please," all the while she was bleeding and shivering.

I was shocked with what I saw. Especially as a young child at my father's medical work, I'd witnessed many people who were sick and bloodied, but this woman was different. It wasn't an illness or an accident that caused her injury, but man-made, inhumane, brutal violence.

Realizing I was disturbed, Miguel wanted me to go back inside, but I insisted, "Miguel, I am okay. Please let me help. I'll be fine."

We helped her to her feet. With Miguel and Phil on either side of her, and me watching, they slowly made their way to our small apartment above the shop. Miguel gave her a warm towel for her face and head wounds, and tried to reassure her, "You are safe with us now. Let me apply some light pressure to your scalp to stop the bleeding."

Once inside, I could see she looked to be in her late twenties. She was a beautiful young woman with hazel green eyes, long eyelashes, light brown hair, and her skin was slightly dotted with freckles.

"The bathroom and shower are back here. We'll go downstairs, so you can have your privacy, but if you need anything, let us know."

"Well, I don't know that privacy matters at this point seeing as you've seen everything," she dryly replied.

Miguel, Phil, and I waited downstairs in the shop area to give her maximum privacy. While she was showering, we were trying to figure out what do next.

Miguel noted, "The Lamberts are generous, but I don't think we can have her here. We don't know much about her. We don't know what happened to her or why. We don't know the people she's involved with. We don't even know her name . . . I'm thinking we should ask Carolina for help. What do you think of that?"

Carolina was a Mexican woman illegally in the Phoenix area whom Miguel was helping with her immigration papers. Miguel wasn't certain Carolina would be happy to take in this woman simply because Carolina had made it apparent that she wanted to be romantically involved with Miguel, but he hadn't reciprocated the feeling. Miguel wasn't into Carolina in that way, and on top of that, he wasn't in a place where he wanted to date or marry. His focus at that time was on working to earn the money required to immigrate the rest of the family and renovate the house. Even still, Miguel continued to help Carolina navigate the green card process to get her papers. She was working as a waitress, but the restaurant owner wasn't willing to act as her sponsor, so she and Miguel were on the lookout for a sponsor for her.

Carolina lived with two other Mexican women who were in the US illegally, Ernestina and Juana, who also worked as waitresses at the same restaurant as Carolina. Phil and Ernestina were dating, and Miguel and I predicted they'd get married. Because of that, we felt confident Ernestina would get a green card through her marriage to Phil. However, like Carolina, Juana needed a sponsor. Miguel was helping her too.

Fortunately, Carolina agreed to come over and help us out.

In the interim, the hurt woman called down to us that it was now okay for us to return upstairs to the apartment.

When we arrived upstairs, we found her wrapped in a blanket and her hair still sticky though she had showered. She had two large abrasions on her face, one on her left cheek and the other on her forehead. The parts of her legs and arms that were visible showed scrapes.

"What's your name?" Miguel asked her.

"You don't want to know my name," she answered. "Trouble follows me—or else I bring it with me—so it's probably better that you don't tell me your names either. If you could just let me stay here tonight and maybe I could borrow some old clothes, then I'll be on my way tomorrow."

Miguel was taken aback by her response. He told her, "We want you to rest and heal completely—as long as it takes. We're worried about you, and we want to help."

"I've had worse happen. This is nothing," she declared.

Miguel was stunned at her attitude. All of us were. She was minimizing the severe violence she'd endured. We still didn't know what had happened—had she been kidnapped? Raped? Hit by a speeding vehicle? We didn't know.

"Okay, you don't need to tell us your name, but I think you should stay for a while. I promise not to call the police," Miguel said.

"What about him? Your friend over there? Looks like a cat's got his tongue?" she asked,

referring to Phil.

Miguel assured her, "He won't call the police either. Don't worry. We will help you as you wish, and you don't have to tell us what happened unless you want to."

"Let's just say it's something that will pass," she muttered.

Confused and uncertain if he should ask, Miguel dared to ask anyway, "Do you have family?"

"Family—who needs 'em? Nope, never," she responded.

"I have some antibacterial ointment we keep here for scrapes and burns. It should help your wounds," Miguel explained, handing her a small jar.

"You think it'll help heal the wounds inside of me too?" she asked.

While waiting for Carolina to arrive, we decided to move downstairs to the shop area. Once down there, the woman asked, "What is this place? It smells weird—smells like farts."

Phil giggled, and I laughed at her comment.

She was right, the "liver of sulfur" that the silversmiths used to stain silver to give it an antique-looking patina around the turquoise stones had a rotten egg and fart-like smell.

The woman, still wrapped in the blanket, strolled around the benches, very curious and observant. She touched the torches at each bench. Moving from bench to bench, she noticed the many tools, rings, buckles, and bracelets. We all watched as she swiftly moved around the shop.

Phil still did not know what to say. At times he wanted to smile but was still shaken and struck by her brash personality.

I looked at her wondering how she could be striding around the shop, wrapped only in a blanket, after she had been involved in such a horrific act of violence. I also could not understand why she was not showing any signs of pain. What had happened to her? Who was she? Where was she from? What was going on in her life?

Though obviously beaten up and injured, she was beautiful and charming, radiant and magnetic.

She asked Miguel, still not knowing our names, "Where is the area you work at?"

"My bench, it's there," he answered, pointing to his particular bench.

She moved to it and sat on Miguel's swivel chair. Immediately she began pushing herself around in complete circles. After a few seconds, she stopped and looked at Phil. He stared back at her wide-eyed but then realized she wanted to know where his bench was. He simply pointed his out but didn't say a word.

I asked her, "Please, ma'am, tell us your name."

She answered, "Kid, let's just say I'm grateful to all of you because you just saved my life. I was a dead woman less than an hour ago, and now I owe you. Don't worry, I'll be outta your hair soon, and you can forget all about me."

Miguel looked at her and said, "You will need more than a night to recover. We are willing to shelter you for as long as you need—a week, a month, longer."

"You have anything to eat?" she asked.

"Yes, we'll make you a hot dog if you like," Miguel offered.

"Yes. Great. Do you have a beer?" she asked.

"No, we don't drink any alcohol. Not here," Miguel answered.

She laughed, saying, "Are you kidding me? You got an Indian here"—referring to Phil—"and you say there's no alcohol?"

Phil stayed silent as Miguel stated, "We don't drink here. None of us." Then he went on to explain, "I will get a shirt and a pair of pants for you. Here's a little cash, so you can buy some more clothes tomorrow. Know that you are free to leave when you want, but I've made a call to a friend of mine who is coming over, and you can stay with her as long as you like to recover."

Looking at Miguel, she asked, "What are you? Who are you, people?"

Miguel answered, "You may not want to hear this, but we are your brothers. Each of us is allotted a certain amount of time in life, and we are here to help each other during that time."

She laughed and said, "So I thought I never had a family, and now I learn that I have a bunch of brothers, one an Indian and the other—whatever you are. What are you?"

"I am Miguel Hernández, and this is Edgar, my brother. We are

Mexican," answered Miguel, "This is Phil who is a Navajo Native American, and we are your brothers. You don't believe us yet, but someday when you meet us again, you will know."

In saying this, Miguel looked her right in the eyes. It was his soul-penetrating, sincere, and honest gaze. In response, she looked down and then looked around and said nothing. Then she began to weep.

There was a knock on the door, so I went and opened it. It was Carolina, well wrapped in a thick, puffy coat. After she stepped inside, she took her coat off and saw Phil, Miguel, and the lady wrapped in a blanket.

Carolina was a short lady, a little on the chubby side, with a wide jaw and nose, and thick lips. She had very nice manners.

"Who is this?" the injured woman asked, referring to Carolina.

Miguel said, first to Carolina, "*Gracias por venir*, Carolina." And then to the woman, "This is Carolina. Her English is getting better by the day. She is a waitress and practices her English every chance she gets."

"Wish I could speak Spanish," the woman said as she was eating her hot dog.

Carolina told her, "You can stay in my apartment. There are two other women living with me—Juana and Ernestina—but we can make room for you. What happened to you?"

Phil, Miguel, and I all held our breaths, waiting to see if she would answer this time.

Finally she replied, "Good thing I have good lungs because screaming as he was strangling me is what brought these angels to help me. He was choking me, but because these two angels came, he got into the truck and took off. It all started in the bed of the pickup. That's when I bit him, and he threw me off the back. Then he jumped off too and started to strangle me. Next he jumped into the truck, and his buddy who was at the wheel, hit the gas and sped away. That's 'cause you two showed up."

Phil managed to speak, saying, "I only saw dust and the sound of a racing vehicle when I got there, and thank God for that."

"From our fight in the back of the truck, to me getting thrown out and strangled, and then these angels showing up to save me—it was probably only three minutes" the woman added.

Miguel told Carolina, "She does not want you to call the police no matter what, so please keep that in mind. Let Ernestina and Juana know."

Carolina told him with a smile, "Miguel, you have nothing to worry about because if there is something illegals do not want, it is to be visited by police officers."

The injured lady commented, "Great, so now I'll be staying with a bunch of illegals."

Carolina told her, "Yes, the other two ladies living with me also have no papers, but they will not know anything about you."

"What is your name?" asked Carolina.

Again, all of us waited with interest. I looked at Phil, Phil looked at Miguel, and then Miguel looked at me as the woman answered, "If I told you my name, you would know something about me and that would not be good. You all should not have told me your names."

"Why?" Miguel asked.

"It's for your protection. It's because those men are bad people, and now they know where I am. But luckily, they did not see you. They are really bad people and I want to shake them off, but I haven't been able to."

"Why not?" Miguel asked.

"It was my half-brother driving. His best friend and I were in the bed of the truck. My half-brother was drunk and wanted to rest, so we parked in that alley, thinking it was safe to hide there. That best friend guy was bothering me, and I wanted him to leave me alone, but he wouldn't stop. That's when we started to fight. I bit him and he threw me off the truck and started strangling me."

Miguel told her, "I believe I understand. You don't have to tell us your name. It's okay. I know many people who are here illegally that also don't want to use their real names, so I understand. We only want to help you if you'll let us. And once you leave, we can forget we ever saw you, I promise. Carolina and her two friends won't ask you anymore about your name or what you do or where you are from. We just want no harm to come to you."

She started to cry and came over to Miguel and hugged him like she never wanted to let go.

Miguel tried to reassure her, "Don't be afraid. We will never harm you. Let's get you into some clothes, and then you can go to Carolina's apartment and get some sleep."

She muttered, "I just want to warn you that they know where I am."

"They don't know us, and you will not be here," Miguel responded while gently bringing the hug to a close. "You will be living with three illegals who every day are in hiding from immigration officers and even the police. I only tell you this, so you can be certain that no one will call the police about you. However, I don't know if you have committed any crimes or anything of that sort, but I must ask you one thing and I beg for your honesty: have you or your friends ever recently or in the past hurt someone? Because if that is the case, at some point we will have to contact the police, and we will have a certain obligation to turn you over to them."

She looked down and didn't speak.

Miguel continued, "I immigrated in 1951, and my brother Edgar in 1960. Carolina and her two friends are illegal but otherwise have committed no crimes. Edgar and I are trying to bring his mother and the rest of our family to the USA, so we can't jeopardize that by getting involved with someone else's criminal offenses. Phil, as you know, is a Navajo and my brother, and he will never harm you. I think you are safe with us. But, I need you to answer the question—have you or any of your friends committed any crimes that we should know about?"

She was facing Miguel, and he looked at her with his trademark deep, penetrating gaze. She locked eyes with him and then embraced him again, answering, "No, we have never hurt anybody. But they have stolen cars and forged checks, and they drink too much. On my part, short of stealing petty stuff, I have not hurt another human being."

She began crying again. Then she told us that she should describe the two men to us, so if they came looking for her, we'd be prepared. "My half-brother is named Jeremy. He's about five-foot eight, brown hair in a flat-top, skinny, blue eyes, and a thin face. Also he wears glasses. He can't see without them. He's easy to recognize. The other guy is Stan. He's stocky, with blond thinning hair, a goatee, long sideburns, crooked teeth, and a scar on his upper lip. They are small-time thieves and drunks, and can be dangerous when they're drunk. Otherwise, I swear they aren't criminals, but they have the potential to get wild and maybe hurt someone. They've threatened people twice when they were robbing a couple of convenience stores just to get a few dollars. They've slapped people around before, but no serious violent crimes. Please, Miguel, I'm sorry to have landed here, and I don't want to cause any of you problems."

"No, there's no problem," Miguel told her in a calm voice, "You arrived here and are with us for a reason."

Miguel always referred to difficult situations or events as "opportune" times in our lives. He didn't just say this; he truly viewed them as such. He believed there were important reasons for even the most challenging of things that happened.

She went upstairs and put on a pair of Miguel's pants and a shirt. Because she'd lost her shoes during the struggle in the back of the pickup, before she was thrown off, Carolina took her own socks off and gave them to the woman, so she'd have a bit of protection for her feet.

Before departing with Carolina, the woman hugged Miguel one more time and asked, "Will I see you again?"

"It depends on how long you stay with us."

She waved at Phil, Miguel, and me, and then she and Carolina left.

Miguel called out, "Drive very carefully, Carolina! Don't speed!"

It was midnight when finally we all went to bed. While in bed, I asked Miguel, "What's going to happen to her?"

"She will be fine. Whether she knows it or not, she has family now, and we will help her—as much as she allows us to."

———

Two days later, on his lunch break, Miguel visited Carolina at the restaurant where she and her two roommates worked. "How is the injured woman doing? Is she still with you all or has she gone?" he asked.

"She's still with us. She hasn't left the apartment once, because she's afraid to go out. Her wounds appear to be healing slowly. She's trying to remove the gravel pieces from her cuts. Apparently that guy Stan dragged her and flung her around like a rag doll in that alleyway. Something else—I find her staring out the window. I don't know what she's looking at. I think she's checking to make sure those fellows aren't outside."

"Do you think I should come by? I could bring more antibiotic ointment," Miguel asked.

"Yes, I think that's a good idea."

Once back at work, Miguel found himself reviewing the woman's situation. He knew he'd like to help her stay in Phoenix and start a new life with people who would show her kindness and support rather than violence. He worried for her. She seemed lost and confused about right and wrong, both in terms of how to behave herself but also how she deserved to be treated. If she would let him, he knew he'd like to help her.

Miguel arrived at the small apartment where Carolina, Juana, and Ernestina lived. All three of them worked at the same restaurant, one of the best Mexican restaurants in Phoenix that was owned by a man of Lebanese descent. Restaurant work tended to be a stepping-stone for illegal workers simply because most restaurants really could not sponsor waitresses. Waitressing was considered temp work. Miguel was trying hard to convince the restaurant owner to sponsor all three ladies, but he hadn't committed. As already mentioned, we hoped that Ernestina and Phil's relationship would lead to marriage, so Phil, as her husband, could serve as her sponsor.

After Carolina handed over a cup of sweetened *café con leche*, Miguel asked, "How's the guest?"

"She's still sad and scared. Everything scares her, but we are starting to see her smile occasionally. She hasn't spoken a word about leaving, which is good. Let me go get her," Carolina said.

A minute later, the young woman emerged, alongside Carolina, wearing Miguel's shirt that she'd borrowed two days before and a Mexican flowery skirt.

Miguel was surprised at how attractive she looked despite the many abrasions and bruises on her face.

Softly, she said, "Hello, Miguel. I'm sorry about everything," and she started to cry. Then she moved to hug him in a tight embrace that she seemed reluctant to release him from.

"I'm very happy to see you are safe. Carolina told me she's happy that you are still here. She hopes you'll stay for a long time," Miguel assured her.

"Why are you all doing this for me? I'm a worthless person, totally unworthy of this kindness," the woman answered, still embracing Miguel in a tight hug.

Miguel gently removed her arms and motioned for the young woman to sit down on the sofa next to him. He looked her pointedly in the eyes, held both her hands, and said, "I'm here for you and so are Carolina, Juana, and Ernestina because—just like you—we had people come into our lives and help us when we most needed it. I truly believe in my heart that it is meant to be for you to be here with us. It was meant for all of us to meet in this way."

Juana and Ernestina had joined them at this point, so when the young woman turned her head, she saw the three women nodding their heads and looking at her to show their agreement and support.

Miguel gave her a sponge and some more antibacterial ointment, and then together they drank more coffee and ate some Mexican pastries. There was even some light laughter and smiles.

"How is your little brother doing? And also Phil?" the woman asked.

"They are good. When I left to come over here, Edgar was doing his homework and Phil was watching television. He loves the *Huntley–Brinkley Report* and the *Dick Van Dyke Show*."

Sheepishly, the woman stated, "Will you please tell Phil that I had no right to insult him when I said I was surprised he didn't drink?"

Miguel smiled at her, saying, "He's heard worse. Please think nothing of it. Phil took no offense at what you said."

She looked at Miguel and said, "Thank you," and turning to Carolina, Juana, and Ernestina, she stated, "and thank you all for everything."

Miguel stood up, telling them, "I must leave now. But this Sunday I'm having my monthly barbecue get-together at the 206 N. 9th Street property. There'll be *carne asada*, beans, and other food, as well as cold *horchata* to drink. I hope all of you will come."

Chapter 11

REVELATIONS

As he approached the entrance of Emily's diner, Miguel was pleasantly surprised to see that the sign was no longer in the window. With a smile on his face, he opened the door and walked inside.

Emily quickly came over to greet him, her freckled face stretched in a wide grin. "Miguel, it's wonderful to see you! How are you?"

"I'm good. What about you?"

"We're good here. I want to tell you—Jaime is fabulous. He's an excellent cook and a fine person. A few weeks ago, he got his green card."

"That's great news, Emily. I'm happy to hear it," Miguel replied. "I'm here to meet with Mr. Howard Jones, the man you contacted me about."

"Terrific. Before you sit down with him, let me go get Jaime real quick. I think he'll want to say hi to you."

Jaime emerged from the kitchen. After exchanging greetings, Miguel invited him to come to his Sunday afternoon barbeque.

"*Claro que sí.* Of course, I'll be there and my wife too," Jaime promised. "And we have a surprise to show you too."

Emily then walked Miguel to a booth where a man was already seated. This was Howard Jones. Miguel shook his hand warmly, looking him deeply in the eyes, and took a seat opposite of him in the booth.

Mr. Jones began, "Thank you for meeting me here, Miguel. You're probably wondering why I asked Emily to arrange this meeting."

"Yes, sir," Miguel replied, "What can I do for you?"

Mr. Jones explained, "I've been told by a good many people, Emily included, that you are a man who knows about the immigration process."

"I know something about it, but by all means I'm not an expert," responded Miguel.

Mr. Jones said, "I went to the immigration office to ask about immigrating a few of my workers. However, when I inquired about it, the people there started interrogating me. Because I didn't know any better, I admitted that I wanted to immigrate a worker already in the US. That's when they ramped up their questioning. I realized I'd made a mistake. It was stressful. Bad. I managed to make it out of there without revealing my name or the name of my business, but it made me realize that I needed help. Seeing as I've known Emily for years, I talked to her about it, and she told me about you and how you helped Jamie with his papers and helped her to act as his sponsor. And she told me that you've helped a number of folks get their papers."

Miguel noted, "Yes, Emily is a wonderful and a generous lady."

Mr. Jones explained, "It's been a struggle for Emily hiring Mexican and Mexican American workers over the years. Emily is a fair business owner. She only hires people that she respects. Her workers are like family to her. The problem for her has been her business partner. To put it mildly, he's a horse's ass. This guy viewed those workers, whether illegal or legal, as 'wet backs.' He was constantly undermining them and insulting them."

"Perhaps he was the one responsible for the sign I used to see in the doorway," Miguel offered.

"Yes, he was the one behind that sign. Last year, Emily and her husband asked me for a loan to buy the partner out. The decision to split with him had a lot to do with the sign. Not only did Emily consider it insulting and humiliating to many people, but also people complained to her about it all the time. She was happy to get rid of the partner and the sign—and I was thrilled to be able to help her to do it."

Mr. Jones continued, "I'd like to talk to you about helping me sponsor a few of my great workers who are living in fear of deportation. I'm concerned about them, and I'd like to learn how I can sponsor them, so they can be here legally. I have a business that manufactures aluminum roofing, awnings, and ductwork for heating and cooling. It's actually my business that put on the new roof here at Emily's. I have twenty-five workers total, just five of them are illegal. Two of the five illegal workers hold positions of responsibility and leadership. I hate thinking of how deportation could mess up these men's lives as well as my business."

Miguel responded, "Mr. Jones, I'm confident that we'll be able to get green cards for all five of these men."

"Miguel, I have to tell you a few more things though. First, while they're hardworking and honest men, they don't speak much English. And that worries me."

Miguel told him, "I've been working regularly with people over a period of several years, helping them immigrate. While a person isn't required to be fluent in English to get their green card, I encourage everyone I help to start taking English lessons. As I see it, they'll be happier and more integrated and have even better job opportunities if they can speak English. But the point is, Mr. Jones, your five workers can still get their green cards even if their English isn't great. In the meantime, I can set them up with good and free lessons."

Mr. Jones responded, "Miguel, that's good news. Real good. You see, I want them to be able to move up into managerial and client-contact positions, but I know they'll have to speak English to do that. Another important factor is my son. He'll soon be graduating from the University of Kansas with a master's degree in architecture. Eventually he's going to play an important role in hiring, developing, and modernizing the business. I worry that he'll want to let go of these workers if he can't communicate with them. For them to have a long-term place with us, especially when my son takes over, they are going to have to get their papers and learn English."

"I understand, Mr. Jones," Miguel said. "And I'll be able to help you with the immigration process as well as connect these men with good English teachers."

"Miguel, that would be wonderful. Ideal. My son is coming here in a few weeks, and I hope you can meet him."

"Mr. Jones, it would be a pleasure to meet your son."

Mr. Jones then asked, "Now, just to be clear—you aren't afraid that you'll get in trouble for helping these guys? Emily told me you never seemed worried, but I just want to make sure."

"Don't worry, it's not an issue. I'm happy and willing to help. I have no concerns about myself. My concern is helping these good, hardworking people, who came to the USA to start better lives for themselves and their families, and who live in constant fear of deportation."

Mr. Jones pressed, asking, "You do know they broke the law, right?"

Miguel answered, "Of course, I realize that. Let me tell you a little about me—I was blessed enough that a generous but random couple who owned a business in Phoenix took the chance to sponsor me in 1951. That's how I got here. My younger brother was here illegally for almost a year in 1959. He escaped raids several times, and it was incredibly frightening. We went back to Nogales to immigrate him legally, and not until a year later did his papers finally come through for him to get his green card. Along the way, kind people—who had no prior connection to us at all—chose to help us. They were instrumental in my little brother finally getting his green card.

"Currently, I'm working really hard to bring in the rest of my siblings and my step-mother to the US. In order to pull it off, I'm going to need God's help as well as the help of many more supposedly random angels on Earth. The way I see it—all people, we're just one big family. Whether we are aware or not, we depend on one another to make our lives better. So just as seemingly random other folks have played key parts in helping me and my family get green cards, I want to provide all the help I can to others in need. So, helping you and your workers is just me doing my part."

"Emily did say you are an extraordinary human being—a 'super human.' I now see what she means," Mr. Jones responded.

The two men talked about the specific papers that Mr. Jones could begin getting in order. Miguel gave Mr. Jones the name of the head coordinator at Friendly House as well. Also they set a date to have dinner when Mr. Jones's son would be visiting.

———◦◦◦———

The first person to arrive for the Sunday barbecue at 206 N. 9th Street was Jaime. His wife was with him, and he held a baby in his arms.

"Who is this?" Miguel asked Jaime, referring to the baby.

With a proud smile, Jaime introduced the baby, "This is the surprise I was talking about. Her name is Emily Ann Montez."

"Wow. Congratulations to both of you!" Miguel told them. "She is beautiful. Tell me, what does Emily think of baby Emily's name?"

"She's crazy about the baby and delighted to have a namesake and a goddaughter. And look, she's the one who gave her these shiny little shoes!"

Jaime also brought all the fixings to make *tortas*, which are a kind of Mexican sandwich. You take a short oval bread roll, sort of like a little baguette, cut it in half, and stuff it with meat, sauce, and anything else to make it taste amazing. Jaime and his wife started to set up the table and get the *torta* fixings ready.

Phil and Ray Fasio came too. Miguel invited another Ray as well, Ray Provencio, a new friend who was also a jeweler from central Phoenix. We had a new guest arrive recently, Benjamín, who had jewelry-crafting experience, and Miguel was hoping that Ray Provencio would consider sponsoring him.

Around forty people came to the barbecue that day, including the Davises from across the street, filling the entire property. The house itself was still under construction, but the tall trees, cool weather, and fenced-in outdoor space made for a fun gathering. There were plenty of places to sit, eat, and converse.

Carolina, Ernestina, Juana, and the young woman whose name we still didn't know showed up. Ernestina immediately found Phil, as they were going out together. The young woman gravitated to Miguel's side and stood next to him. It was apparent she was nervous. Her eyes showed fear. However, the many scratches and bruises were fading, and she was looking healthier and prettier by the day. It had been almost three weeks, yet we still didn't know her name.

As I was sitting and enjoying a bean burrito, the young woman approached and sat beside me on the long, wide wooden beam we'd set up to for seating. I couldn't help but admire her beauty, her light brown hair, hazel eyes, and very fine freckles.

"So you came to the USA in 1959?" she asked me.

"Yes," I confirmed.

"Miguel came in 1951?"

"Yes."

"Where's your mother and father?"

"Did Carolina tell you anything about me and Miguel?" I asked her.

"No, she didn't tell me much, but the little I know, I find fascinating. Your brother Miguel is . . . well . . . I don't know how to describe it. I get this feeling I've met him before. I know it sounds creepy or impossible, but it's something that's been bugging me. A lot. After you all found me that night, I was going to leave the next morning, but something told me I shouldn't. I don't know, maybe I don't know what I'm saying, but there's something about Miguel—maybe he's an angel."

"An angel?" I asked.

She explained, "Like there's some outside force propelling me towards him. I feel protected and unafraid when I'm with him. When I hugged him the first time, well, I didn't want to let him go. It's a weird feeling, something I haven't experienced before. Edgar, I feel like I've seen him before, like in a dream. Okay, maybe not like in a dream. Maybe a long time ago when I was chased by a guy who was trying to attack me. I was running, and I think I might have run into Miguel, and I fell to the ground, looked up—but he was gone. At the same time the guy chasing me disappeared, so it's like Miguel saved me . . . Do you think what I'm saying is strange?"

"No. I think it's more spiritual than strange," I replied.

She continued, "You know something? What I don't want to do is leave, but I know soon I'll have to."

She started to cry. I didn't know what to say, so I kept quiet.

In her now raspy voice, she asked, "How about you—how did you get here?"

"My father died in 1959, and Miguel brought me to Arizona right after his death. There were many obstacles along the way, but we managed to overcome them, and now we're here. Together. My mother and siblings are still in Mexico. But my brother Pedro and sister Olivia live in Cave Creek up north. They take care of a family there and can't leave very often."

"I see. You, Phil, and Miguel live upstairs in the jewelry store?"

"Yes, but this is the property Miguel is fixing up. We hope it will be done in a few years, so that our whole family can live here together. Tell me something about your family."

"My family?" she questioned.

"Yes, your family," I repeated.

"Well, you know about my half-brother who was going to let Stan kill me. That's the type of family I have"—with bitterness in her voice—"How much more do you want to know?"

I said, "Whatever you want to tell me. If you don't want to tell me anything, that's fine too."

"Edgar, you now sound like Miguel," she said, with a twinge of a smile, and at the same time looking across the yard at Miguel, who was now talking with some other people.

"Okay, let's start with your name," I suggested.

"My name is Charlotte. I was born in El Paso, Texas. I was born to an alcoholic mother and a thief for a father. They say my mother was drunk when she delivered me, and my father was in jail, so I was immediately taken away to live with another family as ordered by the courts. I reunited with my parents at the age of two when the courts deemed them to be 'suitable.' The courts and the judges were full of shit!

"Everything we had in our home was stolen, and no one ever talked about it, no guilt whatsoever. My father showed off about how easy it was to steal something and would show me how he stole things. He talked about how he stole furniture and silverware from the Ramada Inn. Because I heard about it so much and it was what I knew, after a while, it became perfectly acceptable. Normal. I accepted all he said since I knew no different. Growing up, when I'd talk, they would call me stupid and kick me or slap me."

I sat quietly and continued to listen.

"I was always, as long as I can remember, being told I was stupid every time they talked to me. 'Hey, stupid,' they referred to me. It's incredible that the courts ever saw them fit to be parents. Edgar, you know who is fit to be a parent?"

"Who?" I asked.

"That beautiful man out there who looks and moves like an angel. You know—Miguel," Charlotte said.

"Oh yes, my brother. He's like a father to me. I have loved him since I was seven years old. That's when I met him for the first time. That was 1957. I know no man greater than Miguel."

"I wish he was my father," she said with tears in her eyes. "I left my parents when I was fifteen and went to live with one of my mother's half-sisters. This auntie had two sons and one daughter. All sloppy and trashy. They never took a bath and rarely bushed their teeth. I couldn't wait to leave them. I dropped out of high school after just a couple months and went to live with friends, but I was still in contact with the two boys. I could never shake them off. My half-brother Jeremy and my repulsive boyfriend Stan are nothing but thieves and lowlifes who got me in a lot of trouble in Texas. We've been living in a run-down, filthy trailer in East Phoenix. All they do is smoke, drink, and steal. God knows why they haven't, as of yet, committed a violent crime. Miguel asked me if I had ever committed a crime. The honest truth is no. A flat no. I have a record in Texas from an attempted robbery of a liquor store, but I don't think it amounts to much."

Miguel came over to check on us and asked, "How's the food?"

"Great as always," I said.

"How about you?"

"Charlotte, my name is Charlotte," she revealed to Miguel.

"'Charlotte'—now that is a beautiful name, and it fits you well."

"Thank you, Miguel."

"So, Charlotte, what do you want to do when you are healed up?" Miguel asked her.

"I very much would like to stay here."

"Here?"

"Here, yes—with you. If it's okay." She stood up and got close to Miguel and said, "Miguel, I'm scared to leave. This is my only opportunity to escape a life with no exit. A life of destruction and total failure. You are the one that has given me a sense of hope. I don't know, but I feel like I've met you before. I just think I've known you. I know you now, and I love you and all these people around you. Yes, for certain I know I've seen you before—years ago."

She hugged Miguel and left to mingle with Carolina and the other ladies.

I asked, "Miguel, do you think she'll leave us?"

"No, she's just settling her thoughts and her spirit. I'm sure this young lady has been through a lot that we don't know about. Without knowing the details, I'm certain that her life has been rough," Miguel answered.

"Yes, she told me some about herself, and she hasn't been treated well."

"Edgar, when I meet again with Howard Jones, the man who owns the aluminum business, I'm going to see if he'd consider hiring Carolina, Ernestina, Juana, and Charlotte. They are all hard workers, and maybe he could sponsor them—not Charlotte, but the other three ladies. Well, not necessarily Ernestina because she and Phil will hopefully get married."

"Miguel, that's a great idea!" I told him.

Miguel's barbecue was a success. In addition to meeting Jaime's new baby and Charlotte opening up to us, Raymond Provencio and Benjamín hit it off really well. In fact, that very night Mr. Provencio had Benjamín come to live in a small guesthouse on his property. Mr. Provencio acted as Benjamín's sponsor, and a year later, Benjamín got his green card.

Another Sunday barbecue several months later also proved an incredibly special affair. Miguel didn't host it. Instead, Calvin, a goat farmer in the Chandler area, hosted it at his farmhouse. Calvin entered the USA from Mexico in 1952. That's when he bought the farm near Chandler and started raising goats for milk, cheese, and meat. He usually employed about eight workers, and Miguel leaned on him several times to hire and sponsor illegal immigrants seeking green cards. The man was an excellent sponsor and boss. At Calvin's barbecue, a number of business owners and their families attended. It was a party celebrating the green cards that four of these business owners had finally attained.

Before the celebration, Miguel, Olivia, Pedro, and I had dinner together—something that was significant because it was rare that Olivia and Pedro were allowed time away from their caretaking responsibilities. At this meal Miguel revealed something incredible about Calvin, business owners, and immigration, something the rest of us had never known before.

Miguel said, "Did you know that here in Phoenix there are, to my knowledge, at least twelve Mexican-owned businesses that employ people who are legal and illegal, yet the owners themselves are not legal—the owners themselves don't even have green cards?"

We were shocked at this revelation.

I challenged him by asking, "How can that be? How can they own a business and even sponsor others if they don't have a green card themselves? And if their business gets raided, what do they do?"

Based on his friendships with these owners, Miguel explained the intricacies of this little-known phenomenon. First, because they owned their business, they took for granted that when raids occurred, the officers would assume, naturally, that as the owners they had their green cards. It was this incorrect assumption that had shielded them, so far at least, from getting deported. For example, an auto body shop owner had nine employees. He, himself, had no papers. When a raid occurred, three of his employees were deported, but since he was identified as "the owner," the immigration officers assumed he must be legitimate and legal, and nothing was asked of him. Miguel knew firsthand many other similar owners whose businesses had been raided, but the owners were left untouched.

Interestingly, the employees didn't even know of the boss's illegal status. In fact, the employees took it for granted as well that the boss/business owner was legal, especially because this person often would sponsor their own employees.

The more successful the businesses became, the more difficult it became for the owners to deal with their illegal status. They couldn't get another business owner to sponsor them because they, themselves, were the business owners. They, themselves, acted as their employer. And they weren't going to quit their successful businesses or jeopardize their business just to get a green card.

While these owners broke the law by entering and living in the US illegally, they contributed a lot to the community and the economy by employing people, offering services and goods people needed, and paying state, and federal taxes. Many also acted as sponsors helping employees gain legal status. Actually, those who acted as sponsors put themselves in very vulnerable positions because part of being a sponsor entailed presenting information about yourself and your business to prove its solvency, which, in turn, showed the capacity to hire and sponsor the person applying for the green card.

Among the information the business owner had to present to be a sponsor included their social security number so that their tax information could be accessed. However, these business owners didn't have real social security numbers. Theirs were fakes—either total fakes, those of deceased people, or that of one of their American-born children. If an immigration officer discovered the number was fake, the business owner would get in trouble. In this way, it was a testament to their devotion to helping fellow immigrants that these business owners would act as sponsors and put themselves and their businesses—and really their whole lives in America—at great risk (or, rather, greater risk, seeing as they were illegally in the US, they were already at risk).

Miguel, himself, felt challenged to figure out how he could help his business-owning friends gain legal status. One of these friends, Abelino, ran a successful concrete business. Abelino sponsored several of our guests, so when he and Miguel finally figured out a way for him to gain a green card—and not jeopardize his business—they were both overjoyed. What Abelino did was incorporate his business with silent partners, and it was one of these partners who acted as his sponsor. Miguel then walked him through all the parts of the immigration process, so he finally got his green card. Miguel was able to help Calvin, the goat farmer, in a similar manner.

In addition to celebrating that Abelino and Calvin had obtained their green cards, the barbecue would also commemorate Solomon and Esperanza. They had come to the US at around the same time as Pedro and Olivia. Initially, when Miguel had immigrated Pedro and Olivia, Solomon and his wife, Esperanza, could not get into the country legally because they lacked the necessary papers and had no sponsor. Miguel told them to be patient and that he would help them. They, however, didn't want to wait and decided to cross illegally. When they arrived, they stayed with a family in Mesa, Arizona. These people owned an upholstery shop but could not (or would not) sponsor Solomon and Esperanza because though they had a business, they did not have their papers. They too were in the US illegally and were too afraid to act as sponsors because of the added scrutiny and vulnerability it would expose them to. Finally, after living and working in the US for over ten years without papers, Solomon and Esperanza had new jobs with business owners who would sponsor them. They had then gathered all the necessary papers and attained their green cards.

We cooked four goats to celebrate the hard work, hope, and endurance that Abelino, Calvin, Solomon, and Esperanza, in particular, had dedicated to finally attain green cards. Other guests included a bakery owner, a framing company owner, Evelyn and Glen Davis, Ray Fasio, other farmers and their families, Miguel, and me.

It was a commemoration of our hopes and dreams—for ourselves, for our families, and for future generations that we hoped would enjoy prosperous lives in the USA. We talked about our home countries, our decisions to depart, and our struggles, as well as the good luck we'd encountered in our quests to get green cards. Everyone had unique tales of fortune, misfortune, generous people, surprise obstacles, and unexpected angels.

Now that we all had green cards, we discussed our dreams of eventually attaining citizenship—actual American citizenship. We pondered together what that might look like and how uplifting and gratifying it would be when we could be more than just legal in the USA—when we could be American citizens.

First, a green card and next, citizenship—both required effort, planning, work, commitment, and the persistent pursuit of a dream—and we knew that especially with the support network that Miguel had spearheaded, we could achieve our biggest dreams. It wouldn't be easy, but together we could do it. We made plans to have future celebrations like Calvin's barbecue because such gatherings provided important opportunities for the exchange of uplifting personal stories as well as practical tips and advice.

It was an unforgettable barbecue.

Chapter 12

CUPID'S ARROWS

I was preparing a presentation for my role in a school play, an adaptation of scenes from John Steinbeck's *The Grapes of Wrath*. I was studying the part where the main character, Tom Joad, along with his family stopped at a gas station-diner to get gas and buy a loaf of bread. The bread was for the grandfather in the family who had no teeth.

The true price of a loaf of bread was fifteen cents, but the waitress told Tom Joad that it only cost five cents because she realized that was all the family could afford to pay.

"I think you're going soft," a customer who frequented the diner told the waitress.

I had so much work to do learning my part in the play that when Miguel went out to eat, I stayed behind. He was going to have a meal at Jordan's Mexican Restaurant, one of the many Lebanese-owned Mexican restaurants in Phoenix. The owner, Mr. Ames, was very nice and had sponsored a few of Miguel's guests, even though he had limited resources.

Before departing Miguel told me, "I'll be back a little later, and I'll bring you something to eat."

After eating, Miguel was walking back to his car when he heard someone calling out to him from the alley that ran alongside the restaurant. Miguel looked over to see a disheveled white man. He wore a tattered coat, torn hat, overalls with holes, and very used boots.

"What's that you said?" Miguel called back.

"You got something to eat? I'm real hungry and so is my family," the man said.

"What's your name?" Miguel asked.

"Frank, Frank Cooper. I'm from Oklahoma. My wife and child are hungry. Our truck done run out of gas. We're flat broke. At the end of our rope."

Miguel realized Frank Cooper was referring to an old beat-up, rusted-out pickup truck in which sat a red-headed lady holding a baby. The pickup looked ready for the junkyard.

Miguel questioned, "Mr. Cooper, what are you doing here in Arizona?"

Mr. Cooper was thin, tall, with an unkempt beard and scarring on his face. His teeth were gnarly and rotted. Initially he'd been chewing tobacco and spitting out bits, but with Miguel staring into his eyes so intently, he suddenly wiped his mouth as if it had dawned on him that it wasn't polite to be chewing tobacco.

Mr. Cooper replied, "Sir, we just need a little help with food and gasoline, so we can get to Sacramento, California. My little lady in the car has a sister out there. We're heading there to join the brother-in-law who works with wrought iron. I'm a wrought iron worker, but I'm outta work. We're good people, sir, just down on our luck."

"I understand, and I'll help you," Miguel told him.

Miguel headed back inside the restaurant to speak to Mr. Ames about getting the family some food. When he returned outside, he said to Mr. Cooper, "Why don't you have the missus and baby get out of the truck and have something to eat? Your food will be ready soon."

Both Mr. and Mrs. Cooper talked about their hard times. They told Miguel about the tire blowout that had damaged the truck. Luckily, the ensuing accident only resulted in them getting a few scratches and bruises. The baby, a three-month-old and also a red-head like his mother, was not harmed.

Mr. Cooper asked, "What's your name, sir?"

"My name is Miguel Hernández."

"That's an interesting name," Mr. Cooper remarked.

Miguel smiled, saying, "In Oklahoma my name might sound unusual, but here in the Southwest it's as common as 'Smith' is in your area."

"I'm sure, but 'Miguel' is new to me," Mr. Cooper said.

Miguel smiled again.

The two of them lined up a few wooden crates to act as seats and a table. Miguel brought them a traditional Mexican meal that the restaurant offered: beans, rice, tortillas, *barbacoa*, and salsa. Two cooks and a waiter came out with drinks and more food.

They were silent as they ate. On occasion as they sipped their *horchata*, they would look at Miguel.

All the while, Miguel was considering where he could find housing for them and if he could find work for them too. His mind was turning, cranking away. The seven bays at his residence were full, and the house itself was in no state for anyone, especially a baby. "Who can I go to? Who can help these people?" A swirling of possibilities came to mind.

That's when Miguel thought of Carl Long, a giant of a man who stood six feet eight inches tall and weighed around 290 pounds. Carl wore his hair in a crew cut and had a heart of gold. In the past Carl had hired illegal workers when Miguel had asked him for help, and he'd even sponsored them. Carl owned a small mom-and-pop hotel with twenty units. At the hotel's front desk Carl displayed Miguel's jewelry to sell on consignment. Carl had an old trailer behind the hotel that was somewhat neglected but otherwise livable.

Miguel decided to call Carl to see if he could help out the Coopers, until they could get back on their feet.

Carl said, "Miguel, anything for you."

The Coopers lived in Carl's trailer for six months, and even when they moved out, they stayed on in Phoenix. They worked at Carl's hotel, and later Frank became the second non-Navajo (after Miguel) to work at the jewelry shop. As he was an expert at polishing wrought iron works, the Lamberts hired him to polish jewelry, a role that the silversmiths had asked many times to be filled.

Mrs. Cooper worked at a Mexican restaurant, and their son, Anthony Miguel Cooper, went to Monroe School, the same elementary school I attended. Mr. Cooper had all his teeth pulled and got dentures.

Though Mrs. Cooper was extremely shy, I was there the time she confided in Miguel, "When we were in such dire need of help, I imagined someone in the streets reaching out to us, extending a hand to help us. I imagined and wished for a miracle for my baby. Then you came into our life." She cried as she spoke.

Miguel hugged her and said, "It's destiny. It was meant to be."

Once, I came upon Mr. Cooper and realized he had been crying. He patted the space next to him and asked me to sit down. After I sat, he tapped my shoulder twice and asked, "Do you know how lucky you are to have a brother like Miguel?"

I replied, "Yes, very much. I am here because of him."

Frank Cooper was a gentleman with much emotion. He cried, hugged me, and confided, "An hour before I met your brother, I was angry and saw death before me. But then, I heard something in my ear that said, 'Don't give up, don't give up, look at your son.' Then we saw Miguel getting into his car. Edgar, I tell you, most people would have run away from me. I looked scary. I had a desperate and dangerous look in my eyes. I wonder if I would've hurt someone if they refused to help me. But Miguel wasn't afraid of me. And, as I neared him, I realized that I held no more anger, and I felt an odd sense that he was the very person my wife had imagined extending a hand to help us."

Mr. Cooper placed his hands on his face and bent forward to bring his head towards his knees. Holding that position he said, "My wife and I prayed for someone to reach out to us as your brother did, thank God."

To this day I am moved by the meeting between Miguel and the Coopers—how their lives came together and how it coincided with the my own studies of hardship that people from Oklahoma endured in the novel *The Grapes of Wrath*. To me there seemed a lot of factors playing into the destiny of our coming together.

———※※———

The same week that Miguel met the Coopers, Miguel had dinner with Mr. Howard Jones and his son. Their dinner meeting was also at Jordan's Mexican Restaurant. As I was still working on my part for the theater rendition of *The Grapes of Wrath*, I again stayed at home to study.

Before going to Jordan's, Miguel made a quick visit to see Charlotte at Carolina's apartment. They talked for a bit, and Charlotte asked him where he was going next.

"I'm going to a dinner meeting with some men who own an aluminum business. I'm going to help them with some immigration issues, and I hope they can help me too. It's an important meeting."

"Where's Edgar?" she asked.

"He's preparing for a play and couldn't come with me."

"Miguel, it would mean so much to me if you could let me go with you. You have no idea how much this would mean to me. I am lonely, I have been so lonely for such a long time. I never had a father or mother to cling to as a child, to go to a movie with, to go out for an ice cream or to a restaurant with"—she broke down and cried—"Miguel, I'm sad inside. Please let me experience just for a bit something I've been longing to do for many years. It'll make me feel special and loved. Please, Miguel, do this for me."

Miguel, in turn, started to cry a little. "Yes, of course, you can join me," he told her.

"Miguel, it's like I'm born for a second time. This time—with love and affection, like a human being should have," Charlotte told him.

Later, when Miguel told me about this conversation, I too couldn't help but cry. For me, living with Miguel as my father was a dream come true. A dream come true for just about any child. He was warm, smart, full of wisdom, gentle, and at times funny. I could well understand why Charlotte felt a strong attachment to Miguel. Though she was older than me by fifteen years or so, I understood that for her, Miguel was the father she'd never had.

It was evident to everyone—to me, Pedro, Olivia, Carolina, Juana, Ernestina, Phil, the other silversmiths, and the Lamberts— that Miguel and Charlotte had a heartfelt attachment. A true bond. Almost like they were related by blood. Like a lost, forgotten daughter and father reunited. Charlotte had now been living with the girls in Phoenix for several weeks, and she had also been working as a waitress with them at the same Mexican restaurant they worked at. She would regularly visit Miguel at the shop. If he was busy, she would sit and wait for him. By now everyone at the shop knew her well.

Sometimes when Miguel would be sitting and talking to people, she would sit on his lap like she was a child. At first, many of us found this odd, but we came to realize that Charlotte was living out a second childhood—the happy childhood she'd never had—with a new father figure who provided the familial-like love she'd always wanted—someone kind, who showed her love, respect, and attention. I, personally, could understand her need to sit on Miguel's lap. When our father was alive, while he had been supportive, he'd never been affectionate and hardly ever touched me and my siblings, so I, too, very much loved to sit on Miguel's lap when I first met him. It felt natural and an act of fatherly love.

Those of us who knew and loved Miguel—even Carolina who'd had a crush on Miguel—never felt any jealousy in regard to Charlotte. Charlotte was charming and smart. For us, it was like she was some kind of mentally suppressed prisoner who had never hoped for freedom, but had suddenly found it. She was experiencing a rebirth with a new father and family. She was figuring out what it meant to be a reborn person with unlimited potential.

As Miguel and Charlotte were entering Jordan's Mexican Restaurant, Charlotte promised, "Don't worry, Miguel, I won't say a word."

"It's okay, Charlotte. Be yourself, say whatever you want, whatever comes into your mind." Charlotte held Miguel's hand as they neared the table where Mr. Jones was sitting. Next to him sat a young man with a crew cut and glasses. He was well shaven and wore a suit. Mr. Howard Jones (the father) was wearing a cowboy hat and cowboy boots, his typical attire.

Mr. Jones stood and said, "Miguel, so nice to see you. This is my son, Michael, and this is your?" looking at Charlotte, whose stunning beauty did not go unnoticed.

Before Miguel could say anything, Charlotte replied, stumbling a bit, "I am his . . ." She stopped and then restarted, simply saying, "My name is Charlotte."

Both Mr. Jones and his son, Michael, invited them to sit down.

Mr. Jones asked, "Would you all care for a drink?" And to the waiter, he stated, "I'll have a double scotch and water."

Michael stated, "A beer for me."

"Can I please have a Coca-Cola?" said Miguel.

"And for you, young lady?" Mr. Jones asked Charlotte.

"I will have the same, a Coca-Cola, thank you."

Mr. Jones then launched into the meeting. "Miguel, Michael will be taking over the business around the first of the year. He just earned his degree in architecture, and he already knows a lot about the business. I think he will do an excellent job at it. After he takes over, I'm going to retire and leave Phoenix. I'm seventy now. I've bought a small place in Portugal, and I plan to move there after the hand-over is complete."

"Oh, I see, that sounds nice," Miguel commented.

Mr. Jones added, "Michael has some good ideas about making our business more modern and more efficient."

"What is it you do?" Michael asked Miguel, very businesslike.

"I'm a silversmith."

"Yes, Michael, he makes jewelry—the traditional jewelry of the Navajo Native Americans—like what I'm wearing," Mr. Jones explained, looking down at his belt buckle, which was hidden by his large belly.

"Yes, I see," said Michael. "Do you also do work for an immigration service?"

"No, I'm only a silversmith," answered Miguel.

"But I understand you help people immigrate. So how is it that you do that?" Michael asked.

Mr. Jones, by that time, was signaling the waiter for a second drink, and then he said, "Oh, yes, Michael, Miguel has helped quite a lot of people immigrate."

"How—or why—do you help people immigrate?" Michael asked, somewhat confused.

Miguel answered, "I understand firsthand the struggles of people who come into the USA, both illegally and legally. However, I have a very special place in my heart for those who live here without papers. I sympathize with all the uncertainties and terror they experience having to live here with that part of their lives hidden."

Michael questioned, "They broke the law, didn't they?"

"Yes, they did, and they know it. Believe me, when I say, they also wish to God they could correct it. And given time some will be able to," Miguel answered.

"Are these people alone?" Michael asked.

"You mean are they here in Phoenix or in America alone?" Miguel asked for clarification.

"Yes," Michael answered.

"It's most typical that they've left their families back in Mexico. They work very hard, and they send money back to feed their children. Sir, these are good people. They are very hard workers and want to do great things. But being here illegally keeps them on their toes—it's very stressful. They live in hiding and are always at risk of deportation. I try to help them pursue the immigration process and at the same time, get good jobs, take English lessons, and find reliable sponsors. That's what I try to do."

Though they were conversing with Miguel, Mr. Jones and his son kept their eyes on Charlotte, noting her every move. It was apparent that they found her beautiful and that they were intrigued by her attachment to Miguel.

"I see, but they aren't related to you. Or maybe some of them are?" Michael asked.

Miguel answered, "I have immigrated several of my relatives already and have more who will come over soon."

"Illegally?"

"No, legally, but it's a long, costly, and sometimes complicated process. I'm working on those details and saving money for them to come here, hopefully in a few years from now. They will immigrate legally for certain."

Michael stated, "We have twenty-five workers. Twenty legal workers who are citizens, and five illegals. I want all of our workers to be legal. I've told my father so on many occasions, but he insists these five are valuable workers, so we shouldn't just let them go."

Mr. Jones commented, "Yes, they are important, and I want to keep them. That's why I wanted us to talk to you, Miguel. Michael wasn't so sure about this and wanted me to get rid of them. I told him that we should wait and hear you out first."

All the while, Charlotte was listening as she ate her food. Miguel would look at her on occasion, and they would exchange a smile. At times, she would lean over and place her hand on his forearm.

As Miguel hadn't yet met their five workers who needed green cards, he said to Mr. Jones, "Tell me more about the five workers—their names and something about them. I would also like to meet them."

Miguel was particular about the people he helped with the immigration process. He wanted them to be good future citizens and loyal to their sponsors, have no criminal records, and be caring and concerned about their families. In order to immigrate them they would have to access many official papers from Mexico, but some might not be able to for various reasons, which would be problematic. Another issue was if any had police records in Mexico. Once, Miguel had tried to immigrate someone with a good sponsor, but his records indicated problems with the police in his hometown in Mexico, so he would never make it through the process. It would be pointless to try to get him a green card because with a police record in his country of origin, the US would never grant him one.

Miguel said, "Mr. Jones, I need to meet them sometime. In the meantime, I need a notarized letter from your accountant that you are financially solvent and that you guarantee each one by name a steady and secure job. Once we get all their information from Mexico, we can review and proceed. Those five men are lucky to have you as a future supportive sponsor."

To Michael, Miguel asked, "Will this be okay?"

"Oh, yes, of course," Michael responded.

By this time, Michael had become a bit distracted by Charlotte though she remained quiet. Miguel continued regularly checking in with her, asking if she wanted anything else. She always touched his forearm when she answered him.

Miguel went on to ask Michael, "What are you doing to make the business more modern? Your father said you have some ideas."

"Yes, first, I want to change the way we order supplies. We have an old lady in charge of this. She has known my father since they were children. She doesn't bargain on prices with vendors. We are losing money because of her. Another problem is poor discipline with workers."

With proudness Mr. Jones sat listening to his son. After Michael finished speaking, Mr. Jones stated, "Yes, I'm sure Michael will make the business better. I'm behind the times."

By the end of dinner, Michael ended up conceding, saying, "Miguel, if you and my father want to help these people, I agree to it." As he said this, he was looking at Charlotte, who smiled and nodded, showing her approval.

Mr. Jones asked, "Charlotte, darling, what do you have to say about my brilliant son?"

Surprised, Charlotte answered, "Oh—I think Miguel, I mean Michael, is going to do very well."

"So how are you two related?" Michael asked her.

"Who?" Charlotte asked.

"You and Miguel," said Michael.

"Yes, how are you two related?" Mr. Jones asked as well.

Charlotte answered, "I've known Miguel all my life, but we just recently reunited a few weeks ago. He is my life's angel, the only person in my life, the only person I trust, and I love him like no other." Tears streamed from her eyes as she said this.

Though Mr. Jones commented, "That says it all," both he and Michael were still puzzled about their relationship.

Miguel smiled and said, "You have twenty-five men working for you and an elderly woman who is apparently on her way out, right?"

"Yes, that's correct," said Michael.

"Do you think there might be room to add some women to your crew?" Miguel asked.

"Women?" Mr. Jones asked as he tightened his bolo tie. Then, straightening out his shirt collar as well, he repeated, "Women? Never thought about it until now."

Meanwhile, Michael asked Charlotte in a low voice, "Where are you from?"

She whispered, "Here, there, everywhere."

Intrigued but mystified, Michael leaned back and did not say anything.

Miguel said, "It seems the type of aluminum work you all produce can be done by most anyone who has dexterity and a desire to learn and work, right?"

"Yes, of course, naturally," Mr. Jones answered.

Miguel went on to say, "Well, that's something I'd like you to think about, employing some women that I want to recommend. One of those women is Charlotte here. In the meantime, Mr. Jones, I want you to know that you and your son impress me very much as kind people with big hearts. My compliments to you, sir, you have done a great job raising Michael who no doubt has made you very proud."

"Why, Miguel, that's a fine thing to say, and I will certainly get back to you on hiring some women, especially if it includes pretty Miss Charlotte."

"Thank you, sir."

The Joneses looked at each other and smiled.

Miguel knew very well that it was a golden opportunity that they not only sponsor five men but three women as well—and also hire Charlotte. Mr. Jones worked with various people in town and was quite influential. He was a "shake hands" type of guy, meaning he did business with a handshake, which he said meant more than a written agreement. Miguel thought Mr. Jones would help to find sponsors for Carolina, Ernestina, and Juana. It was a bold move for Miguel to ask this of them and to try to get Charlotte a job with them too.

Mr. Jones then stated, "I'm flying to New Jersey soon."

Charlotte asked, "Why New Jersey?"

Miguel and Michael looked at Charlotte as she asked the question.

"I own a home in New Jersey that belonged to my mother, and I am thinking of selling it. It's a beautiful home on a large piece of land with tall trees. Hate to get rid of it, but the people renting it now are pigs, and I need to evict them. Then I might fix it up and sell it."

The four stood up to make their way out of the restaurant. Michael and Charlotte were chitchatting as Miguel waited for Mr. Jones to ready himself. First, he placed his Sam Houston hat on his head. Next he straightened out his shirt collar and readjusted his bolo tie. He pulled up his pants and adjusted his belt buckle to accommodate his bulging belly. He looked down at his boots and then looked at himself on a wall mirror and smiled.

Once everyone was outside, Miguel said, "Thank you for dinner, Mr. Jones. Michael, it was nice meeting you as well."

"Yes, thank you, and it was also nice to meet both of you," Michael replied, still curious about the relationship between Miguel and this mysterious beauty.

Back at the apartment, Miguel sat down to speak to Carolina, Ernestina, and Juana. With a twinkle in his eyes, he said, "How would you like it if I found you good work and a sponsor?"

"Oh, Miguel, *gracias*," Carolina said.

Looking at all three, Miguel clarified, "I mean for all of you."

They started screaming with joy.

Charlotte, who had been watching this scene, quietly walked away.

Before departing, Miguel found Charlotte and asked, "Are you okay?"

She said, "Something I find amazing is that even though those three wonderful ladies have less security than I do in this country, they are happy and joyful. I was born here, and did bad things to myself, and have only myself to blame for what's going on in my life. Those women are in hiding and appreciate the little they have— their friendship with one another and with those around them and especially with you."

"Charlotte, I know a lot about you," Miguel told her, "and I totally agree with what you said to Mr. Jones and his son. You and I have known each other for a long time, yet we've only just reunited. That's true in my mind, spirit, and heart."

She looked at Miguel and hugged him and told him a bit more about the bad relationships she'd had in the past with the cruel people that had surrounded her.

She said, "Miguel, please keep me here, I don't ever want to leave. These weeks with you and those three ladies have helped me heal from many wounds far worse than the scrapes and bruises I had. And I am so grateful that you asked about getting me work at the Joneses' business, especially if it means I can continue working with Carolina, Ernestina, and Juana."

"I understand, Charlotte. And I will do all I can to help you."

"Miguel, I'm so glad you are trying to help those ladies and those five men that you don't even know with their papers. I never realized the things that are going on in other people's lives. How can we be so ignorant, unaware, and unappreciative of what we have? So many Americans like me throw away our lives, yet these people are seeking a way to have the life, opportunities, and liberty we take for granted. I think this is so ironic"— again emotions overcame her—"Now I know why you do what you do. What I find really interesting is how people ask you: 'Why are you doing this for people who are not even related to you?' I totally agree with you, Miguel: we are all related. I see it, and I hope more people will too."

———

A few weeks later Miguel met with Mr. Jones's five illegal workers. This time I was present at the dinner meeting that took place at Miguel's house. Miguel prepared an amazing *carne con chilé* with white rice and beans.

All five men had been working for Mr. Jones for a number of years. One for eight years. Three for five years. And one for a single year.

After Miguel told them he was going to help them immigrate, it was apparent that they were skeptical about the whole thing. It was surprising to them that this random person would help them.

To the man who had been in the US for eight years, Miguel stated, "It's very important you try to learn English. You have been here for eight years, so English now should be your second language."

The man responded that he spent almost all his time with Spanish-speaking people. The others admitted that they too did not speak much English.

Miguel explained to them how important it was to Michael Jones, who would be taking over the business, that the workers be able to speak English with him and with clients. Miguel then talked to them about Friendly House and helped them set up lessons with the volunteer teachers there.

I took down their names and other information about where each of them came from in Mexico as well as relevant details of their pasts. Miguel gave them lists of the official papers they would need to get from their home states in Mexico and tried to communicate the urgency of their situations. Miguel believed that Mr. Jones was on their side, but he was not convinced that Michael Jones's support would hold out for very long.

Miguel told them, "You need to tell me if you committed any crimes in Mexico. A clean police record is something the immigration office will be looking for. If yours isn't clean, it's highly unlikely you'll be able to get a green card or that the Joneses will want to sponsor you."

They all said they understood. Four months later when most of them had collected the required papers, one of the workers presented Miguel with a police record from Mexico, showing he'd committed an assault against a shop owner. This record was still open, thus unresolved. A second one also produced a police record that showed he'd committed spousal abuse.

The two men begged Miguel not to tell Mr. Jones. "Please, don't say anything. Just leave it alone."

Miguel reminded them, "You remember when we met, you all told me you agreed to proceed because you wanted to be legally immigrated to help your families. Do you remember?"

"Yes," they confirmed, the two of them looking down at the floor, demoralized.

Miguel told the two men that he would not be able to lie for them and would have to disclose their records to Mr. Jones. "It's going to be difficult for me, but it's the right thing to do," he said. Plus, he knew that the immigration process required police records, so there would be no way to avoid disclosing these details when their green card applications would be submitted.

The other three men were in full contact with their families in Mexico and sending them money as well.

Carolina, Juana, and Ernestina, who were also gathering their papers for the immigration process, all had clean records. They were sending money back to their parents too.

Michael Jones ended up inviting us out to dinner several different times. This included Miguel, Charlotte, and me. I was impressed with Michael. I thought he was sincere, and although a man of few words, he pretty much told you what was on his mind. He also met Carolina, Juana, and Ernestina, and got to know them.

Michael explained to Miguel, "I have two supply vendors in Tucson, who will hire and sponsor Carolina, Juana, and Ernestina. They will be doing manual aluminum piping. It's a good job with some heavy work. The owner is a man of his word."

Michael, himself, would keep all five workers for now and proceed with sponsoring the three with clean police records. He wouldn't terminate the other two, but it was understood that in a few years, when he sold the business, those two would have to go their own way.

Charlotte got a job working at the Joneses' aluminum business, a job she worked for the next three years.

About six months later, Charlotte's half-brother, Jeremy, showed up at the jewelry shop. He asked if anyone had found a watch he'd lost in the alley. It was likely he was using this as a pretext to look for clues of Charlotte. Miguel never saw him, but from the way Nellie described him, Miguel knew it was Jeremy. He never told Charlotte about it.

Charlotte ended up marrying Michael Jones. Eventually, they sold the business and moved to New Jersey. The last time I saw Charlotte was in 1967 at the funeral of Mr. Jones, the father of her husband. Miguel stayed in communication with her. She even returned to Phoenix three times in 1970, 1974, and the last time in 1980. Charlotte died in 1982, at about the age of forty-four. She and Michael never had children.

The last time Miguel saw her, during her visit to Phoenix in 1980, she looked very run-down, deteriorated, and decades older than her actual age. It was a very sad and emotional visit for them both, one that Miguel never forgot. Charlotte told Miguel that a doctor had told her that her blood was "distressed," and there was probably nothing they could do to help her.

I started practicing surgery in 1983, a time when there were many mysterious cases of "distressed" blood and immunosuppression. By 1984 the medical community understood the disorder better and identified it as AIDS. It was at this time that I determined that Charlotte had likely died of AIDS. The consolation is that she and Michael Jones had an incredibly happy marriage, and Michael was devoted to her in those last few very difficult years of her life.

During that 1980 visit Charlotte told Miguel, "Now I'm sure I met you a long time ago. It was when I was very young. I was near a river, and a man was chasing me. He wanted to rape me, but you appeared, Miguel, and you protected me. I can't remember all the details, but when we meet again in another life, I will know for certain."

They embraced, and Miguel told her, "You are forever one of the brightest parts of my life, dear Charlotte."

While Miguel didn't exactly play Cupid to connect Charlotte and Michael Jones, in certain cases Miguel actively played the part of the matchmaker. Often his matchmaking skills didn't just result in love and marriage, but also allowed one party to obtain a green card. Let's turn to Miguel's most amazing example of cupiding.

It was Nellie's birthday, and the silversmiths decided to buy her flowers. Whenever Nellie received flowers, she would dry them, put a glaze on them, and hang them on her windows as decorations. Miguel was the one who would go to the flower shop to pick up Nellie's birthday flowers.

At the flower shop, Miguel was served by a dark-skinned lady with thick ears, thick and protruding lips, who was slightly balding. She was slightly heavy-set and wore a long-sleeved white shirt. Her skin was shiny, her heavy hands were smooth, and her nails well groomed with red nail polish. Miguel often passed by the flower shop on his way to the bakery, but he'd never before seen this unique-looking lady.

She was very kind and spoke with elegance, eager to share all she knew about flowers. She had specific flower recommendations based on the occasion. For high school proms: yellow roses; for graduations: red, yellow, and blue lilies; for birthdays: something bright and cheerful like orchids or else the person's favorite flower; and for condolences: gladiolas, white carnations, or white daises.

After he purchased the flowers, she asked him, "I don't want to impose on you, but would you mind coming next door to the ice cream parlor, so we can sit, have an ice cream, and talk?'

"Yes, I would be delighted," Miguel told her. Then he added, "My name is Miguel Hernández."

She told him, "I am Petra Rosa Vasquez."

Over ice cream, they talked, speaking at times in Spanish and at times in English. Petra told Miguel, "I'm from Monterey, Mexico. What about you?"

"I'm from Michoacán."

Petra then said, "A lady named Carolina who buys flowers at the shop pointed you out to me once before when you happened to be walking by. She told me too that you might be able to help me immigrate. I have been in the US now for five years, but I don't have any papers. My parents are still in Mexico, and they are very old."

Petra was about forty years old herself.

"Yes, I think I can help you," Miguel told her.

"I have a son named Carlos who is also illegal. He's going to school here. He's in the seventh grade."

"Where does he go to school?" inquired Miguel.

"He's at Emerson School in West Phoenix. I feel secure working at the flower shop, but I'm afraid for Carlos and desperately want to immigrate him to protect him. I worry more about him than me," Petra confided.

"I notice you speak English well," Miguel observed.

Petra admitted, "Yes, I've been trying hard. I try really hard to communicate with people in English when they ask me questions about flowers. I'm not afraid to make mistakes. It seems to me I learn from my mistakes, and people are happy to help me. I met a teacher lady who has been teaching me, and in exchange I teach her how to make Mexican food."

Miguel told her, "It's great that you are learning to speak English. By speaking English you can compete for better jobs. Also when it is time for your interview to get your green card, it will prove how serious you are about integrating into American culture."

Miguel then made a list of the specific papers for Petra to gather, mostly from Monterrey, Mexico. When they met again, Petra had collected almost all the needed papers, everything but the police record from Monterrey. Her boss was willing to write a statement of offer of employment but was reluctant to hand it over to her. The boss feared that since Petra was working without papers, somehow this would cause a problem for the flower shop.

Miguel then assured her, "Don't worry, I have an idea for finding you a sponsor."

At the jewelry shop, Miguel went over to talk to a fellow silversmith that we all called Big Tom. He was about six feet four inches tall and had large ears, wide cheekbones, and a contagious smile. Big Tom's wife had died of cirrhosis of the liver, and they'd had no children. Big Tom was a brilliant silversmith, and he was always trying to get Miguel to teach him Spanish and how to cook Mexican food. Miguel had the idea that Big Tom and Petra might make a good match. They both were quiet but smiled a lot and loved cooking. However, Miguel realized it wasn't just about making the match between those two; he would also need to make sure Carlos, Petra's fifteen-year-old son, and Big Tom got along.

After discussing some jewelry designs with Big Tom, Miguel suggested an outing to the movies. Miguel also invited Carolina as well as Petra. Big Tom agreed to go. The plan was for everyone to go to a movie and afterwards eat dinner at Petra's house.

The movie was great. They went to the Azteca Theater in downtown Phoenix and saw an old classic starring the Mexican comedian Adalberto "Resortes" Martínez. The dinner was sensational as well. It could not have been better planned.

Petra and Big Tom really hit it off. They ended up courting for three months. Big Tom learned to cook some sensational Mexican meals, and he started conversing in Spanish. He and Carlos became close too. When the two got married, both Petra and Carlos got their green cards. Later they both became American citizens. Miguel always said Big Tom was the easiest sponsor he'd ever found.

Although Miguel had been successful at introducing Petra and Big Tom, typically he was very cautious about playing Cupid when the intention was to help someone get a green card. For one thing, it wasn't uncommon for an immigrant man to pursue marriage with an American woman when in reality he was deceiving her, acting like he was in love with her, when in fact he already had a wife and children in Mexico. After he got the green card, the man would abandon one of the parties, either the American wife or his (secret) family in Mexico.

There were also "iffy" cases, where, say, a man in need of a green card paid an American woman to marry him. Then the woman ended up falling in love with the man for real, so she didn't want to divorce—even though the man was already married and had a family in Mexico. Because it could get complicated and there were many examples of unhappy endings in green card marriages, Miguel was very careful when it came to playing Cupid.

When Miguel found a match for Erlinda, a young lady who was our guest for a few months, it ended in success and happiness. He introduced her to Alex, a chef and father of two children from a previous marriage. Erlinda and Alex ended up getting married. Erlinda got a green card, and she also became like a mother to Alex's two children. Everyone's lives improved because of the marriage.

However, when Miguel helped Rosa, it ended in disaster. Miguel connected Rosa with an American man named William. Rosa was twenty-five, and William was sixty-seven. They began dating and eventually made the plan to marry. William sustained an injury in his bowels that happened from his military service in World War Two. Because his body could no longer eliminate body waste (feces) naturally, he had a colostomy. This is a surgery in which an incision is made in the abdominal wall. The end of the person's colon is connected to the incision or hole. A pouch—on the outside of the body—is then connected to the hole, and the pouch collects the person's feces.

When Rosa discovered this about William, she couldn't handle it, but she figured that over time she would become comfortable with it. So, she married William. However, she could never get over her unease with the colostomy and the bag, so she ended up divorcing him and returning to Mexico to care for her mother.

While it didn't always end well, when Miguel played the part of Cupid to help people find love and to get green cards, more often than not, the results were good. In the case of Petra and Big Tom— Miguel hit a homerun.

Chapter 13

THE ELEMENT OF SURPRISE

Hodges Barbeque was a hole in the wall with the most delicious homemade smoked ribs and sandwiches. One of the unique things about Hodges was that on each table you'd find a bucket containing jars of whole pickles of different sizes and brands. You could choose the kind of pickles you wanted to eat with your ribs or sandwich.

Miguel knew the owner, Herschel, a pleasant man with polished manners. Herschel came from a long line of experts in barbeque. His father and grandfather in Atlanta had run barbecue restaurants as well.

Despite the ups and downs of the barbeque restaurant business Herschel managed to be a good boss. He even sponsored at least five of our guests. Miguel and Herschel became good friends. Two of our guests, Leodegario and James Groom, worked for Herschel from about 1960, when he opened Hodges, until 1979, when they moved on to other work.

Miguel and I had been eating at Hodges from the time it opened. It was a place that held a special history for us, through our friendship with Mr. Herschel, through our guests who had worked there, and for the other friendships we had fostered there over amazing barbecue and pickles.

It was 9:30 pm on a Sunday night in early December. Miguel was having difficulty lighting the burners used to heat the partially renovated house on 206 N. 9th Street. We needed to use flashlights to figure out what the problem was, but the batteries were dead, so we decided to go and buy some new ones.

Leodegario, Vicente, Erlinda, and James Groom were the guests on the property at that time. Leodegario accompanied Miguel and me on our quest to buy batteries.

We went from store to store, but everything was closed except Sam's Convenience Market, located at 20th Street and Broadway. Because of the gang violence in our neighborhood, people generally did not visit this area after 6:30 pm. Once it got dark, muggings and assaults increased in frequency in the neighborhood around the store. Everyone knew about how dangerous the area was.

Only because all the other nearby stores were closed did we decide to go to Sam's.

From the backseat, Leodegario questioned Miguel, "*Estas loco*? Are you crazy? Let's go back. I'd rather freeze to death than die in that store."

Miguel insisted, "We'll buy the batteries quickly. It will be fine."

"No, Miguel. No, please don't go there, please," Leodegario begged.

Miguel wasn't afraid. Miguel often would say that we are afraid of fears that we've created for ourselves. However, fear was only in the imagination. It was not physical, and it only became tangible if you let it.

Miguel parked in front of the store. Six men stood outside in the cold in front of the store. They were shadow-boxing and goofing around.

Again Leodegario pleaded with Miguel not to go in.

Miguel said to him, "There is nothing to fear," and then he went inside.

Leodegario and I waited in the car. I was reading a comic book while Leodegario sat totally still, frozen with fear.

Miguel was gone for forty-five minutes. When finally he came out, a tall man—about six-foot five—came out with an arm on Miguel's shoulder. Miguel waved for us to get out of the car. I got out, but Leodegario stayed back. Reluctantly, he eventually followed.

"This is Sam," Miguel told us. "Sam's grandfather owned a convenience store in Georgia, and his father owned one in Milwaukee. He used to crawl under the counter at his father's store."

Sam wasn't just very tall; he was also large with broad shoulders. People would say to him, "Sam, you could be an alligator wrestler! The alligators wouldn't stand a chance with you." He would just smile. He was slightly balding, had a beard, a smile, and a chuckle that was contagious.

Leodegario stood silent. Petrified.

I looked up at Sam, and Sam looked down at me, asking, "Who might you be?"

Miguel answered, "Sam, this is Edgar, my brother, and this is Leodegario, who is a guest at our home."

"Would you like an ice cream cone? Sam asked.

"Yes, I would very much," I replied.

"Go ahead and help yourself," he said, pointing to a freezer inside his store. "And you too," he added, referring to Leodegario, who remained statue-like.

"Sam, I'll bring you back your watch tomorrow at 6 pm. I'll replace the turquoise stone that's missing in the band and make it look like new," Miguel said.

"That would be great," Sam replied, "And I better get back inside because there are customers to attend to."

Sam gave Miguel a big bear hug and then returned inside the store. We got into the car. As Miguel was starting the engine, he turned to me and Leodegario and said, "Isn't he wonderful? Sam is a fine and kind man. He trusted me with his Bulova watch and his watchband, yet I've only just met him."

I smiled at Miguel. Leodegario remained stunned.

This was the start of Miguel and Sam's friendship, one that was to continue for years to come.

It was about 9 pm when we heard the knock accompanied by screams of pain. I opened the door to find Jimmy, bloody and in anguish. Jimmy was seventeen, and I was thirteen. Apparently his father had beaten him up, so Jimmy had fled. He worked part-time at Hodges Barbecue, where we had first met him, so initially he'd gone to Herschel's, but Herschel hadn't been home.

Next Jimmy tried Miguel's (not the jewelry shop apartment but the property), and that's when I opened the door for him. It was lucky because Miguel and I weren't living at 206 N. 9th Street at that time, so we often wouldn't be there so late at night. However, on this night, that's where we happened to be.

As Jimmy came inside, I called back to Miguel, "It's Jimmy from Hodges! He's bleeding and in pain! Miguel, we need to help him!"

Jimmy fell to the ground as he entered the house. He was barefooted and wore a torn-up t-shirt, which was also bloodied. He seemed to be bleeding everywhere. I ran to get towels for the cuts that covered his body. Leodegario, Vicente, and Erlinda emerged and started to help too.

"What happened, Jimmy?" Miguel asked.

"My father beat me with a belt buckle. He was drunk," Jimmy managed to reply.

"Does he know where you are?" Miguel asked.

"No, I ran out of the house."

He was shivering and in pain as he spoke.

When Jimmy saw Miguel go to the phone, he pleaded, "Miguel, please don't call the police. I don't want my father to get in trouble. He's a sick man and needs help."

Miguel explained, "Jimmy, you need help too, so I'm calling Olivia to see if her boyfriend, Dr. Schwartz, can fix you up."

Even though it was nighttime Dr. Schwartz agreed to meet us at his clinic. He attended to Jimmy's wounds, gave him stitches, ointment, and medication to help reduce the pain and swelling. When we brought Jimmy back to the property, Erlinda made soup for him, and we kept him warm.

It took Jimmy about a week to feel better. Two weeks later, he had his stiches removed. However, Jimmy did not want to go home. Miguel decided it would be best to contact his father, but Jimmy did not think it was a good idea because of the man's violent nature.

"Yes, but he's still your father," Miguel said, "and I think the right thing to do is for me to visit him."

Jimmy begged, "No, he will hurt you, Miguel. No, please, let's wait."

Miguel insisted, "I'll be okay talking to him. He won't harm me."

Jimmy argued, "According to Mr. Herschel, my father doesn't know where I am, and I want to keep it that way."

Jimmy was tall and skinny and had nice manners. He was a hard worker, working two jobs. He was an only child. His father did not work because of his drinking habit, and all the money Jimmy earned went to alcohol and cigarettes for the father. Though his mother worked, she too seemed like a prisoner of the father. Intimidation was not in short supply at Jimmy's house.

"Miguel, can we please wait a little longer before we contact him? Please?" Jimmy begged.

Miguel gave in, saying, "Okay, Jimmy, but I think it's better to let him know where you are. Otherwise, it will make him more angry when he finds out later."

"Yes, Miguel, please let's just wait a few more days."

"Okay, in a few days we'll talk," Miguel said.

"Okay, thank you and thank you for all you're doing," Jimmy stated, adding, "It's interesting that all the people who live here are in hiding, just like me, though they are in hiding for a reason very different than mine. Even still, we all feel safe here with you, Miguel."

Miguel gave Jimmy a glass of milk and said, "You can stay as long as you like, but keep in mind, he is still your father and we'll eventually have to mend this problem."

Another two weeks passed.

Miguel was visiting Sam, who was now selling some of Miguel's jewelry pieces on consignment. Miguel discussed Jimmy's situation with Sam, who knew Jimmy and his parents.

Sam said to Miguel, "Jimmy's father is a dangerous man, and we need to be careful with him. Thank God Jimmy is fine, but sooner or later his father is going to hurt him again, and it won't be pretty."

"Yes, I know. That's why I want to talk to him," Miguel said.

Sam warned, "But not alone, Miguel. You'll have to take a police squadron with you."

Miguel responded, "Perhaps, but Jimmy doesn't want the police involved because he doesn't want to hurt his father."

"Well, that may be, but don't you go and make a foolish mistake about going to his house alone."

A week later.

Vicente had found a sponsor, the owner of a mechanic shop, and moved on, leaving our residence. Miguel was trying his hand at matchmaking and was in the process of connecting Erlinda to an American-born chef named Alex. In the meantime, Erlinda, along with Leodegario, continued living at the residence.

Around this time Pedro told Miguel about Crespin, an illegal who was working in a prosthetic limb shop, a shop Pedro frequented when assisting the person with polio he was caring for. Crespin was about forty years old, and he used to work in a rehab stroke center in Mexico City. He knew a lot about limb prosthetics and physical therapy for stroke victims.

Although Miguel was preoccupied at the time dealing with Jimmy and his father, he managed to accommodate Crespin. As long as Crespin complied with the four agreements, Miguel welcomed him to stay as a guest. Crespin had lived in Nogales for six months and had started to learn some English. He was enthusiastic to learn more—and the other three conditions were no problem for him.

Dr. Schwartz used his connections to help Crespin get a job in the therapy section of a hospital. Crespin also helped Jimmy with his wounds and even helped him with therapy for his left arm, which was badly cut. Miguel saw a bright future for Crespin, who was both nice and talented.

Jimmy surprised all of us one night when we found him reading about becoming a physical therapist and learning about the anatomy of the muscles and bones in the body. Apparently Crespin was having a huge influence on him.

Sam informed Miguel that Jimmy's father had somehow learned that Jimmy was living in the area, but that he still did not know where and with whom.

Miguel sat down and told Jimmy, "Son, I know you don't want me to notify your father that you're here, but someone must speak with him—either you with a companion, me alone, or perhaps I can go with Sam. If we ignore this, it will only make things worse, and the situation is not going to go away by itself."

Jimmy started to cry, saying, "Miguel, I don't want to leave here."

Miguel hugged him and said, "I understand, and while we have enjoyed having you here, your safety is a primary concern to me."

"Yes, Miguel, but I want to stay here."

"Yes, I know, but as a young man, you need to understand that ignoring a difficult situation and ignoring a possible solution will only escalate the difficulties and make the problem worse. You know we must confront this issue and correct things with your father and someday make it better, after all he is your father."

"Yes, Miguel. I just don't want any harm to come to him. He's a sick man, but deep inside he's a good man. He just doesn't know it."

"Jimmy, that is a kind and noble thing to say about your father, and I agree with you. It's too bad your father doesn't realize how lucky he is to have a son like you."

"Miguel, I also worry about you."

Miguel responded, "I understand. I will be okay. All will be okay. Can we agree that Sam and I will visit your father? We'll see if we can cut a deal with him and see if he will allow you to stay here for a while longer until things cool off a bit more. This is your home."

When Jimmy gave Miguel his consent for the meeting, Miguel then had to work out a good location for it and then get word to Jimmy's father.

Miguel and Sam asked Herschel for his help. "Herschel, can you do us a favor and get word to Jimmy's father that Jimmy is fine and he's been living at Miguel's? If it's alright with you, we'd like to meet him at your restaurant to talk."

Because Jimmy recommended that they ask his father not to be drinking when he came to the meeting, they also brought this up to Herschel.

Herschel agreed to orchestrate the meeting.

Although Miguel was working his typical long hours—starting at 5 am and going until 5 pm and often later, he made great use of his time and still had the energy to do the additional things he considered necessary—like meeting with Jimmy's father.

Sam let Miguel know that Herschel had been in contact with Jimmy's father. Though the man agreed to come to the meeting and not drink, he expressed his dissatisfaction with Miguel.

Sam added, "It's not good."

Miguel defended the father, saying, "But he's right. We should have notified him sooner that his son was living at my property."

"I just hope this turns out right," Sam muttered.

"Sam, everything will be just fine," Miguel responded.

Miguel did not seem nervous at all. He wasn't concerned about Jimmy's father being angry. He too felt as Jimmy once said—that Jimmy's father was a good man inside and that we must allow time for that goodness to come out.

However, Sam and Herschel were quite apprehensive about the whole thing and still thought the police should be involved.

Miguel stood strong, arguing, "No, the police will likely want to prosecute him, and Jimmy doesn't want him to get in trouble. Jimmy is a good kid. He now wants to go to school and be a therapist."

"A therapist of what?" Sam asked.

"A physical or occupational therapist."

"Wow, that's something," Herschel said. "Miguel, you certainly have a way of molding people."

"No, it's not me," Miguel explained, "It's their desire and hard work. I just want people to have a better life and be legal."

"Amen," Sam and Herschel chorused.

———⊰⊱———

Miguel and Sam were sitting in Hodges Barbecue when Jimmy's father walked in. He was a heavy-set man, about five feet, eleven inches tall, and sported a thin mustache. He wore a white t-shirt and a baseball cap, which he took off upon entering. He had thick hair and a scar on the right side of his forehead that ascended up to his scalp. He had a serious look to him.

As he walked towards the table, immediately Miguel stood and extended his hand, saying, "I am Miguel Hernández, and this is Sam."

"Yep, I know Sam, but I never met you before," the man stated, ignoring Miguel's extended hand. Next he asked, "Where's my son?"

Miguel said, "Please take a seat. Would you like something to eat?

Sam stood up and extended his hand, but the man also refused to shake hands with Sam. He looked down, avoiding eye contact with Miguel and Sam. His eyes were swollen, and he was shaking slightly.

"Yeah, I'll eat something," he said.

Miguel stated, "Sir, your son is quite a man. He is someone any father would be proud of. He is doing very well. He's at a hospital—"

"What? A hospital!" the man screamed. "You, goddamn people! Why didn't you tell me he's in the hospital?"

"Sir, he's not ill," Sam said.

"Not ill?"

Miguel explained, "No, he's fine. He's spending some time there to learn more about the work that physical therapists do."

The man put his head down on top of his fisted hands on the table. He was trembling.

Miguel continued, "Sir, won't you please talk with Jimmy? He worries about you and tells us all the time that he never wants any harm to come to you. The night he came over, he asked us not to call the police. He was bloodied and hurting, and he was only concerned about you, sir."

"Yes," Sam said, "It's God's truth."

"He needs to come home, his mother wants him home," the man mumbled into his hands.

"Where's your wife, sir?"

Still with his head down and talking into his hands, he replied, "At work, she works in housekeeping at a hotel. She sleeps during the day and works all night with only one day off. She's also sick. She has lost weight and won't talk very much. She can come by for Jimmy?"

Sam said, "You hurt this kid badly, and we don't want harm coming to him again."

Miguel reached out to the man and touched him on the forearm. The man, still hanging his head down, looked up at Miguel. Miguel looked at him, locking eyes for a second.

Then the man looked at Sam and asked, "When can I come for my boy?

"Sir, anytime you like," Miguel told him, "In fact, why don't you and your wife come over and have dinner with us? I'll make *carne asada*, and we can also have barbeque ribs from Hodges."

The man stood up and answered, "I'll think about it." Then he walked out.

Miguel and Sam could not tell exactly what had happened.

Sam asked, "He was crying, wasn't he?"

"Yes, maybe," Miguel said.

Before leaving, Miguel and Sam found Herschel, who had been in the back and not present at the meeting. Herschel recommended, "Just call the cops on him. He's crazy. He's going to kill that boy if he goes back home."

"How do you know?" asked Miguel.

"Because all that man knows is cruelty. Have you seen his wife? She's all cut up with scars. She comes in for food and tries to hide her bruises and scars, but the agony in her eyes is something she can't hide."

Back at home Miguel told Jimmy what had transpired. "We're going to sleep on it for a few days. Maybe he will come around."

Jimmy looked at Miguel and said, "God help me. God help him."

———◆———

It was late on a Saturday night. Miguel, Jimmy and I were breaking up and clearing out the rotten floor in the back of the house at 206 N. 9th Street, ready for Monday's complete wood replacement.

We heard a heavy knock on the kitchen door. I opened it, and Jimmy's father stormed in. He was screaming obscene words and was obviously drunk. He was shouting that he'd come to get Jimmy.

Miguel told Jimmy and me, "You two go and sit down."

The man brought his face within inches of Miguel's. Then he put his fist right in front of Miguel's face, but he didn't strike him. Instead, he shouted, "I've had enough of you, Miguel Hernández! You have no right to keep my boy here!"

In a calm voice, Miguel responded, "Calm down and let's talk."

"No, no, no! No talk! He's coming with me!" the father hollered.

Jimmy watched with apprehension as his father screamed at Miguel.

"Sir, it's Jimmy's decision to stay or go. He's been doing well here. He's a fine boy with a good heart and loves you dearly," Miguel said.

To Jimmy, Miguel said, "You know that you are free to go with your father."

"Miguel, please, I'm afraid. Maybe later," Jimmy managed to say.

"No, you come now!" the father commanded and grabbed Jimmy by the shirt collar. Next, he lifted him up and swung him around in the air, like he was winding up to launch a discus. The man released his son, hurling him headfirst into a wall. Jimmy smashed into the wall and crumpled to the ground.

Unexpectedly, the man froze and looked down.

Miguel and I looked to where he was staring: his right foot.

He'd stepped on a nail that had gone right through the sole of his shoe, passed through his foot, and then emerged through the top of his shoe. The nail must have been four inches long. It's pointy end was sticking through the top of his shoe.

At the same time, Jimmy lay collapsed on the floor, bleeding from the scalp.

Miguel stated, "We need to call the police. Things have gone too far, and all our lives are now threatened."

The man was in a daze, looking down at his foot in a state of shock.

Jimmy had heard Miguel, and from his crumpled position, he begged, "No, Miguel. Please, no police. I love my father and don't want to harm him."

Miguel indicated to me that I should hang up the phone. He held my arm and said, "Let's help this man."

"I'm going to pull you away from the nail and free your foot."

The man had remained standing but in a frozen state, his foot and leg locked in place by the nail. Shocked. Jimmy, still bleeding from his scalp and traumatized, crawled over and held on to his father. Miguel pulled the man's leg and foot in one direction to separate him from the nail.

Once the foot was freed, the man fell to the floor.

From the time he'd entered to this point, only about a minute had passed.

The man tried to get up but could not. Jimmy was sitting by his side. Next, with violent effort the man managed to scramble to his feet. Stumbling and swaying, he made for Miguel. He got his arms around Miguel and ferociously began squeezing Miguel's chest to break his ribs and cut off his breathing.

Without warning, a voice roared from outside the kitchen door. The kitchen door burst open, and Sam sprinted in.

"What the hell is going on here?" Sam bellowed as he took in the scene of disarray and bloodshed. Clumps of wood, twisted wires, and linoleum bits were scattered about. And everything was smeared with blood.

Sam had come over unannounced to talk to Miguel about some jewelry he wanted to sell—and happened upon this scene of chaos and destruction.

With haste, Sam pulled the man away from Miguel and wrestled him to the ground. Pinning him down, he declared, "You are an animal and should be caged!"

The man seemed to black out there on the ground.

In the meantime, Miguel called Dr. Schwartz about Jimmy's skull injury.

The next thing we knew, Jimmy's father was gone. He must have left the house while we were attending to Jimmy.

The next morning, Miguel showed the nail to the carpenters. He'd used a solution to clean it.

They asked, "Where did this nail come from?"

They were surprised when Miguel told them it had been in the linoleum in the kitchen floor because the carpenters thought they had removed all the nails already.

"Also," one of them said, "the nails in the linoleum were only one-and-a-half or maybe two-and-a-half inches long, but this looks to be four inches."

Another carpenter pointed out, "It's an unusual nail too. The head is wide and looks to be made of a different metal than the shaft. The head looks like it's made of bronze and the shaft steel. I've never seen anything like it."

Miguel and I viewed the mystery nail as Miguel's savior. Perhaps it had saved Jimmy and me too. Miguel recalled that when Jimmy's father had grabbed him like a wrestler and begun squeezing him, that his strength was fading probably due to the nail puncture wound. Thus, it prevented him from applying a greater force—and greater harm—to Miguel. We figured that he must have been seriously injured when he slipped out of the house.

Four days later, again we were doing work on the property. It was three guests, plus Jimmy, Miguel, and me, scraping the paint off of windowpanes. It was about 10:30 pm.

Jimmy told us, "I think I hear my mother."

"Your mother?" I questioned.

"Yes, my mother," he confirmed. "Yes, I think she's outside."

Jimmy went outside, and Miguel followed. They found her shaking and crying.

"I'm Gwen, Jimmy's mama," she managed to say to Miguel.

"I'm Miguel. Please come inside."

Once inside, Gwen told Jimmy, "We need to go."

"Go where?" he asked.

Miguel asked her, "Where is your husband?"

Very disturbed, she answered, "That's what I mean—we need to leave. Danny is in the hospital with a very swollen leg, and he may very well lose his leg."

Miguel told her, "Gwen, I think you know that Sam called him and told him that Dr. Schwartz would treat him, but he told Sam to leave him the hell alone."

"Yes, I know, I was there," Gwen replied. "Danny is a sick man, mentally, and now on the edge of losing his leg. As I see it, this is the chance for me and Jimmy to leave outta here. My sister lives in Texas, and we need to get away now. I can't deal with his cruelty anymore."

"No," Miguel said, "Please don't do that. Danny needs both of you now more than ever. You just said he's sick. You can't abandon him in this grave time of his life."

I was standing very close to Miguel when I heard him say, "Please, please let me talk to him."

Hearing this, I became frightened and wanted to say to Miguel that he should not go, that it was too dangerous, but I knew very well what his answer would be, so I remained quiet.

He repeated, "Let me go and visit him."

Gwen said what I was thinking, "Miguel, he will hurt you if he sees you."

"No, I don't think so. There is some goodness in that man, I just know it, and it's wrong to leave him like this. I want to go see him. All this is not sitting well with me," Miguel explained.

That night Miguel went to the hospital and asked to see Danny. When Miguel walked into his room, Danny was sitting in a reclining chair. Though he had never given Miguel his name, Miguel called him by name anyway.

"Danny, it's Miguel. I was hoping to talk with you. I want you to know that in the past two months or so while your son has been living with us, I have come to admire him. I feel you are lucky to have him as your son. My brother Edgar, who you saw that night—he and I lost our father from alcohol and the ill effects of smoking. Now I'm like a father to Edgar, but there is nothing better than a son's own father. Edgar suffered as a child like Jimmy, but in a different way. I don't think you realize how much Jimmy adores you. He talks about how fantastic you were as a baseball player and how he looked up to you and how at one time he wanted to be just like you."

Danny had been silent since Miguel walked in. While he still didn't make eye contact, he did start talking.

"He told you about baseball?" Danny asked.

"Yes, he talked about you and baseball and how fantastic you were."

Since Danny seemed to be warming up to him, even though he still hadn't looked at Miguel, Miguel decided to take a seat.

Danny stated, "See this worthless leg? They're going to clean it up again, and hopefully they can save it. The doctor tells me that my fever is gone and that I have a good shot at recovering well."

Miguel was quite surprised that Danny showed no anger—at him or at Jimmy or at anyone else about his leg.

Miguel responded, "That's good. I'm sorry that you are upset at me for keeping Jimmy with us. You know, he was afraid to return back to your house, but now he wants more than anything in the world to be by your side."

"Listen," Danny stated, "It's a good thing he stayed with you because I think if he had come back home, I would have hurt him, so it was probably for the best. Do you want me to tell you why I'm a worthless man? Don't you want to know, Miguel?" Danny started to weep.

Miguel was silent.

While crying, Danny blubbered, "I could have been something, I mean maybe, maybe not, but I wanted a shot."

And then it happened: Danny looked Miguel in the eye. Holding that deep, vulnerable, soul-penetrating eye contact, Danny implored, "Why are you doing this, Miguel? Why are you here?"

Maintaining that sincere and full-on eye contact, Miguel answered, "Many people have been kind and loving to me, and I want to pay back that kindness. I feel that all of us are lucky to be here together in life. I also know that deep inside you are a good man."

Danny began crying again. This time Miguel touched him on the shoulder. Next, much to Miguel's astonishment, Danny moved to hug him and said, "I am sorry, Miguel, I am truly sorry, and thank God we are talking."

A nurse entered the room to see if Danny needed something for pain.

"Pain you asked? No. Actually I feel pretty good," Danny told her.

Miguel was astonished again that Danny refused pain medication. He kept the conversation going, saying, "Danny, tell me more about baseball."

"It's difficult for me to admit it, but when I didn't make it playing baseball, even though plenty of others didn't make it either, I became very upset and depressed and started to resent the people around me. I started to drink and drink—and now, see what I have done to my family and myself? I'm a miserable man with no soul. This has been going on for almost eight years. Jimmy, my only son, used to come with me and play ball, jump on my back, hold my hand. But once I started drinking, he became really sad. Afraid. I wish I could bring those memories back, and I wish I could erase the bad times. I have stolen from my son. I hit my wife frequently and hurt Jimmy, yet they still stick around. You would think they would have left me by now."

Danny did not realize that Gwen was considering leaving him at that moment, and Miguel—still hoping to dissuade them—was not going to mention it.

"May I say something to you?" asked Miguel.

He nodded to indicate yes.

"I wanted to call the police on you, but Jimmy didn't want to hurt you in any way or form. I know that to be the truth, Danny. He and your wife love you very much and are hungry to have harmony and love in your home. Sometime later I will tell you why, the whole story about why my father resorted to drinking and smoking, which took his life, but in brief—my father was thrown out of medical/dental school because of his lack of respect for the code of conduct. He too became depressed and angry. You are young and had several good years of high school education. I heard from Herschel that you were a good student and very much liked by your teachers."

"He said that?" questioned Danny.

"Yes, he did," Miguel said, "He also said you could hit a ball like no other. In fact, he showed us a picture of you batting. It was from baseball tryouts."

The same nurse came in again and informed Danny, "We are going to do your dressing changes now. Your gentleman friend can stay, or he can take off and see you after surgery tomorrow."

"If it's alright with you, Danny, I would like to stay," said Miguel.

Danny indicated that he'd like that.

The nurse asked Danny, "Do you want something for pain, sir, before we start?"

He looked at Miguel with teary eyes and said, "No, just do it. I feel fine."

The nurse looked at him and said, "But you are crying. Are you okay? It's pain, right?"

Danny answered, "No, it's not pain. I don't know, but it's not pain."

While the dressings were being changed, Danny did not react. This baffled the nurse because eight hours earlier, when she'd changed the dressings, Danny was in obvious pain and very vocal about his discomfort.

He smiled as the nurse said, "Danny, your leg is getting better and a good cleanup in surgery will help even more." When the nurse walked out, she looked back several times in disbelief over the change that had come over Danny.

"Danny, may I come tomorrow after work and also bring Jimmy and Gwen to see you?"

Before he could answer, Miguel continued, "Did you know that Jimmy is considering going into the rehabilitation profession? You know, working with people who have injuries like yours? The surgeon told me that if you don't lose your leg, you will need physical therapy. That's the kind of work Jimmy is interested in doing."

"Yes, Miguel, please come tomorrow. I hope they want to come too, but I'm not sure they ever want to see me again," he said.

Miguel could not believe what had just happened. Danny's transformation in attitude, spirit, and demeanor was astonishing. He touched Danny on the shoulder and said, "I think you are wrong. They very much want to see you."

Danny gave a weak smile and then sobbed again.

Miguel said goodbye to Danny with the plan of returning the next day with Gwen and Jimmy. After exiting Danny's hospital room, he was walking down the corridor when the nurse asked him, "What's your name?

"I'm Miguel Hernández and you?"

"Cheryl. How do you know the patient?"

"Danny is my brother."

"I see," she said with evident skepticism.

Miguel commented, "That's a nice bracelet you're wearing."

"Yes, it's a Navajo bracelet," Cheryl told him.

"Yes, I know. I'm a silversmith, and I make many fine Navajo pieces of jewelry."

"Wonderful. Are you Navajo?" she asked.

"Well, yes and no. I work with Navajo Native Americans, and I speak their language. I feel like a member of their family . . . I can see there's a small turquoise stone missing from your bracelet. Did you know that?"

She looked at her wrist and said, "Oh no! I lost a turquoise stone—how upsetting!"

"Don't worry. I can fix it for you," Miguel told her, "You can come to the jewelry store anytime and ask for me, and I will fix it while you wait."

"Really?" Cheryl asked.

"Oh yes, definitely," Miguel assured her.

She was excited and said, "I hope it's not an inconvenience."

"Not at all," Miguel said and gave her a piece of paper with the name and location of the jewelry shop on it.

Cheryl noted to Miguel, "I still don't understand. I changed the dressings on your brother eight hours ago, and he had severe burning pain and wanted me to stop and let him be. He was very vocal about it and showed a lot of pain. But just now when I changed his dressings, he didn't even flinch. I guess it must be the power of the mind. I don't know."

Miguel said, "Maybe or maybe it's more than that." He shook her hand and departed.

Nellie tapped Miguel on the shoulder to let him know that she wanted to speak to him. Miguel stopped what he was doing. He got up from his workbench and met with Nellie on the far side of the workshop where there was a bit less noise.

"There is a lady outside named Cheryl. She said she met you about three months ago at the hospital. She wants to say hello and talk to you about her bracelet. And she's pretty too," Nellie said to him.

Miguel smiled and went to the front area.

"Miguel, how are you?" Cheryl greeted him.

"Good. How are you, Cheryl?"

"I'm good too. I'm here to take you up on repairing my bracelet."

"Yes, for sure," Miguel responded.

Then Cheryl told him, "By the way, I missed you at the hospital after Danny's surgery because I had to leave the following morning to go to Louisiana. My mother passed away."

"I'm sorry to hear that, Cheryl."

"I stayed there for two months. I was told that Danny did very well."

"Yes, he did, thanks to the good nurses like you and, of course, the doctors," Miguel told her.

"Yes, he had a good surgeon. How is he doing?" she asked.

"He recovered, and as you know, he kept his leg."

"Yes, that's wonderful. Miguel, you and only two other men visited him while he was in the hospital, and those men were there for only a few minutes. But you were there almost three hours," Cheryl observed.

"Yes, you are correct."

"I heard his wife and son were there for the surgery. I heard it was quite emotional."

"Yes, it was," agreed Miguel.

"Thank God they were able to see him before and after surgery," Cheryl noted.

"It was meant to be," Miguel said.

Cheryl said, "Tell me, Miguel, you are not really his brother, are you? You two look so different."

"You mean our color?" Miguel asked. Danny was an African-American.

Cheryl nodded.

"We might have different color skin, but on the inside, we're the same color. We're the same," Miguel said. "As I see it, we are all brothers and sisters. We might not know it, but later upstairs"— Miguel looked upwards—"we will meet and regret that we did not greet each other as brothers and sisters more often. Trust me, it's the truth."

Cheryl didn't react. Instead, she simply looked at Miguel.

Miguel smiled and said, "Let's see your bracelet."

Miguel took her bracelet and returned about ten minutes later to present Cheryl with a shiny, expertly polished bracelet with a newly replaced turquoise stone.

"It's beautiful, Miguel. It looks even better than when I bought it. How much do I owe you?"

"Think nothing of it. I'm simply glad to have met you."

She locked eyes with Miguel, and for a few seconds they maintained a direct and deep eye contact like they were peering at each other's very essence.

Cheryl embraced Miguel and said, "Miguel, I am still confused about how fast Danny's pain went away when you were there visiting. And really, how his whole personality seemed to change too. I told people about it, and I still can't figure it out."

Miguel simply smiled.

Chapter 14

Something Special, Something Unique

A s it had been several months since they'd first met—and it had been an emotional and intense first meeting—Miguel contacted Jerry and Gary Johnson to have a leisurely, let's-get-to-know-each-other-better lunch at Jaramillo's Mexican Food. The three men ate and chatted together, smiling, laughing, and catching up.

Miguel let the twins know how the seven guests who'd been staying in the garage-hostel at the time of the Johnson twins' visit were doing. When he told them that Rafael's sponsor—the architect in New Mexico—had come through for Rafael, the twins were astounded. They had thought it was crazy that Rafael would leave Mexico just because an American stranger at a restaurant made a suggestion and gave an off-hand promise. Now they were seeing that when folks got involved with Miguel Hernández, the seemingly impossible suddenly became real.

"And how's Bonnie and the rest of the family?" Miguel asked and was pleased to learn that everyone was doing well.

As they continued talking, they noticed a Latino-looking man cleaning up nearby tables. His manner was noticeably jittery.

Miguel asked the Johnson twins, "Do you two notice how nervous that guy seems?"

"Yes, it's like it's his first day on the job," Jerry replied.

Gary suggested, "Also, there was a raid here at the restaurant about four months ago. It wasn't pretty either. They must've deported sixteen illegals from this area who happened to be here at the time. It would surprise me greatly if he wasn't thinking about it."

"Probably true," Miguel answered. "He spoke to me before you arrived. He asked if I knew of a job of some sort for him. He wants to find something more steady and with more of a future than what he's doing here."

"How did he know to ask you, Miguel?" Gary inquired.

"Well," Miguel started, "I hate to say this, but word gets around."

"Miguel, you're a good man," Jerry assured him.

"We always knew that about you, even from the first minute we met you," Gary added.

After they finished their lunch, they made plans to meet again soon, and they did meet many times over the next several years. Also, it should be noted that as their friendship strengthened, the number of raids in Central Phoenix decreased, though they never discussed this directly.

After Gary and Jerry departed, Miguel remained in the restaurant to speak some more to the nervous man who had been cleaning tables.

"*Como te llamas*? What is your name?" Miguel asked.

"Gabriel, *me llamo* Gabriel Valenzuela."

Miguel went on to tell Gabriel, the whole time speaking in Spanish, "I'll return to the restaurant this afternoon with some of my family members. I will see you back here then, and we can talk more."

———————

It had been almost a year since Miguel had managed to legally immigrate our sister Surama and our brother Jorge into the US. Quickly, both of them settled in to their new lives. Jorge started school and quickly learned English. Surama worked for Mr. Davis in his pest-control business, making all the necessary preparations before the field workers sprayed insecticide. All of us—Miguel, Pedro, Olivia, Surama, Jorge, and I—would contribute the money we earned (even those of us going to school, like Pedro, Jorge, and me, worked part-time or did odd jobs) to a pot that was not only for household expenses but mostly to put towards paying for the rest of the family to immigrate. Our goal was to make that happen in eighteen months.

It was hard because the house on 206 N. 9th Street still wasn't complete. We had one room in a livable state, so we could sleep in it, but the kitchen wasn't ready. There was a functional stove, but the floor wasn't complete and there was no refrigerator. In the meantime, Miguel would prepare meals in the small kitchen in the apartment above the workshop and then bring those meals to the rest of us at the house. We also ended up dining out together at restaurants, which is why we all were eating out at Jaramillo's that evening.

At dinner, Gabriel was able to sit with us and talk. He told us that he'd been working at the restaurant for six weeks. He entered illegally two months earlier and was living in a small home with seven other people who were working on a day-to-day basis. His wife and two daughters were waiting in Nogales while he worked in Phoenix. They were all hoping for a miracle to happen—that Gabriel would find good-paying work and a sponsor—but currently he was earning barely enough to pay for his own food and housing, and sending just a few dollars back to the family. Gabriel was about forty-five years old, his wife forty-four, and his daughters twenty-two and twenty-four.

Miguel asked him, "What type of work did you do in Mexico? And what did your wife do? And why did you all decide to leave?"

Gabriel explained, "I worked with Sofia, my wife, in a small hospital, preparing food and cleaning patient rooms, and doing overall maintenance to the building and grounds. Our two daughters, Ernestina and Josefina, were going to school. I did all the trouble-shooting and fixed just about anything in the hospital.

"That seems like a good job," Miguel said.

"Yes, but we had to leave," replied Gabriel, and suddenly he started to weep.

All of us looked at Gabriel with sympathy and also concern.

Miguel asked him, "What's wrong? *Que pasa?*"

"I can't tell you. *Yo no puedo decir*. I can't say it."

"Why?"

Unable to look at any of us at the table, Gabriel answered, "Because I need to tell you privately, Miguel. Alone. It's too hurtful."

"I understand," Miguel assured him.

Jorge, Surama, and I were shaken by Gabriel's emotional reaction. Though we didn't know exactly what was going on with him, we knew it was something horrific that had happened to him or his family that made them leave their hometown in Mexico. We weren't sure we wanted to know what he would tell Miguel.

Miguel suggested to us, "How about we eat and then I'll take you all to Dairy Queen for ice cream? I'll come back and talk to Gabriel and then return for you afterwards?"

We agreed.

After leaving us at Dairy Queen, Miguel returned to speak to Gabriel at the back of the restaurant.

Miguel began, "*Con confianza*, trust me and talk to me."

"It was the administration, the hospital administration," Gabriel said and then started to weep.

Though Miguel still did not understand, he knew that

something serious must have happened to this family. Miguel touched Gabriel on the should and said, "Please let me help you."

Gabriel took a deep breath and began again, telling Miguel what happened. "My daughter, Josefina, worked part-time at the hospital, helping comfort patients with her music. She plays the violin beautifully. People start to cry when they hear her music."

Miguel, still perplexed, said, "Okay, so what happened?"

"Every day she showed up after school to comfort patients and their families. Josefina played just about anything. Her violin was her life, and through it, she gave happiness to those around her. At seventeen, she was playing in a symphony as well. Plus, she played at funerals. People loved her music."

"That's wonderful," Miguel commented, all the while quietly gripping the seat of his chair with both hands to steady himself. Gabriel's talk of his daughter's moving violin playing brought to Miguel's mind the haunting and mystical violin cries that Santos Ortiz, the enchanted hermit of La Mira, used to play at children's funerals. Santos Ortiz's violin "music" was jarring, rather than soothing, and full of deep sadness.

Miguel maintained his grasp of the seat of his chair, for his recollection of Santos Ortiz had him anticipating the great tragedy to come in Gabriel's story. Fearing the worst, he encouraged Gabriel to continue.

Gabriel explained, "The hospital administrator . . . he raped my sweet, loving Josefina. He got her pregnant, and she is now three months along. He threatened me and my family when I confronted him. He was a well-respected man with a family of his own and did not want his violent misdeed—and my daughter's ensuing pregnancy—to embarrass him and ruin his stellar reputation. He threatened that if I spoke a word about it, something terrible would happen to me, my wife, or our daughters. When he made those threats, three bodyguards accompanied him, each with a pistol strapped to their waistband. The *pistoleros* surrounded me and gave me evil smirks to show the pleasure they'd take in hurting me and my family if given the chance."

Gabriel wept while sharing this with Miguel. He continued, "We had a small home that we sold at a loss, so we could leave the area. I paid a *pollero* about a hundred dollars to bring me across the border. They hid me amongst rolls of textiles in the back of a big truck. My wife and daughters stayed behind in Nogales. Within two hours of arriving in Phoenix, I found Jaramillo's and started washing dishes. We only have a small amount of money from selling our home, and my pay is negligible at this restaurant. I am so scared for our future. What are we going to do?"

Later, when Miguel told me what Gabriel had related, he confessed that he could hear the young woman's violin playing as her father spoke. Not only that, he could hear Santos Ortiz's crying violin as well. Miguel told me, "It's like the sound of those two violins were trying to tell me something, Edgar. It was like musical angels were circling inside my head. Like something from the heavens was inside me and telling me not to be outraged at what had befallen this family, but to channel my outrage into helping this family start a new, good life."

Miguel had never helped a whole family get their green cards before. And on top of that, it had to be accomplished quickly. Because Josefina was pregnant, if she had the baby or even if her pregnancy was made known to the immigration officers, the paperwork for her visa would get very complicated, perhaps too complicated for Miguel to help her do it successfully. For those two reasons—that it was a whole family and that Josefina was due in six months—accomplishing the immigration process quickly was a priority.

Getting green cards for Gabriel and his family—which also meant finding them sponsors—would prove a major challenge for Miguel. He would have to dig deep and consider new channels in his fairly vast network of business owners to pull it off.

Miguel ended up becoming good friends with Cheryl, the nurse who'd cared for Danny while he'd been in the hospital and whose bracelet Miguel later repaired. Actually, Miguel went out to lunch and dinner several times with Cheryl and her husband Allen, who was an anesthesiologist. Over the course of those meals, Cheryl and Allen got to know Miguel, and he told them, though not in great detail, how he helped illegal immigrants that he met in the Phoenix area.

In fact, Cheryl called Miguel about a patient named Veronica to see if Miguel could provide some assistance. Veronica was twenty-eight and landed in the hospital after a *pollero*, whom she'd hired to cross her illegally into the US, attacked her. The *pollero* tried to rape her, but she resisted. He ended up beating her up to the point that she needed medical attention.

Cheryl told Miguel, "Veronica has no family in Phoenix and no place to go. Miguel, because you told us that you help illegal immigrants, I was wondering if there was anything you could do for her. I'm worried for her."

Because he knew people in many types of businesses, there were a few options for securing employment, sponsorship, and a green card for Veronica. He did his best to avoid temporary jobs for illegals because he most wanted to find them sponsors, so they could get their green cards.

Miguel was able to get Veronica situated in our garage-hostel, and he helped her get a job at a nearby hotel. Within three months she fell in love with a plumber at the hotel, an American citizen. They got married, and through this marriage Veronica got her green card. Cheryl and Allen were amazed at how Miguel found such an ideal situation for Veronica. This was simply another example of the mystery and magic of Miguel Hernández.

Even still, Miguel's enigmatic abilities and resources were going to be put to the test in finding sponsors and legally immigrating Gabriel and his family.

Cheryl and Allen had recently decided to start their own business, an upscale caretaking home for elderly people. Cheryl and Allen borrowed money to buy two homes and began refurbishing them to make them suitable facilities for elderly clients. However, they still needed to staff the place. They hoped to open in about six months, and they already had clients who'd signed on for spaces once it was opened.

Miguel figured that Cheryl and Allen and Gabriel and his family would make an ideal partnership. Cheryl and Allen needed high-quality and experienced staff. Gabriel and his family had years of experience working the many different aspects of a small hospital in Mexico: patient comfort, kitchen work, janitorial work, and such. Gabriel and his family needed an American business owner who could sponsor all four of them.

The biggest "glitch," so to speak, in pulling off the partnership was the baby. Cheryl and Allen would also have to take in a baby and have a baby on their business's premises. Even with the baby factor, Miguel was convinced that it would work out between the two parties.

Miguel started off by telling Cheryl and Allen about the Valenzuelas, minus the violence and pregnancy that had forced them to leave Mexico. He told them about their experience working at the small hospital in Mexico and how they were seeking a new life in the USA and how Cheryl and Allen and this family would make a great fit.

While Cheryl and Allen were somewhat interested in the Valenzuelas, they admitted that they didn't know anything about hiring and sponsoring illegals. So, even before they heard about the rape and the baby, they were skeptical.

Miguel assured Cheryl and Allen that he would help them navigate their side, as sponsors, of the immigration process and how he'd already begun working with the Valenzuelas to gather the needed papers. Though he'd already explained why he, himself, helped illegals to get their papers, Miguel tried to articulate how rewarding they too would find it to help these good human beings.

He told them, "It would be a courageous act of spiritual human kindness for you to work with this incredible family. I even imagine that you would be rewarded with heavenly dividends as well. It's a powerful thing to help our brothers and sisters in this way."

Cheryl and Allen agreed to at least consider it. They would think about it.

While Miguel had confidence that Cheryl and Allen would pull through, because of Josefina's pregnancy, timing was critical. It needed to happen sooner rather than later. Every week counted.

I still remember when Cheryl and Allen came to one of our Sunday barbecues at 206 N. 9th Street. They walked into the backyard and saw four men and two ladies (our guests at the time), as well as Surama, Jorge, Olivia, Pedro, and me. Miguel introduced them to everyone and served the fine meal he'd prepared. Miguel was a quite a cook. He could cook up just about anything with anything, either inside the house or outside on a grill, it didn't matter. We had quesadillas, refried beans with chicken, chorizo, *carnitas*, roasted peppers, and Mexican cheese. Along with *agua de tamarindo* and *horchata* to drink.

As Miguel had already explained to Cheryl and Allen that he aided and housed illegal immigrants, the two understood that the six folks at the barbecue were our current guests. Thus, as illegal immigrants, these six guests were in precarious positions in the US.

At the barbecue Miguel told Cheryl and Allen about the four agreements he had with each guest: work hard, pursue legal immigration, participate in English language classes, and never drink or smoke.

Miguel continued, "Remember with Veronica, the young woman you called me about, how I wasn't looking for just any job for her?"

"Yes," Cheryl confirmed. "I thought you wanted to find her work with a boss who was responsible and reputable and also work that would pay her decently."

"You are correct," Miguel replied, adding, "But also I was looking for a business owner who would be willing to act as Veronica's sponsor, so she could get her green card through her work."

"But Veronica got her green card when she married Byron," Allen pointed out. Cheryl also had a puzzled look on her face.

"Yes, true. And while I always hope that romance and marriage with an American citizen will happen with the guests I help, I know it's not something to rely on. I set Veronica up at the small hotel because I've known the owner, Carl Long, for many years, and he's proved a good boss and a sponsor for past guests of mine. Carl had actually agreed to sponsor Veronica, but he held off when we saw how she and Byron hit it off."

"Business owners as sponsors for people that work with them— that's what you asked us to do with that Mexican family, so they could get their green cards. Correct, Miguel?" Cheryl asked.

"Yes, exactly. You see, as an employer or business owner, you would accompany them to the immigration office in Nogales. There, you'd provide the necessary papers to show that indeed you are the owner of a business, your business is solvent, and you have the ability to hire and pay a salary to the four members of the

Valenzuela family, so that they can become self-sufficient, productive American residents."

"I know you've done this before because you told us about it already. But are you certain that we won't get in trouble for sponsoring these people, especially since the father is already here illegally?" Allen asked.

Miguel answered, "I've done it a few times. Several. I helped Olivia, Pedro, Edgar, Surama, and Jorge get their green cards. Even before that, I helped two of my nephews, Luis and Daniel 'Boli,' and my niece, Blanca, get their green cards. And I've helped a number of guests too. For the people I helped who were already in the US illegally, none of their sponsors faced problems."

"So you have good and solid experience helping business owners act as sponsors and helping applicants, whether they are already in the US or still on the Mexican side?"

"Yes, I have experience. Of course, much of what I know real experts have taught me. For instance, Aurelio, a wonderful, generous, and highly capable immigration expert in Nogales, worked with me a lot. Then there is an actual immigration official who has helped me many times."

"What? An immigration official? Does that person know you are helping illegals get their papers?" they asked in disbelief.

"Yes, he knows. He and I happen to be good friends. He had a turquoise stone missing from his belt buckle, and through that, we became friends. Not the first time I've started a friendship over a missing turquoise stone," Miguel told them with a smile.

Cheryl and Allen smiled back at him.

Miguel explained, "What I have found is that these people who start out illegal—once we find them good work with a responsible employer who will sponsor them—they become outstanding and loyal employees and ultimately patriotic citizens. Trust me, I have seen it. I can refer you to two-dozen business owners who can vouch for me on this. I have seen previous guests get their green cards, and then they begin working towards buying a home, a car, and helping immigrate their sisters or brothers still living in Mexico just like I'm doing. I came here in 1951 and, with the exception of our current guests, I've immigrated everyone you see at this barbecue. In a year or so, I'm planning to immigrate the rest of our family as well. Well, as long as God grants me the strength and helps me open the door, then it will be done."

Cheryl and Allen stood stunned and silent, in awe of all Miguel had accomplished as well as his declared goal for the rest of our family.

Cheryl then asked Miguel, "Have you heard that Danny hasn't touched a drop of liquor since he left the hospital?"

"Yes, I did hear that. It's such great news. After the family moved to New Orleans, Jimmy sent me a letter. He told me the same thing, and also he wrote that he's in school there and he loves his parents very much."

"Miguel, Danny said that you saved all their lives," Cheryl said.

"I didn't do much. Jimmy did it all. That Jimmy will be someone great, I just know it."

As I'd been sitting by Miguel during this whole conversation, Miguel then pointed to me and told Cheryl and Allen, "Edgar too will do something great."

"Yes, Miguel tells us you want to be a surgeon," Allen said to me.

"Yes, I do very much," I said.

"If you want it that bad, you will do it," they told me.

Cheryl turned back to Miguel and said, "You told us you wanted to talk to us more about Gabriel Valenzuela and his family and the possibility of Allen and me sponsoring them and employing them at the caretaking home. Allen and I talked, and we aren't opposed to it, but we also aren't convinced. Can we discuss it more right now?"

Miguel replied, "Thank you, Cheryl, for bringing it up. I realize that it's among the biggest favors I could ever ask of you. They are a very special family. Gabriel and his wife Sofia used to almost single-handedly run a small hospital in Mexico. They are very talented, they did the cooking, maintenance, cleaning, and were very good with patients. They have two daughters, Josefina and Ernestina, who also worked at the hospital and went to school. They are well educated. Josefina plays the violin and used to entertain patients in the hospital. As I see it, this family needs a sponsor, and you also need stellar staff when you open your business. They are good people, and they will be loyal to you. Trust me, I'm sure about them."

Cheryl did not know that Miguel had only met Gabriel about ten days earlier. However, Miguel was certain he somehow had known the Valenzuelas for a long time, for that was how Miguel looked at people. He felt we all knew each other, but our paths may not have yet crossed.

"What do we have to do to be sponsors?" Cheryl and Allen asked.

"I told you about my good friend who is also an immigration official? This friend will give me applications and a rundown of all the requirements for their immigration. All you need to have is a bank statement of your business's assets, an accountant who can provide tax forms showing your ownership of your business and need for employees. You have to show they will be employed from day one after receiving their legal papers. And you will have to come to their final interview in Nogales."

Miguel was quite convincing and assured Cheryl and Allen that it was safe to sponsor the Valenzuelas and that no harm would come to them.

"Allen and I have been thinking about this since you briefed us about it last week," Cheryl shared.

"Thank you," Miguel told them. "You see, it's not every day that you get such an opportunity to challenge yourself to do something so unique and profound for our sisters and brothers. This, I believe, offers a tremendous opportunity that only a few people get in their lifetime to fulfill the heart's need for connection and generosity. Most people go through life and never do anything consequential to help their brothers and sisters. So often those that have the means miss out on sharing those means with others who would benefit most. It's such a wonderful opportunity for you two and for the Valenzuela family."

On my part, I thought Miguel sounded like a top salesman or perhaps just a very charismatic and unique man in the way he presented the sponsorship to Cheryl and Allen.

Allen said, "Okay, tell us more about these people."

"Gabriel, the father, works at a restaurant here in Phoenix, and his wife and daughters—Sofia, Josefina, and Ernestina—are in Nogales. Their savings will soon run out though the women are working now in a private school and earning a little, that is still not enough. I was hoping to get them across within the month since they soon will have all the needed papers. Also, I've encouraged them to start learning English while they are waiting in Nogales."

Looking at Miguel, Allen asked with a grin, "So this is going to make us feel really good?"

Miguel said with a smile and a wink, "I guarantee it."

"Why are you doing this Miguel when these people are not even your relatives? And when you have such limited time and so much work to do to get your blood relatives in Mexico up here in the USA with you?" he asked.

"Allen, I've told you and Cheryl before why I help my guests. As I see it, all people are related though most of us just don't know it. So, we all need to do all we can, especially those of us with means, to help others. In our great future, I believe that you too will come to find my belief to be valid."

Allen was intrigued by Miguel's explanation. He looked at Miguel, and the two men locked eyes. A soul-penetrating gaze was exchanged for a brief moment.

Allen smiled and said, "Miguel, Cheryl and I are thinking that we want to do it, we want to sponsor the family."

Miguel knew that he had to reveal the family's whole story—and that now was the time—so Cheryl and Allen would have a complete picture. He continued, "There's something more you need to know, and this will require a deeper spiritual effort on your part. It's something very special and something that will ultimately challenge your goodness, your spirit, your faith, and your devotion to life itself. It's a secret that will make us feel that we all have done something special. It will make us feel that by helping and sponsoring this family, we earned every bit of goodness we have within our hearts."

Cheryl and Allen looked at each other. As Allen turned back to Miguel, he asked, "What is this special thing?"

Miguel replied, "Actually, it's not a thing. It's a human being. It's . . . a baby."

"A baby? What baby? You said four people—husband, wife, and two daughters—right?" Allen questioned.

"Yes, but one of the daughters is pregnant," revealed Miguel.

"Pregnant?" Allen asked.

Cheryl jumped in, declaring, "Miguel, we can't do this. A baby—oh no, we can't do this. It is too much responsibility. We agreed to help them, but one is pregnant. No, I don't think so. We need to rethink this."

Miguel, looking at both of them, said, "I understand. It will be a great gift to them, trust me. Won't it be wonderful having a young child around to brighten all of our lives, and at the same time you will have wonderful people working for you? Having the baby will be no burden. The Hernández family will help you and the Valenzuelas with the baby."

Allen noted, "Really, Miguel, the young woman shouldn't be fleeing to the US. She should inform the father and raise the baby with him. It seems to me that the family may have made the situation more difficult by leaving, instead of having the young man responsi-ble for the pregnancy own up to his responsibilities."

After Allen said this, Miguel told them what had happened to Josefina at the hands of the administrator and also the resulting threats of violence against the whole family.

Cheryl and Allen were stunned into silence. Cheryl began crying.

Miguel ended the conversation by saying to them, "Please, let's do something good for these people. I promise they will bring high-qual-ity work and ethics to your business, and you will feel deep satisfac-tion for providing them this life-changing opportunity."

Cheryl and Allen refused to commit. Cheryl, instead, contin-ued weeping.

Allen and Miguel tried to comfort her, but Cheryl simply wanted to go home.

On the way to the car, Miguel told Allen, "Let me know as soon as you reconsider."

Miguel hugged Cheryl and Allen, each in turn. Then they got into their car and left.

Miguel felt certain by this point that they would agree to sponsor the family. He figured they just needed a little more time to digest ev-erything. But, in light of Josefina's pregnancy, time was of the essence.

———

A few days later, Cheryl showed up at the jewelry shop. She wanted to speak to Miguel. While waiting for him, Cheryl began talking with Nellie.

"I understand that Miguel is your son's godfather?" she began.

"Yes, he is," Nellie replied. "Sampson is now eight."

"Sampson—like Sampson in the Bible?" Cheryl asked.

"Yes, exactly."

Cheryl then asked Nellie, "How is Miguel as a godfather?"

Nellie told her, "Truly, he is the best. He visits Sampson all the time. Look at these pictures I have of them together. Here's one where they're both wearing head feathers."

Cheryl looked at the photographs and smiled.

"Oh, yes, Sampson loves his godfather. Look at this one, this is Sampson at the age of one, hugging Miguel."

"Who is the man on the left?" Cheryl asked, pointing.

"That's my father, Ben," answered Nellie.

"Wow, Sampson looks so much like your father," Cheryl observed.

"Miguel says the same thing all the time."

When Miguel entered the reception area, he greeted Cheryl with a hug.

Cheryl simply asked him, "Miguel, can we talk later today when you get off work? Can you meet Allen and me at the new business?"

"Yes, that sounds good. I'd love to see how the refurbishments are going."

"You will be impressed, Miguel. Everything is looking great," Cheryl told him.

Allen and Cheryl had been using some of the contractors Miguel had recommended, who were also remodeling his home, so he was very happy to hear that Cheryl was pleased with their work.

In the late afternoon, Miguel showed up at Cheryl and Allen's new business. Indeed, Cheryl had been correct. Miguel was impressed with the remodeling work.

"It was a major feat, Miguel. You see—they joined the two houses together with this corridor-type room."

The space built between the two houses featured shiny, tiny square tiles on the floors, and the walls were covered in exquisite wallpaper. The resulting home could now house more than ten clients.

"How do you like it?" Allen asked Miguel.

"It's quite a place. It's impressive, yet it also feels cozy, like a home," Miguel answered, all the while looking at the ceiling, floor, windows, and fixtures around him. Taking in the thoughtful design and the high-end materials that had been used.

"Yes, we wanted it to have the comfort and feel of a real home," Allen replied, "The backyard is like a picnic area with tall trees."

"Yes, it's great. And you already have some clients signed on?" Miguel asked.

Cheryl replied, "Yes, we have commitments from the families of three lawyers and two doctors, as well as two well-to-do types. When they came over to view the home, they immediately gave a deposit to reserve places."

"Wonderful," Miguel responded.

Cheryl hugged Miguel and then asked, "Why are you so desperate to help this family when you've got so much else going on, what with bringing your own family here and remodeling your home? I know we've asked you this before, but Allen and I want to understand better."

Miguel gave a simple and honest answer, "I want to do something important in life that will last forever."

Cheryl continued, "These people, from what you said, have very little money, so you won't get any kind of payment from them. Also, I could never understand your relationship with Danny and Jimmy. What I learned about Danny, only after he left the hospital, was that he had been a very violent man. It was while he was in the hospital, and before my very eyes, that his temperament changed so completely. I remember when you visited him in the hospital. That's something I have never forgotten, how you could spend so much time with a man who was so nasty and who had tried to hurt you physically. Before your first visit, he'd been such an uncooperative patient, yet you called him your 'brother'—why? I just want to know why, and I realize it's got nothing to do with money. But what you are doing is so time-consuming. What you do for your guests, for Veronica, for so many people—it's time-consuming. And I know you work long hours and don't have a lot of free time. Also the reason you seek out sponsors for the people who you house in your unfinished home, that is also a mystery to us. I have to admit to you, at one time, we were suspicious of you."

"Really?" Miguel asked with a twinkle in his eye.

"Yes, but no longer," said Cheryl. "I guess we are not used to such unusual and profound human kindness."

Miguel responded, "Cheryl, what I try to do is just what every human should do for others. I feel it isn't practiced enough, but I also think you and Allen are now trying to practice these wonderful things that all people should be doing."

"You mean helping the Valenzuelas?"

"Yes, that's exactly what I mean. Cheryl, most people would have run away from even listening to me, perhaps out of fear of violating the law or just plain fear of getting involved. You have said nothing to the contrary, and for that, you too are doing these small and unique things in life to help your brothers and sisters. That's kosher. That's legitimate."

Cheryl smiled. Allen smiled too.

"Do you remember how I told you that Danny was my brother? And that someday you would find out I was right and that he is your brother too?"

Cheryl nodded her head as she looked at Miguel.

With her eyes locked with his, looking at him intently and unflinchingly, she announced, "Miguel, we will help you with this family, but there's something that I need to talk to you about first. Please sit down."

Allen then left the room.

Cheryl began, "Miguel, my sister and I grew up with abusive parents. Both of them. Our parents had no business having children"—tearing up, she held on to Miguel's hand—"I very much want to help this family. For two reasons: number one, because it's the right thing to do and because your sincere efforts can't be ignored. As you point out, it's an exemplary act of human kindness.

"Number two: for me, it's personal and important to do something for this family, more so now because there is a young woman who has been raped and is pregnant. I'll admit to you that I really didn't want to hear about her because it brought back to me so many terrible and hurtful times from my past."

Cheryl paused. Then all at once, her composure returned. She cleared her eyes and told Miguel, "I don't know why you had to come into my life and wake up such terrible fear and anger within me. A hatred I have had towards life and people. No, please, Miguel, listen to me, it's not meant in a bad way but a good way. You are giving me and my lonely soul a gift. Perhaps even more importantly—perhaps you are healing a hurt from my past."

Miguel, though slightly puzzled, was moved. He stayed silent and continued listening.

"My sister was raped by a neighbor. My father knew it was happening, but he did nothing. She went to a lady to have an abortion. I took her myself, and we held on to each other as we walked into the room where the procedure would happen. I'll never forget how that lady was standing there in the doorway with her hand out, demanding payment before she would help my sister. The woman told my sister to make herself comfortable and that it would be quick. I held her hand tight, and she looked me in the eye, a look that I still remember. My poor sister suffered so much mental anguish and was scarred forever from that experience. I share this burden with her to this very day. A burden that no one should suffer. We survived physically but mentally, as you can now see, it is still within me. I did not want to marry anyone and did not want to get pregnant for many years. I have never had a child though now I long for one. To this day that horrific event from the past has stayed with me.

"I want more than anything to help you with this family, so this young lady has some better options available to her than my sister and I had. I know you said that an abortion is being contemplated because immigration may be easier, so know that I am willing to help her and her family as a sponsor. I don't want her to have an abortion. Allen and I will go to Nogales to get them all immigrated as soon as you tell us to—whether that be tomorrow or next week. We will prove our financial solvency and job security and housing. I just don't want this young lady to do something awful at this young age."

Miguel sat in complete silence. He was upset that Cheryl had experienced such pain, but at the same time he was happy about her generous desire to help.

Miguel told her, "It hurts me to hear of this event in your life, but healing comes in various and sometimes mysterious ways."

"Yes, Miguel, I agree. And I understand how you feel about doing something special for people. Perhaps more of us should do unique things like this in life."

"Cheryl, unique opportunities to help are probably around us all the time, but we just don't know it. It's faith in what you do, both within your heart and every day of your life, that is important. Believe me, someone is keeping count, you just don't know it at the present time. We are here for a reason. Living a long time is not the reason. So many people live long lives but do very little that counts. We are here for a special reason, and that is to do something that counts in our life and the lives of others. And, yes, it's assisting our brothers and sisters that I'm talking about."

Cheryl smiled at Miguel's words. They hugged and then made their way to find Allen.

When they approached him, he was tearing up too and said, "Cheryl, thank you for making me happy with all you do for me."

He looked at Miguel and explained, "Miguel, at first Cheryl did not want to start this new business, but I insisted. We talked about it a lot, and finally she agreed. This has made me happy. It will be a good business, and at the same time hopefully we can do something special for the special people that will stay here."

"Yes," Miguel replied with a smile.

A few days later Miguel had lunch with Rex Thompson to discuss the immigration applications for Gabriel and his family. Miguel even told Rex about Josefina's pregnancy.

Rex responded, "Miguel, I don't know of any pregnant young lady. All I know is you are helping a husband, wife, and two daughters—one skinny and one fat."

Miguel smiled at him.

Rex looked over the applications and papers from Cheryl and Allen regarding their business and assets. Their business would hire Gabriel as the handyman, his wife as the chef, and the two daughters as attendants and entertainers.

Within fourteen days of that lunch meeting, the family had their interviews in Nogales and got their green cards.

The Valenzuela family lived in our garage-hostel briefly. Then they moved into the staff lodging at the caretaking home. They were responsible for all the maintenance of the buildings and grounds.

When Josefina gave birth to a baby girl, she named her Cheryl Allen.

Cheryl and Allen's business ended up being so successful that they expanded, hiring an additional five people, all of whom they sponsored. Their business closed after twenty-five years due to new government regulations and bureaucracy. Basically, it became too expensive to run. However, during the years of its operation, Cheryl, Allen, Gabriel, Sofia, Josefina, and Ernestina worked as a tight-knit team and family.

After its closing, Cheryl and Allen retired and moved to the Midwest. Gabriel and Sofia went to work at the Hilton. Ernestina became a nutritionist, and Josefina became an accountant. Cheryl Allen, Josefina's daughter, ended up becoming a teacher.

About five years later, in 1969, when I was about to graduate from high school and start college, Cheryl invited me out to lunch. She also gave me a generous graduation gift of one hundred dollars. By that time, the rest of my siblings and my mother had been living in the US for more than three years, for in 1966 Miguel had successfully arranged to immigrate them.

At lunch Cheryl told me, "Edgar, I have no children and always wanted to have a son or daughter, but I was also afraid. Miguel changed our lives by encouraging us to sponsor Gabriel and his family. At that time, I wasn't totally sure if we were doing the right thing, but I quickly realized that more people should be generous like your brother Miguel. And frankly, I don't understand that feeling that happens inside me when Miguel and I talk. It's inspiring to listen to him. It's like anything is possible, and everything is joyful. The world really becomes our oyster, and all people truly feel like one giant family. That's what he brings out in me—an overwhelming feeling of great possibility and love. And I find it incredible that just like he said he would, he managed to immigrate everybody in your family to the US."

"Yes, Cheryl, I agree—Miguel is a mystery. He's an amazing and mysterious man. Thank you for recognizing this and for talking about it with me."

She continued, "I know that even now, Miguel and your mother still house people in dire need, and it's inspiring. It's something I want to tell the world, but I know Miguel is very private and doesn't want any accolades or anything else in return."

"That's certainly true. He walks away from people when they want to thank him. He tells them, 'Think nothing of it.'"

Cheryl and I were in agreement—and there was a mass of others in agreement with us as well—Miguel Hernández was beyond human. Beyond real. A phenomenon of persistent human kindness and compassion. A mystery and a mystic.

Chapter 15

GOLDEN OPPORTUNITY

Miguel sat in the waiting room at Dr. Flores's clinic. Dr. Flores was a well-respected doctor of Puerto Rican descent whose clinic was a short walk from our 206 N. 9th Street property. A few weeks earlier, Miguel accidently cut the outer area of his left palm when using an X-Acto, a knife-like instrument, to shave a bevel on a ring. The cut required four stitches, and now it was time to get those stitches removed.

In the waiting room with Miguel sat a man, an elderly woman with a baby in a chair near her, and two young women. The baby was crying relentlessly, and it was evident from the odor that it had soiled its diaper. Actually, the baby was covered in its own excrement too. It was quite a mess. Eventually, Miguel decided to approach the elderly woman. As she appeared to be a Latina, he let her know in English and then in Spanish that it would be a good idea to change the baby's diaper and clean the baby up as best as possible.

Strangely, the old woman ignored Miguel. She didn't even acknowledge his presence. It appeared that she couldn't hear him. When Miguel gently touched her on the shoulder, she tilted her head up as if to look at him. However, her face held no expression, and both of her eyes appeared clouded over. Encased in a milky white coating.

Miguel was taken aback. The old lady remained immobile and oblivious of both the crying, feces-covered baby and of him. It was as if she—or perhaps Miguel—was operating in another space and time. In fact, the other people sitting in the waiting room also seemed to exist in another reality, for they too appeared to be completely oblivious to the baby's incessant crying and the smell of feces. Like they couldn't hear or see or smell what was happening. Eventually, they simply left the waiting room, exiting the clinic.

It was too much. Miguel decided he needed somebody on staff to help get the old woman to care for the baby in her charge. He stood and made his way to the receptionist's window. He tapped on it.

When the receptionist opened the window, Miguel said, "Excuse me. I'm sorry to bother you, but I'm concerned about the baby that's crying—"

"We'll be with you in a minute," she interrupted him and then closed the window.

Miguel remained standing before the window. Waiting for her to return, he examined his hand, for blood had started oozing a bit through the gauze.

As he gazed at his hand, he felt confused and even shocked at how no one showed any concern about what was happening with the baby. The other folks had preferred to leave rather than acknowledge there was a problem. The old lady sat there impassively. And surely the staff could hear the baby's incessant crying through the door, wall, and glass though they chose to do nothing. It was all so strange.

The receptionist opened the window again and asked, "What is it that you want?"

Again, Miguel stated, "The baby that's crying," and he turned to point back to it. Then Miguel suddenly stopped speaking.

The receptionist prompted him, "Yes, what about it, sir?"

Miguel turned back to the window to face her as he said, "She's not here. The old lady sitting near the baby—she's gone. The baby has been left by itself. Everyone disappeared."

Taking in Miguel's words and state of shock, the receptionist realized something serious was wrong. She got up and came out to the waiting room. Pointing at the crying baby but looking at Miguel, she asked, "Oh dear, what is this?"

Miguel looked at her wide-eyed.

"Is this your baby?" she asked him.

"No, it's the old lady's baby," Miguel answered.

"What old lady?"

"The old lady who was here," he replied.

"I saw two people waiting, and two patients are currently with the doctor, but no old lady," the receptionist explained.

The baby was still crying, and it was apparent it was unhappy and uncomfortable in its soiled state, so Miguel asked, "Can we change the baby and comfort it while we figure out what's going on?"

Without waiting for her reply, Miguel went over and picked up the crying baby. In doing so, his bandaged hand and shirt became soiled with feces.

"Come inside and clean up. Let's change the baby," she said and then, "Oh no! You soiled your bandage!"

"Yes, but it's okay. Not a problem. One thing at a time," Miguel responded.

They took the baby into an examination room where there was a sink, soap, towels, and such.

"I'm going to check to see if any of the patients with the doctor are the parents," the receptionist told Miguel.

Miguel didn't wait. He went ahead and washed and changed the baby. It was a little boy with black hair, wide eyes, and two tiny lower teeth. The baby continued to cry as he was cleaned and changed, though shortly after he calmed down a bit.

When the receptionist came in again, Miguel was down to his undershirt, having taken off his soiled shirt to wash it. She was pale and silent. Stunned and temporarily mute.

Miguel asked, "Did you find the mother or father?"

She took in a breath and then answered, "No. They both said no."

Miguel again felt like he was dreaming. Like it couldn't be real. Then he glanced down at his hand to see the blood dripping out of his bandage and onto the floor.

The receptionist also noticed the blood. She reached for a roll of fresh gauze to apply to the wound area all the while looking at the baby.

As the door was propped open, Dr. Flores—who was about to walk past the room—turned and entered, saying, "There you are, Melinda. Can you schedule Mrs. McGrady for a follow-up next week and the other patient, Mr. Leverenz, needs an appointment in three weeks?"

As Melinda didn't reply, Dr. Flores looked up from his clipboard. That's when he noticed Miguel and the baby in the exam room with her.

The doctor asked, "What's going on here? Whose baby is that?"

Melinda replied, "That's the thing—we don't know. I think the baby's parents left him here."

"Left him here?" Dr. Flores, confused, replied. "Please schedule those appointments and come right back."

To Miguel, he asked, "So, let me get this straight—you are not related to this baby?"

"No, sir," answered Miguel, "I only came in to have my stiches removed. In the waiting room, that's where I saw the crying baby. It had soiled itself and was covered in feces. Sitting near him was an elderly woman. I tried to talk to her about the baby, but she ignored me. When I went to speak to your receptionist, the old lady disappeared."

"Disappeared?"

"Yes, Dr. Flores, in an instant. There were three other people in the waiting room too, but they also left."

"Ridiculous, this is ridiculous," Dr. Flores replied and abruptly left the room.

Miguel was about to walk out to follow the doctor, but the baby started to cry. Then the crying started to intensify, so Miguel picked him up and carried him as he walked out of the exam room.

The secretary found Miguel in the corridor and she commented, "This is crazy, isn't it? Let's see what Dr. Flores wants to do. He's in his office."

"Do you have milk for the baby?" Miguel asked.

"Yes, in the back. I'll get it," she replied. She soon returned with a cup of milk.

Miguel, still carrying the baby, realized he'd have to make do without a bottle, so he got some gauze, rolled it, and saturated the rolled gauze with some milk. The baby sucked the milk from the gauze.

Miguel was on his own, feeding the baby, for about fifteen minutes when finally Dr. Flores returned to ask him, "Are you sure the baby doesn't belong to you or someone in your family?"

Masking his amazement at the doctor's question, Miguel simply answered, "Yes, I am sure. I have no children of my own."

"This is very strange to me," the doctor muttered, and then he asked Miguel, "Are you sure someone didn't drop him off and leave him in the waiting room?"

Miguel replied, "That's possible. The old lady sitting near him took no notice of him or of me, so maybe the baby wasn't related to her. Maybe someone did drop him off."

Dr. Flores asked, "Did you talk to anyone in the waiting room about the baby?"

"I tried, but no one listened. Because the baby was crying for so long and it was evident from the smell and from the mess that he needed changing, I tried to talk to the elderly lady. I assumed the baby was with her, but she ignored me. I thought she might be hard of hearing and perhaps blind too. Her eyes looked like they were covered in egg yolk."

The doctor commented, "I haven't seen a patient matching that description today."

As if trying to prove that indeed the baby belonged to Miguel, the doctor, clearly frustrated at this point, questioned, "You said you don't have any children, so how is it you know how to feed a baby, especially when there's no bottle?"

Miguel, ignoring the doctor's frustrations and suspicions, replied calmly, "Dr. Flores, I have many brothers, sisters, and godchildren. I've had lots of practice feeding babies over the years."

It was now 10:00 am. Miguel's appointment was for 7:30 am, and he was supposed to be at work by 8:30 am. He realized he needed to call the jewelry store about being late.

Miguel repositioned the baby, so it rested on one forearm and his chest. With his free hand, he picked up the phone's receiver, dialed the shop, and informed Nellie that either he would be late or might not be able to come in today.

When Miguel finished the call, Melinda, the secretary, informed him, "Honestly, we don't know what to do with the baby. Dr. Flores suggested we call a church or a hospital to see what they do when a child is left on their doorstep. But we don't know what to do, and we have patients to attend to. Oh and I found this"—she handed Miguel a baby bottle—"It'll be easier than the gauze."

Abruptly Melinda left Miguel, so she could attend to a patient.

About thirty minutes later the doctor emerged from his office to find Miguel. Melinda was by his side.

Dr. Flores told him, "You can take the baby to the hospital on Durango Street today or to the church on Van Buren Street tomorrow morning."

"Tomorrow morning?" Miguel asked, looking at the secretary for some sort of reaction or sign of support—surprise, commiseration, confusion, or even an offer of help.

Melinda was stone-faced. It seemed that both she and the doctor simply wanted to get rid of the problem. The inconvenience.

Miguel never for a moment thought they were bad people. He simply realized they had other priorities. So, he decided that he would take responsibility for helping the baby.

As Miguel was departing the clinic, Dr. Flores called out to him, "Good luck! Don't forget—the hospital on Durango or the church on Van Buren!"

Miguel stopped and turned back to ask the doctor, "And who is it that I ask for?"

"Anyone. Anyone at either place will help you," answered the doctor.

———

Miguel took the baby and gently held it on his left arm and against his chest while opening the car door. Again, very carefully he placed the baby on the passenger's seat. From the trunk, he removed a Kellogg's box that had contained eight boxes of cornflakes, and he found some towels as well. Miguel tenderly wrapped the baby in the towels and placed him in the Kellogg's box that would serve as a crib for now.
After he sat himself down in the driver's seat, Miguel prayed, "Help me, God. Help me and help my little brother, this innocent angel visiting our earth." Then Miguel started the car.

The baby was sleeping soundly in the Kellogg's box crib when they arrived at the hospital. With the box in his arms, he approached the hospital's receiving desk.

A woman with a nametag that read "Ava," was working the desk. "How can I help you?" she asked Miguel.

Miguel said, "I have a baby in this box. I would like to leave the baby with you because he has no family."

She asked, "You want to leave a baby here?"

"Yes," Miguel confirmed, "He has no family."

"Let me get someone to talk to you," she told Miguel.

A short time later, a heavy-set woman came to the front desk. Ava pointed the woman over to Miguel.

With no introduction, she questioned Miguel, "Where's this baby?"

He answered, "Hello, my name is Miguel Hernández and you are?"

She responded, "Never mind my name. Where's this baby?

"Here," Miguel answered her.

"Where?"

"In the box," Miguel replied, pointing at the box sitting in the chair next to where he was standing.

She peered at the baby, who was smiling at the sound of Miguel's voice. As she looked at the baby, Miguel was explaining to him, "We are looking for a home for you and some good home-cooking. We may have found someone to help you."

The baby continued to smile, but the woman wasn't happy. With her face scrunched up, she muttered, "It won't be here," and stormed away.

Miguel was playing with the baby's feet and the baby was giggling when another hospital official approached.

This person immediately asked, "Where did you get the baby?"

Miguel responded, "I am Miguel Hernández and you are?"

"Oh, my name is Tom Hamilton, and I run the emergency service. So, the baby is not related to you?"

Miguel answered, "Sir, we are all related. Just as you are my brother, this baby too is my little brother."

Tom Hamilton questioned, "Yes, but he is or isn't your real brother?"

"I found him up at a Dr. Gustavo Flores's office this morning.

He has no one but me, and he has been with me since this morning. When I was at Dr. Flores's office, we thought his parents were there, but everyone denied being his parent. I asked the doctor and his receptionist about what to do with him, and they told me to bring him here or to a church."

Tom Hamilton suggested, "Probably the police would be better, at least from my standpoint. Or a church." Looking inside the box, he added, "He's charming. Seems to laugh a lot!"

"Yes, he's a good boy," Miguel said and then asked, "So I should take him to a church?"

"Correct. They will certainly help you," answered Tom Hamilton.

Before Miguel departed Tom Hamilton asked, "Tell me, honestly—is he your son? Your brother? Nephew?"

Miguel answered simply, "Yes, you are correct, for in the eyes of the Lord we are all family."

As Miguel left, carrying the box with the baby in it, he wondered, "Perhaps if the baby was sick, they might've helped me?"

He decided not to wait until the next morning but to go immediately to the church on Van Buren Street. He set the box with the baby in it on a step, and he knocked on the church's door.

A woman opened the door while at the same time demanding, "Can't you see the sign, 'No salesmen or solicitation'?"

Miguel explained, "I'm not a salesman. I have a baby here that I want to leave with you." He reached down to pick up the box and show her.

The woman looked at the baby in the box and asked, "Who does this baby belong to?"

"I don't know."

"You don't know?"

Miguel explained, "I found him alone in a doctor's office, and the doctor said for me to bring him here—the church on Van Buren Street. He even called. Someone is expecting the baby, but they might be expecting him tomorrow morning. I decided to come today instead."

"I can't take in that baby. It's not my place. I need to speak to the head," she stated and then asked, "So, he has no family?"

"No. Really, it's only me," answered Miguel.

"So he is or is not related to you?" she asked.

"We are all related—in the eyes of God. You too are related to this baby and to me as well."

The lady's eyes narrowed, showing her annoyance at Miguel's choice of words. Then she said, "You should go. Take the baby. I'll call you later and let you know what the head says."

"Well, let me give you my phone number then," Miguel stated. When she returned with paper and a pen, he gave her his phone number.

"If you don't hear from me, then I guess you should come back in the morning. Early," she said and then closed the door.

No one was home when Miguel and the baby arrived. Jorge and I were at school, and early that very morning, Surama had left for a five-day business trip to Los Angeles. She and another colleague were going to a convention to learn about the latest innovations in pesticides for the Davises' business. Miguel stayed near the phone all day waiting for the call.

When Jorge and I got home from school, we found Miguel sitting by the phone with a baby by his side.

As Miguel was telling us the whole story of his day, Jorge and I watched him feed the baby and then replace his diaper with one he had made himself from a segment of a towel that he cut up. Jorge and I were impressed and moved at how gentle Miguel was with the fragile baby.

Jorge and I took turns holding and watching the baby while Miguel went across the street to talk to Mrs. Davis about the baby and to use her phone to call Olivia. Miguel didn't want to tie up our phone with a call in case someone from the church called us. Jorge and I were at the ready to answer the phone.

Over the phone Miguel explained to Olivia what had happened that day, and Olivia was very upset that she couldn't help. As already mentioned, she and Pedro had a very demanding job. It was rare that they could leave the premises of the family's property where they worked. They actually lived in a small shed at the back of the property and had to pay rent to live in it. The family wanted them on call and ready to help at any moment—day or night—should their family member with polio need unexpected help. So there was no way that Olivia could leave to help Miguel with the baby.

Mrs. Davis offered to help care for the baby, but she needed to be in her house to supervise some pesticide-related business. In the back, several workers were cleaning pesticide spray guns, tubes, and tanks. When she and Miguel thought about it more, they realized it probably wouldn't be a good idea for the baby to be around those chemicals anyway. Before he left, Mrs. Davis gave Miguel extra milk, two large safety pins, some more towels to make into diapers, and some talc.

Early the next morning Jorge and I were awoken by the sounds of Miguel cooing and softly singing to the baby as he attended to him. We got up to keep Miguel company and to help him out.

"I'm going to take this little fella to the church at 7 am, and then I'm going to head to work," he told us.

All of us knew that making the most money possible right now was the goal. In three weeks, Pedro and Olivia would be leaving their jobs with the family outside Phoenix and moving in with us.

We also had the plan to immigrate the rest of the family in three to five months' time. But all of this depended on our reaching a particular financial goal by a designated time, and while we all contributed, Miguel's earnings were the most substantial and, thus, key to making it all happen.

So when Jorge asked Miguel, "Usually you start work around 5:30 in the morning. You missed yesterday, and today you won't be starting until 8 am. Are you feeling stressed about it?" we were amazed at Miguel response.

He answered, "No, not at all, actually. As I see it, this was meant to be. God wanted us to have this special time with our little brother. I'm simply grateful God selected us for this honor."

We smiled at Miguel, in awe of his conviction and fortitude. We also felt grateful that Miguel was our older brother and had become like a father to us.

Jorge and I even talked together about the possibility of keeping the baby and having him become part of the family. But we knew that Miguel was the one to make this determination, and as of yet, he hadn't brought it up.

Miguel admitted to us, "I wonder if I should've insisted Dr. Flores take responsibility for the baby. Maybe if he were in charge, the people at the hospital or the church yesterday would have done something? I got the feeling, especially at the hospital, that they thought it was my baby and I was shirking responsibility. I wonder if the police will be like that too. If Dr. Flores had the baby, they might not be so skeptical. After all, he is older than me and has his own clinic. No matter, I have faith that we are meant to be with this little guy and that everything will work out beautifully. In the meantime, we've got some places to go! First the church, and if there's an issue there, then I'll see if the police can help."

Jorge and I walked with Miguel and the baby to the car. We placed the baby, happily asleep in the Kellogg's crib, onto the passenger seat. Jorge and I tucked a blanket around him, and we gave Miguel the bottle of warm milk for when the baby awoke.

We looked on with pride as Miguel drove away.

At 7 am sharp Miguel rapped on the church door. Miguel had to keep up the knocking for about a minute before he could hear someone on the other side unbolting the door.

Before the door even opened, Miguel heard a woman's voice, different from the woman's voice from the day before, muttering, "Now who is it knocking on the door so early in the morning? This better not be a salesman!"

Upon opening the door, Miguel could see that, indeed, this wasn't the same person from yesterday. She looked at him and asked, "Why are you knocking on the door so early?"

Miguel responded, "The lady from yesterday told me to return early this morning with the baby. That you would be ready for us."

"What are you talking about? What baby?" she asked.

Miguel pointed to the box at its feet. That's only when she noticed it. She looked inside to see the baby. His eyes were open, and he smiled at her.

She looked up at Miguel, confused. "I'm sorry. I don't know what's going on. I don't know anything about you or a baby."

Miguel tried to explain to her how the woman from yesterday told him to return to the church early this morning and that someone at the church would be ready to help him with the baby. However, it was apparent that this woman knew nothing about what he was talking about. So, he had to start from the beginning and tell her the whole story. Even then she seemed stunned. Confounded.

Though he'd sufficiently explained the situation, the woman was having difficulty wrapping her head around the strange reality of it, so she asked questions that he'd already answered. "Now who exactly does the baby belong to?"

Patiently, Miguel answered, "Yes, that's the thing—no one knows who the baby belongs to. Dr. Flores recommended I bring the baby to this church because you all would be in a position to handle an abandoned baby. The woman at the church yesterday told me that she would locate a person of authority in the church who would be ready to receive me and the baby early this morning and help us address the situation. That's why we are here."

She replied, "This is terrible. You picked the baby up at a doctor's office, and now he is here? Why the doctor's office? Is he sick?"

"No, I was sick. Well, I was injured, and that's why I was at the doctor's. The baby just happened to be there. We don't think the baby is sick."

"But who was the baby with?"

"The baby was alone. Abandoned. Alone and abandoned in the waiting room at the doctor's," he explained again.

"Alone. Alone," she repeated almost as if irritated.

Miguel gently asked, "Can I come in and discuss with you what happened and why I have the baby?"

The woman shook her head vigorously and explained, "No, that's not going to be possible. No indeed. I need to prepare for the morning services. Come back around noon."

Miguel ventured to suggest, again very gently, "Perhaps it would be the most holy of services for us to discuss this together and for us to help this baby together. You see, I need help to find a good family that will adopt him or help to locate his birth parents. Wouldn't that be the ultimate service for us to accomplish this morning?"

The woman immediately responded, "You should have left him with the doctor's people. Why are you getting involved? You should have the doctor take care of him. This isn't a good morning for us because we have dignitaries coming to the church this morning."

Miguel suggested to her, with a gentle calm, "We could seize this as a golden opportunity. Think how engaged and impressed those important people will be when they see us, together, doing God's work by helping this abandoned child. Such important ministry, helping our little brother together."

"Sir, don't lecture me about what is best for us all. I only work here," she replied.

"Very well, ma'am. I'll move on with the baby. May I give you my work number? You could call me if you have any open time in your day, and we could talk more about helping our little brother?"

She looked at Miguel and stated, "I keep hearing you say, 'Our little brother.' I thought you weren't related to this baby—so?"

"Oh, but I am. You are too. In fact, the three of us are related. In the same family together. You might not believe me now, but soon enough you'll understand," Miguel said.

For the first time, her eyes rested directly on Miguel's. Intent, deep eye contact.

This honest looking into each other's eyes motivated Miguel to say, "Please, ma'am, this is our brother. I need your help to find him a home or to find his birth mother. He needs love and nurturing, so he can grow strong and smart. Someday, he will be the one to care for you and me."

However, she remained impassive.

Miguel was able to convince her to write down the jewelry shop's number when he promised that if she did so, he would leave with the baby.

As Miguel was gently placing the baby, in his Kellogg's box crib, back onto the passenger's seat of the car—the baby smiling and making baby sounds all the while—he looked over towards the church door. He saw the lady had opened the door a crack and was watching him.

———◦◦◦———

Miguel decided to go to the shop. He needed to let Margaret and Doc and his silversmith colleagues know what was going on and why he might not be able to work for a few hours.

When Miguel got to the shop parking lot, he parked his car and rested his forehead down against the steering wheel. He sighed and then lifted his head. In a quick flash Miguel saw an image of Santos Ortiz. This frightened him, but only for an instant.

Miguel took another deep breath. He got out of the car and then went around to the passenger's side to retrieve the baby. When he picked up the box and looked inside, the baby was sound asleep. Miguel gently moved one of the baby's little hands to make sure he was breathing.

Miguel released a sigh of relief. Then an idea came to him, "Maybe I shouldn't let this baby go. What if he ends up in the wrong hands? What if they hurt him?"

Suddenly Miguel's thoughts were interrupted by Big Tom.

"Miguel, what are you doing out here? Late start for you today!" he hollered.

When Big Tom reached the car, Miguel asked him, "Tom, do you want to see something?"

When Tom walked around to the passenger's side, Miguel pointed to the cardboard box inside the car. Big Tom looked in, and a massive smile spread across his face. Then he asked, "Miguel, what are you doing with a baby?"

Miguel answered, "I don't know myself, but soon he will have a home, and I want it to be a good home."

Big Tom opened the back door, and Miguel entered the

workshop carrying the cardboard box. The shop was noisy as usual with the silversmiths working at their benches.

Big Tom started telling everyone, one by one, "He has a baby. Miguel has a baby."

Heads began turning and looking at Miguel and the box. Next Margaret entered, and Big Tom told her the news too.

"Baby? What baby?" she asked.

"It's in the box," answered Big Tom.

Margaret walked to Miguel's bench and stood before the box. She pulled back the blanket to find the baby with a smile so big that she could make out his two tiny teeth.

"What's going on, Miguel?" she asked, concerned and curious at the same time, all the while watching the smiling baby.

By that time Miguel was exhausted from having told the story so many times, so he gave Margaret the short version: "Yesterday morning when I went to get my stiches removed, this baby was in the waiting room crying and covered in his own feces. No one was paying attention to him. No one around claimed him either. The receptionist and the doctor were busy and didn't want to get involved, so they had me take him, hoping I could find someone to help locate his birth parents or get him adopted."

"Miguel, say no more. I trust you completely."

Doc joined them. He looked in the box and commented, "Cute baby! New silversmith?" Then he smiled wide and talked to the baby, "Goo, goo, goo."

Everyone laughed.

"Where's the mother?" Doc asked.

"You're looking at Mama," Margaret replied.

"You?" Doc asked, looking up with wide eyes.

"No—Miguel," she answered, and everyone laughed again.

Miguel told everyone, "I feel like Joseph and Mary going from place to place, but there's no room at the inn." Then Miguel explained what had happened at the doctor's office, the hospital, and then twice at the church.

"Hey, Miguel, let's keep him here," someone suggested.

"Who will be changing him and feeding him?" someone else asked.

"That's a big chore, feeding and changing. Time-consuming, and you have to be very gentle. Only the most talented people can pull it off, and I'm not certain any of us have the talent!" Miguel joked.

The whole morning was consumed with the baby. Everyone seemed more light-hearted and happy to have the baby in the workshop. The noise did not seem to bother the baby either. It seemed to soothe him. He slept most of the morning. Then Miguel fed him, and Margaret helped to change his diaper.

While everyone else felt greater joy with the baby at the shop, Miguel was brainstorming the next step for finding the baby a proper home.

Margaret sat down next to him to ask him in seriousness, "Miguel, what's your plan for the baby because I know very well he's not staying with you, right?"

"Yes, you are correct. And thank you, Margaret, for being so understanding. You are the finest person."

"You too are a rarity, Miguel. Most people would have walked away from this situation," she pointed out. "I knew you were special when I met you in 1951. I remember when we were in that crowded room at the Consulate in Nogales, and you told us, 'I worry about these people and their families and what could happen to them.' I will never forget how sincere and concerned you were about them."

"Thank you, Margaret, and thank God, and, of course, Doc too."

"Let's talk strategy," Margaret said.

"Margaret, this is what I'm thinking. I will take him to the police department this afternoon. But first I want to consult with my very good friend. You probably heard me talk about William 'Rex'

Thompson. He's a fine man and a good friend. I will call him during the lunch hour and run everything by him before I go to the police."

"Isn't he the man who works at the immigration office? One of the higher-ups?"

"Yes, that's him," Miguel answered.

"Good, I think that should be your plan."

Miguel then remarked, "I'm going to miss my little brother. I don't even know his name."

Margaret pointed out, "Maybe he doesn't have one."

Because the baby needed three changings over the morning, Miguel had to wash the homemade cloth diapers outside with the water hose. He hung them, so they'd be dry and ready for use later in the day.

When Big Tom saw Miguel doing this outside, in a way he wanted to laugh, but, instead, he cried. He was amazed by this mystery man Miguel Hernández.

Rex Thompson arrived at the shop around 3:00 pm. When Miguel introduced him to Margaret, she said to him, "Mr. Thompson, I just want to thank you for helping Miguel with his family's papers. He is almost ready to bring Edgar's mother and the rest of the children across, a plan he has talked about since I first met him in 1951. It's been almost fifteen years now. Now that his property is ready, they have a place to live. Did you know that Miguel lived upstairs till about six months ago? He lived up there since 1951."

Rex replied to her, "Yes, I know. I know just about everything about Miguel. He doesn't like to show off or be thanked, but I will tell you, there are a lot of illegals who are now legal because of Miguel's dedication. They have a lot to thank him for, those 'brothers' and 'sisters,' as Miguel calls them. Without him many, and I mean a whole lot of people, would have been deported and never would have gotten a green card. I've never met a man like Miguel Hernández."

Then they focused on the baby. As Rex already knew the whole story, they only needed to make a plan on how to proceed. They decided it would be helpful for Rex to accompany Miguel to the police station with the baby and to be there when Miguel explained the situation.

Before leaving, Rex picked up the baby and commented, "Boy, would I like to keep him. I have no grandchildren of my own. God has been stingy in that department."

An hour later they arrived at the police station. Miguel carried the baby in its box into the building, with Rex at his side.

A sergeant at the receiving desk greeted them and asked, "What can I do for you two gentlemen?"

Rex answered, "My name is William Thompson, and this is Miguel Hernández. We have a baby we would like to give to you. I will let Miguel, who found the baby yesterday morning at a doctor's office, tell you all about what is going on."

"What baby?" the sergeant questioned.

Miguel placed the box on the counter and indicated that the sergeant should look inside.

"Yes, there is a baby," the sergeant said, almost to himself. He looked up at Miguel and said, "Okay, let's talk."

Miguel gave the sergeant a detailed description of the situation. The officer listened intently, and once Miguel finished, he said, "I need to make a phone call. Please wait right here."

Miguel and Rex only waited a few minutes until a female police offer came to the reception area to speak with them.

Rex explained his presence to her saying simply that he was a friend of the family. The officer was fine with him staying while she gathered all the needed information from Miguel.

She had Miguel and Rex move to a private room inside the department. The three adults sat at a table, with the cardboard box holding the baby atop the table. She was there to collect more information from Miguel, both about the baby and about Miguel himself. She wanted all the details about how Miguel came to meet the baby, but also everything about how, when, where, and why Miguel came to the USA. What he'd been doing since he came in 1951. His occupation. Whether or not he'd had any previous encounters with law enforcement. She wanted to know everything. All the while she was professional and polite.

"So, let me get this straight—you found him at a doctor's office, then went to a hospital and then to a church twice, and they could not help you?"

Miguel explained, "They were very nice people, but they were busy with other pressing matters."

"Why didn't the doctor's office help you?" the officer asked.

"They did," Miguel told her. "The doctor directed me to go to the hospital and the church."

Rex sat listening calmly. As he already knew the story well, he would occasionally look towards the baby.

After Miguel answered her questions, she said, "Let's talk about the baby"—pausing she stood and then leaned over to look at the baby in the box and then to smell him. The baby smiled and giggled back at her—"He looks happy and smells clean. Can you tell me—who has changed him and bathed him, what has he been fed, and who has he been with since yesterday?"

"My two brothers and I have been caring for him," Miguel said. "We've been warming milk to feed him with a bottle, and we change him as needed."

"Who else helped with the baby?" she questioned.

"No one really. Mrs. Davis from across the street made diapers for us and supplied some additional milk. She also gave us some talc for after we bathe him or change his diaper."

"What is Mrs. Davis's full name?"

"Evelyn Davis, she lives across the street. She is wonderful, and her husband Glen is as well," answered Miguel.

The officer asked Rex again, "Who are you, sir?"

Rex told her, "As I said before, I'm a good friend of the Hernández family, and I'm here to assist Miguel in any capacity."

She then asked Rex, "Is there anything you want to add to what is going on with this baby?"

Rex stated unequivocally, "All I can say is that this little one is lucky to be cared for by Miguel Hernández. Miguel has the utmost integrity and good intentions. As you can see for yourself, the little one looks clean and well-fed and very content."

"Yes, sir, I can certainly see that," she told Rex. Then she said, "The next step is finding his parents. Are they around here? Did they lose him or abandon him? These are questions I need to find answers for."

Miguel told her, "I do not know anything about his birth parents. I too have been wondering about them and also about how to relocate my little brother with someone who is kind and can nurture him to become an educated and respectable man. That's been on my mind, and it's why I brought him here."

The officer told Miguel, "That's a very ambitious goal, sir. Right now we should look to find someone that will first give him a crib and food to soothe his tummy. And it's going to be up to a judge to determine the family that takes him in—whether temporarily or for adoption."

Miguel explained, "I need to know where my little brother will be staying. I would beg that I, at least, get to know what conditions, with who, and where he will be staying. I don't want anything to happen to him."

"I hear you and understand you, sir," she replied. "I have an idea of someone to call. But there's one more thing I want to ask you. You refer to him as your 'little brother.' What do you mean by that?"

Miguel answered, "Yes, indeed, he is my brother, and you are my sister as well."

Upon hearing these words, the officer looked at Rex, then looked down at the baby, and looked back at Miguel to say, "I've never heard a stranger refer to me as their sister. That's a new one."

"Perhaps you may think differently, but I can assure you that at one time or another in the future, you will agree with me. You and I are brother and sister, and everyone is related though most people don't realize it," Miguel commented.

Rex then spoke up, telling the officer, "I don't mean to speak out of turn, officer, but I have heard Miguel say this many times before—that we are all brothers and sisters, and those of us who don't understand that now will understand it very well later on in the afterlife—and I used to be skeptical, but now I believe that Miguel might very well be right. Don't ask me why, it's just what I feel when I think about it."

The officer nodded her head and gave a thoughtful smile. It was apparent that she was moved by these words.

After a reflective pause, she spoke to them, saying, "Will you excuse me for a moment? I need to make a call."

Before she left the room, Miguel asked her, "Officer, can you tell us your name?"

"Rose is my name, Rose Tomlin. And I'll tell you something else, when I first came to work this morning I was having a terrible day. A lot of stressful things have been going on at work and at home—and I've felt bogged down and just bad. But strangely, after listening to you and what you have been doing for this baby, all of a sudden my troubles don't seem that big. My heartache has gone, and I feel great. You've made me realize all the good that is possible, even in situations that seem so tragic."

Miguel stood up to answer her, saying, "You are very kind, Officer Rose. Who would not want to have you as a sister?" and then he hugged her.

A few tears rolled down her cheeks. She wiped them off as she walked out to make her call.

Miguel leaned over and checked the baby. As the baby was getting a little irritable, Miguel told Rex, "He must be hungry." Miguel took the bottle that was already filled with milk—but was no longer warm—and dipped it into the cup of hot coffee that another officer had just brought to each of them. Miguel did his best to warm the milk bottle without spilling the hot coffee all over the table. After that, he dripped a few drops of the warmed milk onto his hand to make sure it wasn't too hot. He took a taste, approved, and then gave the baby the bottle.

With one hand busy bottle-feeding the baby, Miguel, with the other, lifted the coffee cup to his lips to take a sip.

Rex, having watched this whole scene, gave a big grin to show he was impressed with Miguel's multiple talents.

Officer Rose returned about five minutes later and said, "Miguel, I think we can help you. This is what we're going to do. I just called a lady at Friendly House—"

"Friendly House? I know that place well. They've taught English to many of my friends. There are wonderful people there with big hearts," Miguel stated with enthusiasm.

"Oh good. They're going to connect the baby with a couple who is looking to adopt. Initially, the baby will only be granted a temporary stay with the couple until a judge reviews the matter and makes things legal. How does that sound to you?"

"It sounds great. Ideal. There's one important thing though— can I meet the couple who might adopt my little brother?"

"I don't see why not," Officer Rose replied.

Miguel explained, "I very much trust the people at Friendly

House, but I would still like to meet the people that my little brother will live with. It's important to me."

"I understand," replied Officer Rose. Then she asked, "May I ask you a question?"

"Of course," Miguel assured her.

"It seems like this has been quite an ordeal for you, taking on this baby. Why didn't you just walk out of the doctor's office and let them deal with it?"

Miguel explained to her, "Walking out would have been the easy thing to do, but it also would have been the wrong thing to do. I realized that although they were nice people, they were very busy and weren't committed to taking care of this little guy. Sure, if I had left, they would've had to do something, but I wanted the best for my little brother. I realized that instead of a burden, I should consider it a golden opportunity to do something unique and meaningful for him. It's something that doesn't come around very often in our lifetimes—caring for a brother or sister who is so vulnerable and in such need. As I see it, when a golden opportunity presents itself, we should take it on with gratitude."

Officer Rose was speechless. Rex smiled and once again looked at Miguel with admiration and respect.

With their eyes on him, Miguel placed the now sleeping baby into the Kellogg's box crib and wrapped him in blankets and towels. He gave Officer Rose another hug and thanked her for her help. Then Miguel and Rex left with the baby to go to Friendly House.

Miguel drove. Rex sat in the passenger's seat with the baby, in its box, on his lap. Officer Rose promised them that her contact at Friendly House, a Mrs. Ricci, was ready to receive them there.

Mrs. Ricci was in her seventies and had spent more than half her life working in orphanages.

"So, you are Miguel?" Mrs. Ricci began.

"Yes, ma'am, I'm Miguel Hernández."

To Rex, she asked, "And you are?"

"Rex Thompson, ma'am," he answered.

"Are you related?"

Miguel answered "Yes, Rex is my brother, and here we have our little brother that Officer Rose talked to you about."

Mrs. Ricci commented with a smile, "What an interesting crib."

"Yes, a box that held some boxes of corn flakes. Someday this little one will certainly be eating cornflakes," Miguel noted.

Mrs. Ricci asked, "Now that you bring up eating, where is his bottle?"

Miguel held out a bottle and handed it to her, explaining, "It's empty because he just ate a short while ago."

Mrs. Ricci then reached into the crib box and pulled the baby out, noting, "He is beautiful and smells like talc."

"Oh yes, he gets a sprinkling of talc every time he is changed."

"Good, that's good," Mrs. Ricci said.

She inspected the baby, looked at his hands, arms, neck, face, legs, chest, and abdomen. She told them, "He looks good. We have a couple who have been looking towards adoption for a while now. I have spoken to them already, and this couple wants to take the baby. I expect the judge will approve this decision as a 'temporary stay' until we can investigate more about this baby. If no one comes forward to claim him, then the court will most likely allow the adoption. The couple has been praying for a child."

Miguel asked her, "Will I be able to meet them before they take him?"

"I'm not sure, but I will tell them you'd like to meet them," she answered.

Miguel questioned, "Are you sure a judge will agree to this couple taking the baby?"

"Yes, the judge knows the couple well. He's been working with them for quite some time in the area of the adoption process."

"If you don't mind, I want to meet them before letting them take the baby. After all, I am his only relative, right?" Miguel said.

"Yes, you could say that," she responded.

Mr. Thompson asked, "Will the couple come here for the baby?"

"Yes, but not until tonight," Mrs. Ricci responded, "They are now in Prescott on business, but you can leave the baby here. I'll make sure that they call you to set up a meeting with you at some point."

Miguel firmly stated, "No, that's not possible. I have to be here to meet them tonight."

Rex agreed, adding, "I don't think that's too much to ask for. After all, the child's been part of Miguel's life for two days, and Miguel only wants to be sure he meets these people."

Miguel asked, "What time will they be here?"

"At 7:00 pm."

"Okay, I will bring the baby back here at that time," Miguel said. Then he took the baby from her arms and placed him back in the Kellogg's box.

———

Back in the car, Rex asked Miguel, "Are you okay with the plan? You seem unsure."

Miguel answered, "I am. I just need to protect him, I want to do right for him. I owe him that much. He is a gift, a gift to share, and I must share him as if giving a part of myself."

Rex took a long sigh and said, "Miguel, you never fail to amaze me. This situation with this baby and what you've gone through.

Looking after this child as if he were your flesh and blood and all you do for everyone around you. Amazing."

Back at the jewelry shop, before Rex departed in his own car, he told Miguel, "You are making the right decision to ask more about those people before you turn the baby over to them. If you need me tonight, give me a call. I'll be at home. And let's have lunch next week."

After Rex departed, Miguel entered the workshop carrying the baby in its box crib. Again, Miguel's colleagues were thrilled to see him and the baby. He told them about the 7 pm meeting and then worked for several hours until it was time to leave for the meeting. Of course, he took breaks to feed the baby and change him, and Nellie and Grace helped as well.

When Miguel returned to Friendly House, he encountered a nice-looking couple about thirty years of age waiting outside. Mrs. Ricci was standing outside with them too.

Carrying the cardboard box, Miguel walked toward them. The couple was looking towards him and whispering.

When Miguel reached them, Mrs. Ricci told him, "Miguel, this is Mr. and Mrs. Gazara."

Mrs. Gazara immediately asked, "Where's the baby?"

"Here, here is the baby," Miguel answered.

Mr. Gazara asked, "Where?"

"Here, in the box," answered Miguel, and he just slightly lowered an end of the box, so they could see the baby sleeping inside.

"Oh my God, in the box," Mrs. Gazara commented. She became very emotional and hugged her husband. Then looking at the baby, Mrs. Gazara commented, "Oh, he is beautiful."

"Yes, he is, and look at the dark hair," Mr. Gazara said.

"My goodness, he looks like you darling," Mrs. Gazara noted.

"Let's all go inside and sit and talk," Mrs. Ricci told everyone.

Miguel kept the baby with him. He'd been with the baby for about thirty-six hours straight at that point, but it felt more like a month. Miguel had grown very protective of him and preoccupied with his future. He wasn't going to let the baby go lightly, not at this point.

As Miguel would always point out to me and my siblings, "The way a person shakes hands tell you a lot about them. How they shake hands, how they carry themselves, express themselves, the way they look at you, the way they smile or don't smile, and most importantly, how they look into your eyes," he knew that he must shake each of the Gazaras' hands and look into their eyes.

Before walking inside, Miguel shifted the box to his left arm to free up his right, and extended his right arm before Mr. Gazara, saying, "Nice to meet you. I'm Miguel Hernández, and I am very happy to meet both of you."

Miguel noted that Mr. Gazara had a fairly good handshake, firm but not too firm, which meant confidence with a tinge of caution. Mrs. Gazara's handshake was gentle and paired well with a kind look in her eyes. Overall, they passed the first "Miguel Hernández test."

Inside, everyone took a seat, and Miguel placed the sleeping baby next to him. The couple asked Miguel to talk about how he came to be with the baby. Once Miguel explained all that had happened, they started to focus on the box. They peered towards it and at the same time asked Miguel questions about himself—where he was from, how he came to the USA, what he did for a living, his family situation, and such.

As Miguel answered them, he reached into the box and lifted out the fresh-smelling baby. As he continued to talk, answering their many questions, Miguel held the baby on his lap, with the baby facing the couple. The baby was awake and smiled several times.

They could not help noticing the tenderness Miguel exercised while handling the baby. They saw every gentle move Miguel made, his remarkable attention to detail. Covering the baby, ironing out the wrinkles on the tiny blanket, layering the blanket over his tiny, fragile feet, and keeping the blanket from blocking his gorgeous brown eyes.

The couple made halting attempts to reach out and help Miguel position the baby, but they managed to resist, forcing themselves to patiently wait until Miguel offered them the chance to hold the baby.

Looking to the wife, Miguel asked, "Do you want to hold him?"

After first getting a nod of approval from her husband, Mrs. Gazara then took the baby in her hands and started to cry.

Her husband put his arm around her and said, "I don't know what to say, but I think this baby was meant for us. Who knows where he would have landed should a church or a hospital have taken him? Thank God for this blessing."

"Yes, this is a gift from God," Mrs. Gazara commented.

Mrs. Ricci said, as she looked at Miguel, "With Miguel's approval we can notify the court that we have a suitable home for the baby and let the legal process take its course, providing there is no claim for him. Do you agree, Miguel?"

Both the Gazaras anxiously looked to Miguel for his response.

Miguel said, "I've told you everything about me, now I'd like to know some more about the both of you."

As they held the baby, they turned to flash looks of surprise at each other, indicating that they were taken aback at Miguel's request.

After some hesitation, Mr. Gazara replied, "Yes, of course . . . The advocacy group and the court have already done all the proper inquiring as to our solvency. I'm a professional architect, and my wife stays at home and would be a great mother to the child . . ."

Miguel listened and looked at them with a serious look on his face.

They then both turned to Mrs. Ricci, giving her a look that communicated that they didn't like what was going on, a look that communicated, "Who is this man? What authority does he have? Who is he to ask us questions?" They did not say anything aloud, but their look said it all.

Mrs. Ricci explained to them, "Miguel only has one vested interest, and that is to make sure the baby has a good home and that he also feels comfortable with the both of you. That is all. What Miguel has been through these couple of days, taking full responsibility for this baby—I think he deserves to know who will be raising him. I think that is most proper—after all, right now, Miguel is truly the only legitimate, or semi-legitimate, brother, father, and mother that this baby has in this world. Do you not agree?"

Mr. Gazara looked at Miguel and asked, "What do you want to know?"

Miguel responded, "I hope you understand that this child is a brother to me, and he may not know what is taking place right at this minute—but believe me—he and I will see each other again, and it is I who will have to answer to him why I let him go with you two. I will be accountable to him. Perhaps you will be good parents, but—maybe not."

They looked at each other in disbelief. It seemed they'd expected Miguel would hand over the baby to them and just walk away. They were mistaken. Miguel wanted to know everything about them and more, and then make a decision.

Mr. Gazara took a deep breath. Released it. Then began, "I'm of Italian descent. My parents came here as immigrants. My wife and I met in high school. We went to college together. I finished architecture school, and she got her teaching degree but only taught for a couple of years. Now she cares for me and the house, and she's a fantastic cook."

Mrs. Gazara added, "I was born in Pennsylvania, and I come from a long line of teachers."

Miguel asked them, "Have you had any issues with the police?"

Mr. Gazara replied, "No, no problems with the police. I have been asked that and more by the advocacy group who is helping us with adoption. We are now at the top of the list for adoption and were told that if anything comes up, we would be called. That's why we are here. They know everything about us, right sweetheart?"

"Oh, yes, we have been well vetted," she confirmed.

"Thank you, but I also need to know about you both since the baby can't possibly interview you," Miguel told them. "I want to ask you something."

"Yes, anything you like," Mr. Gazara responded.

"Are you prepared for the possibility that his birth parents might come forth and claim him? Are you prepared for such a possibility?"

Mrs. Gazara broke out in tears and blubbered, "Yes, unfortunately we understand it's a possibility. We appreciate that it would be devastating once we come to know this baby boy and love him."

Miguel pressed, questioning, "And do you agree that considering the circumstances I've described to you, about how I came to find this baby—meaning we don't know the birth parents or have their consent—that the possibility that his birth parents might appear and claim him is even greater than in a conventional adoption? You realize this, don't you?"

Even Mrs. Ricci showed surprise at the acuteness of Miguel's question, but she too agreed that he made an important point.

The two nodded their heads to show they understood that what Miguel was pointing out was correct. It was apparent that while they still recognized it was true, it greatly upset them.

"And your temperament, Mr. Gazara. Do you think you have the temperament to be able to cope if both this little baby and your wife get very ill? Will you be able to care for the child and your wife, even if it jeopardizes your career?"

Mr. Gazara thought for a moment before responding, "That's a difficult question, and the answer is that I would sacrifice whatever is needed to provide loving care for both our new son as well as my wife, even to the extent of putting my job on hold to fulfill my obligation to my family."

Miguel looked at both of them who were now in an emotional state.

Mr. Gazara asked Miguel, "Sir, why is it that you are so concerned about us and our abilities to care for this young child that you have only known for two days? Why all the questions?"

"Like I said before, right now I am absolutely accountable to this baby and would hope very much that anyone in my position would do the same."

Mrs. Ricci commented, "Frankly, when I first met Miguel, which was today, just a few hours earlier, I assumed he would come here, hand the baby over to me, and leave. But after hearing his concern for the baby's welfare and future, I'm so happy he has asked these questions of both of you. Do you not think this is a healthy and worthy conversation to have? Because if you should think otherwise, I would very much be concerned about your sincerity to adopt this baby?"

"Please, please. It's just that we are overwhelmed by you, sir," Mrs. Gazara said, her voice vibrating, trembling, barely able to speak.

Miguel said, "Imagine carrying this baby around in a Kellogg's box for two days, feeding him, changing him, and going from place to place, the doctor's office, the hospital, the church twice, the police department, and now here—and everyone either saying no or sending me somewhere else. As a result, my devotion to him, my duty to him, has grown and grown. I am his only protector. I am his only brother."

At these words Mrs. Gazara broke down and sobbed. Amidst her tears she blubbered, "This morning when Mrs. Ricci called us about the baby, we never imagined this conversation would take place. But now looking at what we're discussing, I'm forever grateful that it happened this way. Now we have even more appreciation for what we 've been blessed with, a new baby, providing we have total consent from you, sir."

Looking at Miguel, Mr. Gazara pleaded, "I give you my word of honor that this baby will be treated as we would our own flesh and blood and that we will care for and nurture him and love him for the duration of our lives. Miguel Hernández, sir, you have given us faith and an outlook beyond our own belief. Thank you."

They both stood up, Mrs. Gazara holding the baby, and embraced Miguel.

Miguel took the baby in his arms, kissed him, and told him, "Brother, you are now with your new parents and ready for a journey through life to adulthood. May it be one of good health, and remember to always respect, obey, and love your parents. Make your parents proud."

In 1982 while I was in my surgical residency, I had the opportunity to talk to William Rex Thompson. It wasn't the first time I'd met him. As mentioned earlier, I met him for the first time with my mother in 1968 when he intervened to save us from an overzealous immigration officer while we were picking up an immigration application for a guest.

Our 1982 conversation was an eye-opener. He told me that he was always a straight-as-an-arrow immigration officer and never ever would he have dreamed of helping illegals in the way he did for many years after meeting Miguel. He said, "How was it possible that a high official like myself was supporting a sort of 'underground system,' assisting people who'd broken the law by entering the US illegally? Truthfully, Edgar, I don't know what came over me. At that time in my life, I was a sad and miserable man, taking care of my beloved wife who'd developed early dementia, and I was angry at the world. Then Miguel Hernández came into my life. I'll never forget how Miguel said to me that it would be a total waste if these people, who'd sacrificed so much and risked their lives to come to the USA to seek a better life, one with many opportunities, got deported. Miguel likened turning a dream off to the way you switch off a light."

Rex went on to tell me, "Because of Miguel, I was convinced that I needed to do something good instead of being miserable and upset because of my wife's situation. I wanted to do something different, something unique and consequential—that's why I agreed to help your brother with his plans to immigrate those people in dire need.

"About Miguel and the baby and Officer Rose. I couldn't help but agree with what Miguel said to her, that he could just have walked out on the baby at the doctor's office, but it's not every day that a person has a golden opportunity to do something unique in life for someone else. Miguel said those opportunities don't come along every day. It's a challenge to our lives and to ourselves to seize those golden opportunities when they do come along. I'll never forget his words."

Rex then looked at me and said, "Edgar, Miguel was absolutely correct. He has expressed to me that he too hopes you will do something great in life; that the world is out there waiting for you. It seems to me that since you are learning to become a surgeon, that Miguel is right, that you are going to be doing something unique and consequential for our brothers and sisters."

I believe that Rex too was a rare and unique man who provided many brothers and sisters with the vital help they needed.

Chapter 16

WILL POWER

Finally, our home on 206 N. 9th Street was ready. Miguel had already successfully immigrated Pedro, Olivia, Jorge, Surama, and me, and it was finally time for the rest of the family: Mamá, Lupe, Asunción, Reyna, Manuel, and baby Salvador. Miguel had all their immigration applications completed. Timing and money were tight, but everything was ready and in order. It was time to get them to Nogales and proceed with the green card interviews and pray that all went well.

Miguel reminded us, "As has been the plan since I came to the USA in 1951, it's finally time to proceed with immigrating Nena and the children, so we can all live together. I will drive to La Mira to get them and bring them back with me to Nogales five days later, and Pedro you can meet us there. Then we'll leave for Phoenix and meet the rest of you—Olivia, Surama, and Edgar—here at the house."

That's when Pedro spoke up, "Miguel, I think it's a better plan that I am the one to drive to La Mira to get the family. You can meet us in Nogales. This is what I've been dreaming about doing for some time. I've been waiting and waiting for this opportunity. It's my turn to do something for the family."

Miguel looked at Pedro, who was only nineteen years old, and said, "As you wish, Pedro."

Olivia turned and hugged him.

Miguel said, "You will leave next Friday, early in the morning, Pedro. I will meet you in Nogales on Wednesday."

With tears in his eyes, Pedro said, "Thank you, Miguel, for giving me this great opportunity. I haven't seen Mamá for twelve years. I want to go. I want to see La Mira even if it's only for a few hours."

On a Friday morning in 1966, Miguel gave Pedro a leather pouch containing about a thousand dollars. Pedro took a knee, and Miguel gave him his blessing.

As Pedro moved to his feet, Miguel told him, "Be careful not to fall asleep. Take a few hours to rest when you need to. Please don't worry either. You will be fine. There will be many angels around you, looking after you."

Strangely, there was not a bit of worry amongst us. It almost seemed like Pedro was going away on vacation, yet this trip was an incredibly challenging journey with many potential difficulties. Even still, there was a sense of mission and of a dream manifesting, so there wasn't room for worry.

After giving Pedro a final hug, Miguel said, "Be careful on the gravel road before La Mira. Your Mustang has a low-riding carriage. It's short on clearance, so if you go over a ditch or a bump—and there will be many on that stretch—it could do your car in. Drive very carefully there."

Pedro smiled and told Miguel, "I'll be fine, and my car will get me there safely."

Pedro, ready to depart, got into his 1964 orange Mustang and adjusted the rearview mirror. Next he took his comb out to comb his Fonzie-like hair, first the left side and next the right. Looking at himself in the rearview mirror, he gave one of his classic not-bad-if-I-do-say-so-for-myself smiles. He started the car, turned on the radio, and as he drove away, the Marcel's "Blue Moon" was playing. "Blue Moon" was Pedro's favorite song, so it seemed a darn good omen for the start of this important journey.

Pedro made a safe trip to La Mira and retrieved Mamá and the children in good time. The only damage happened on the return, about halfway to Nogales, when the Mustang hit a cow that had wandered onto the road in the middle of the night. The car was very damaged but drivable, at least to Nogales. Most importantly, no one was hurt beyond the cow itself.

As planned, Pedro arrived with the family in Nogales on Wednesday. Miguel was there and helped everyone through the interview process and the final steps for getting their green cards.

Mamá and the children were enchanted by the drive from Nogales to Phoenix and arrived at our 206 N. 9th Street property full of wonder at the new country and city they found themselves in. They marveled at the massive trees adorning the house and with its small gate hidden amongst the trees by which to enter the property. They were delighted by it all, including the large garage-hostel in the rear. For all of us, this reuniting of the family was amongst the most important moments in our lives. That time in our life felt so fresh and abundant, and our future so laden with promise.

As Mamá slowly got out of the car, with baby Salvador in her arms, she was speechless taking in her surroundings. When she stepped over a green garden hose, she finally spoke, asking Miguel in Spanish, "What is this?"

He explained, "*Una pipa de agua para las plantas,*" meaning a water pipe to water the plants.

"*Si, entiendo,* I understand," she said.

When two people emerged from the garage-hostel and approached, Miguel explained to her in Spanish, "Nena, these are our guests. They will be staying here for a while."

Mamá immediately shifted baby Salvador to her left side, and extended her right hand to them, saying, "*Soy* Magdalena Hernández, but you can call me 'Nena.'"

Once inside the house, Manuel ran into a room and jumped onto a bed, and the rest of the girls joined him, laughing and crying at the same time. It was their first time seeing beds and mattresses. In La Mira everyone slept on *petates*, which were circular woven mats about a half-inch thick.

Miguel took Mamá's hand and said, "Nena, this is your house. Let me show you a couple of things." At the stove, he flicked on a burner and explained, "Nena you will never have to use logs to make charcoal to then make a fire again. Now you have a stove to cook on."

Mamá burst out crying.

Miguel next pointed out the refrigerator, a blender, and then for the toaster, he took two slices of bread and placed them inside, saying, "Look—they will toast to your liking."

In disbelief she began crying afresh and hugged Miguel. All of us watched and smiled. Here was our mother whom we watched for many years cook breakfast, lunch, and dinner with only rudimentary equipment, starting with making her own coals from wood.

All of us will always remember seeing Mamá first witness the new American life that was to become hers. It will never be forgotten.

Miguel told her, "I'm sorry it took so long, Nena, but by the grace of God, finally all of us are together again."

Mamá joined Miguel in his efforts to run an underground immigration "service" and garage-hostel that allowed many of our guests to become green card holders. Our mother got to know the many people Miguel would bring to live with us. She loved having them live with us. She became quite involved with assisting illegal people who were experiencing dire times and over time she got to meet both the Johnson brothers and William Rex Thompson.

Everyone in the family remembers the time Miguel brought two men who had worked in a chicken factory to the garage-hostel. The factory had shut down, so everyone working in it lost their jobs. The two men had lived on the premises of the chicken farm, but now had no place to live. The owner asked Miguel if he could help them, for they had been honest and hardworking.

When Miguel brought them to our home, they came upon two other guests who, very diligently and with apparent focus, were clipping and cleaning their nails.

The two men watched the two guests ardently pursuing this task, and then they looked at Miguel and asked, "Miguel, what exactly are they doing?"

Miguel told them, "Actually, you are going to be doing the same thing shortly. Soon you'll meet Nena, and she'll let you know how important she finds personal hygiene and in particular clean hands and nails. Nena is not a difficult person, but she does have certain standards, and one of those is clean hands and nails. As a matter of fact, she only allows those who have clean nails to sit at the table and eat."

The men were nodding their hands to show they understood and at the same time, tucking their hands behind their backs because they realized their nails were not yet up to par.

———※———

September 1971, the evening.

Quite suddenly I started having nausea and acute abdominal pain. Mamá made me chicken soup to soothe my stomach, but about two hours later I vomited. I vomited repeatedly. I felt like I had diarrhea as well, but nothing actually happened while on the toilet. I tried to do my homework, but it proved very difficult because of how terrible I felt and my many trips to the toilet. Throughout the night the abdominal pain continued.

Even still, I went to school the next day. I was an undergraduate at ASU taking a heavy class load of pre-med courses because I wanted to complete college more rapidly than the standard four years. I didn't have a car, so I would take the bus to ASU each day.

Throughout the day at college, I experienced fever, chills, nausea, some vomiting, and bouts of diarrhea, yet I managed to finish up the day, still hoping desperately that it would pass. Again while doing homework and later while having chicken soup, the abdominal pain increased. It was worse than ever.

That night my fever and pain hit the highest level along with nausea and diarrhea. I realized it wasn't going away but getting worse. It could be lethal, so I woke Miguel. I didn't want to do it because he'd put in yet another fourteen-hour workday.

After I explained to Miguel what was going on, he said, "Edgar, I heard you get up during the night last night, but since you went to ASU this morning, I thought you were okay."

"I thought it would pass, Miguel. And I don't like waking you up, but it's getting worse. Dangerously bad. Honestly, I don't know how I made it through the day."

Miguel suggested, "Edgar, you know you are probably stressing your body and mind with all those classes you are taking at college. Do you think that could have made you sick?"

I answered, "Probably not, because if that were the case, this would also happen to you since you have been working twelve- to sixteen-hours days, and you've done that for months at a time over twenty years."

Miguel smiled at my response and then became serious again, saying, "Since it's such great pain in your abdomen it could be appendicitis. Let's go to the hospital."

At Scottsdale Memorial Hospital, a general surgeon wearing a turquoise bolo tie examined me. He was tall and slightly heavy-set. Well-shaven and slightly balding. His round, slightly chubby face resembled the great actor Orson Welles. He was friendly and made me feel comfortable. He introduced himself as Dr. Jack McFarland.

Dr. McFarland said to me, "Edgar, you have the classic signs of appendicitis. Can you tell me how the pain started?"

"Doctor, it started around my belly button, then shifted to my lower right torso, and it continued. It's even gotten worse," I answered.

Dr. McFarland touched me on the left lower quadrant of my torso, pressed down, then pulled his hands off rapidly, and asked, "Where did you feel the pain?"

"In the lower right part of my torso, here," I answered and pointed to the area.

"That's called 'rebound tenderness,' and it's pain from the inflammation rubbing inside the abdominal wall that's lined by the infected appendix. You are going to need an appendectomy. I'm going to call the operating room and get it scheduled."

I thanked him, then looked at Miguel, and remarked, "You were right. It's my appendix."

Miguel asked, "Remember what you said to me when we were driving here and I ran over a bump on the road?"

"Yes, I said that my right side hurt when you hit the bump."

Then Miguel asked, "Do you remember the rough and bumpy road from La Mira to Los Coyotes?"

"Yes, of course," I answered.

He said, "I remember when I accompanied a child from La Mira to Uruapan to get an appendectomy. Can you imagine the pain he must have felt sitting in the back of that pickup going over those bumps for two hours?"

"So much pain. But he did it—with your help, Miguel. You've helped so many people get through pain and discomfort. You've helped me, Miguel. I thank God every day that you are my older brother. My second father."

Miguel hugged me and promised that we would get through this pain together as well, especially with Dr. McFarland in charge. "He's a no-nonsense surgeon. Professional, direct, and experienced. We are blessed that he is here to take care of you."

When Dr. McFarland returned, another doctor accompanied him. Dr. McFarland made the introduction, "This is Dr. Susan Smith. She will be your anesthesiologist and will put you to sleep for the procedure."

Dr. Smith was painfully skinny, her skin very wrinkled and ashy in color, and her lips purple. Her eyes were slightly sunken, and her hair thinning. Overall she seemed jittery and rushed, like she had a hard time being still. She had a distinctive cough, deep and frothy, and strongly smelled of cigarette smoke. It was a smell both Miguel and I remembered well, for it was how our father smelled.

Miguel and I both smiled and introduced ourselves to her.

Before they departed, Miguel pointed out to Dr. McFarland, "Sir, you have a tiny turquoise stone missing from your beautiful bolo tie."

He quickly removed it to see for himself and muttered, "Darn it. I love this bolo. I wear it every day. It must have snagged on something."

"The bevel that holds the stone in place, see that one? It has separated in one corner and that's why the stone came out."

Dr. McFarland looked at Miguel, impressed with his technical understanding, and commented, "Looks like you know something about Navajo jewelry."

"A little. I'm a silversmith," Miguel answered.

"That's wonderful. I love classic Navajo jewelry. I'm thinking about having a turquoise watchband made for my watch." He removed the watch from his wrist and handed it to Miguel.

Miguel examined it and noted, "Yes, it's an exquisite Omega. A band of turquoise would only make it more beautiful."

As he returned the watch to the doctor, Miguel said, "Thank you for caring for Edgar. He's a dedicated student at ASU, and he aims to be a surgeon. Actually, it's been his plan since he was six years old living in Mexico."

With his interest sparked, Dr. McFarland sat down to talk to us more while we waited for the operating room staff to arrive and take me to the OR.

As I was wheeled away, Dr. McFarland took Miguel to the waiting room and explained, "Don't you worry, I've done more appendectomies than I can count. Edgar is going to be just fine. It should only take about forty-five minutes, and I'll meet you back here afterwards."

———✦———

When I came out of the anesthesia, I opened my eyes to find my mother and Miguel looking at me. At first my vision was blurred, but soon I was able to focus enough to clearly see them both. We smiled and exchanged hugs.

———✦———

In the late morning the following day, Dr. McFarland came to see me.

"Wow, I'm told you've been walking around, and you're ready to go home," he said.

"Yes, sir, I feel great," I replied.

After that we talked about medical school, residency, and becoming a surgeon. Even at that time I realized that Dr. Jack McFarland was a surgeon to look up to. He had it all: the highest level of professionalism; a sincere bedside manner; a kind and gentle touch as he addressed the entire family; and overall great personal hygiene, including clean fingernails, which—as already noted—was very important to my mother! In all areas he was a stand-out surgeon and person.

"Dr. McFarland, I would love to be able to return to college tomorrow. Will that be possible?"

"We usually keep patients who've undergone appendectomies for about five days."

"I'm fine. I feel good actually, and I would appreciate it if I could go."

"Edgar, yes, we can discharge you this evening. Know that you are going to be the first patient to go home only fifteen or so hours after an appendectomy," he told me with a smile.

Because I was laser-focused on my studies with the aim of earning both my bachelor's and master's degrees in just four years, I decided to phone my classmates to get any assignments I might have missed. Because Mamá knew me so well—really, everyone in the family did!—she'd already brought my briefcase of books and notebooks to the hospital, so I could study.

Prior to discharge, when Miguel arrived to take me home, he and Dr. McFarland were speaking. Next, the doctor handed Miguel both his watch and bolo tie. They shook hands. Then Miguel gave the doctor a hug.

I returned to classes the following day as if nothing ever happened. I'd managed to only miss a single day of classes. I had no pain and was able to maintain my previous pace of studies.

About a week later Miguel and I met with Dr. McFarland for a post-operative appointment in his office. The office walls were covered in family photos and Navajo crafts. It was both fascinating and welcoming.

After a quick examination and a few questions he determined that my recovery was going well. Then Miguel returned to him his bolo tie, now highly polished with the stone replaced.

The doctor was over the moon. "It looks even better than when I bought it! I can't tell which stone you replaced either. Thank you," he told Miguel, marveling at it.

Next Miguel gave him the watch with the special band that he crafted for it. The doctor was speechless. He studied the silver, gold, and turquoise band that Miguel had crafted, applying his years of experience and creativity.

Finally, Dr. McFarland said, "Miguel, this is beautiful. Absolutely beautiful. I love it."

"I'm very glad."

"Thank you, Miguel. Thank you very much. Would you like me to pay you now, or will you send me the bill? I can do whatever you prefer."

"Dr. McFarland, consider it a small thank-you from me for caring for Edgar."

The doctor was stunned, but no matter how much he insisted, Miguel refused payment.

As we stood to leave, Dr. McFarland told me, "Edgar, keep in touch with me about your career. If you need anything, let me know."

I told him, "Thank you, sir. You are an inspiration to me, and I hold you in high regard."

After leaving his office, we stopped to speak to the administrator in charge of billing.

As we didn't have the money to pay all at once, Miguel suggested that he pay fifty dollars immediately and then twenty-five dollars each month until it was paid in full.

"Well, your appendectomy has been written off," the secretary told Miguel. "Dr. McFarland knew you didn't have insurance, so he wrote off his part. What remains is the payment for the anesthesia."

"No, please, I need to pay you in full. Please," Miguel insisted.

"No, that part's been taken care of. It's already done," the secretary maintained.

We were astounded and humbled. All we could do was say thank you.

The secretary noted, "About paying for the anesthesia on installment, I will need to get that okayed from Dr. Smith. If you could give me a few minutes, I can let you know about that."

While we waited, we took advantage of the time to do as we'd already planned: a short visit with Dr. Susan Smith to thank her and let her know we were working out a payment plan for her bill.

We met with her secretary who told us that we could go in and see Dr. Smith as she was in her office.

Dr. Smith was surprised and delighted that we stopped in. She had us take seats and revealed to us, "Edgar is the first patient that I have put to sleep for surgery that has ever stopped by to visit me. Please take seats. I'm happy to get to speak with you."

Her office already smelt of cigarette smoke and as she conversed with us, with a single hand she rapped her cigarette pack on her desk to knock loose a single cigarette from the pack. Then she picked up her lighter, lit the cigarette, and began to take drags while conversing. Again, her constant movement reflected the overall nervous quality she possessed.

Miguel told her, "We are very aware that you played an important role in helping Edgar. We are stopping in to say thank you."

She smiled and then said, "Most patients think their surgeon does everything. When they get my bill, they call up the hospital and ask, 'Who is Dr. Smith? I never met with any Dr. Smith. It was a surgeon who did everything, not any Dr. Smith.' That's what normally happens." As she was speaking, she pushed her seat closer to the window, opened it a crack, and tried to exhale the smoke outside.

Dr. Smith looked at me and said, "Jack told me this morning that you want to be a surgeon."

"Yes, Dr. Smith, I very much want to be a surgeon," I confirmed.

She looked me in the eye and said, "Son, remember to always be kind to your patients, show compassion. Be like Jack McFarland. He is the most generous man I know. Oh—and always remember to introduce your patients to their anesthesiologist prior to surgery." Then she took a drag off her cigarette and smiled, adding, "Perhaps then your patients won't forget about us anesthesiologists, and we may have a better chance of getting paid."

Miguel and I smiled.

She smoked the cigarette down to its butt, smashed it onto the loaded-up ashtray, tapped out another, and lit it. Then she hastily stood as if to indicate that our conversation had come to an end.

When Miguel asked her, "May I see your lighter?" she then sat back down, acquiescing to a bit more conversation.

He examined it, commenting, "This is pure sterling silver. One hundred percent."

Dr. Smith replied, "Oh, I didn't know that. It was a gift from my ex-boyfriend. He picked it up in an old Native American jewelry shop in New Mexico."

"It's of excellent quality," Miguel said. "You see, you can degut it," and he showed us what he meant. He extricated its lighting mechanism from the sterling silver case and began to inspect the silver case further.

Next Miguel said, "Dr. Smith—actually I'd like to call you, Dr. Sue"—she smiled and nodded her head in agreement—"Dr. Sue, please allow me to take this lighter. I'm a silversmith, and I'd like to make it even more exquisite. I can place turquoise in it and gold."

With a glimmer in her eye, she asked, "Will it make me smoke less?"

Miguel answered sincerely, "Maybe yes. Probably no. Quitting smoking is more likely to help. You are a beautiful lady, Dr. Sue, and quitting smoking is going to make you even more beautiful."

At Miguel's words she slowly and gently stroked her eyebrows and then ran her hands through her hair. She smiled and said, "Yes, I like that idea. Jack has been at me to stop smoking for years. Every time we work together, he tells me, 'Sue, you're going to kill yourself someday.'"

I stayed silent as I listened to them talk. Actually, I was listening to them and at the same time reviewing parts of my physics textbook. As a devoted student with a goal of completing my undergraduate studies in just three years, I typically kept several textbooks by my side, always at the ready, so that I could take advantage when even the shortest of opportunities presented itself.

Miguel next said to her, "Dr. Sue, our father practiced medicine and dentistry in rural Mexico. He was chain smoker, and we lost him when Edgar was only nine-and-a-half years old. It was a tragic loss for our family but also for our pueblo. He was a dedicated healer. Experienced, at the ready, creative with the few tools he had, and devoted to his patients. Just like you. It was when he died that I brought Edgar to the United States. You are a pretty and kind lady, and you do important work. We both want you to live a long and happy life. Do you have a family?"

"I've been married three times and divorced three times. Now I'm only dating. If you're wondering, 'Why three divorces?' I admit—they hated my smoking."

"I'm sorry to hear that," Miguel said, "And I know those men missed out losing you as their wife. Personally, I think they abandoned a wonderful person."

"Why, Miguel, that's a very kind thing to say," she responded.

"It's true, Dr. Sue," Miguel said, "They missed a golden opportunity to have you as a wife. On the other hand, smoking is a significant issue. It would be a serious issue for me too."

She looked at Miguel and stated, "Now I know you're being

honest with me. And I appreciate it. I value honesty. I need it."

Over the conversation, she smoked in the same obsessive-compulsive way as our father. Lighting the next cigarette to have it at the ready when the previous one was only halfway smoked. And just like with our father, we found ourselves wondering how this doctor, who made a career and devoted her life to healing those who are ill, could be such a prolific smoker. It was baffling.

Her voice sounded raspy and even sultry, the way some smokers' voices can sound. Soon after she'd started, she gave up trying to exhale the smoke out of the cracked-open window and instead, leaned way back in her chair and blew the smoke up and out in an arc towards the ceiling of the little room.

"Do you have any children?" Miguel asked her.

"Yes, a son. He's a young engineer in North Phoenix. He has a business that works on refrigeration heating and cooling systems."

Miguel, always thinking of current and future guests, asked, "Does he hire people who are hard workers?"

"Definitely. As a matter of fact, he's expanding his business, branching out, and is looking for more skilled employees. Do you know of anyone?" she responded.

Miguel had someone particular in mind, José Juan Bermudez. He was forty-seven years old and educated with an engineering degree from the University of Guadalajara, Mexico. Currently José Juan was working at a refrigeration repair shop. He was going to night school to learn English and was gathering papers for immigration. Miguel was helping him find a sponsor, either a work sponsor or even a sponsor through marriage. Miguel actually thought it could go either way with Dr. Smith and her son. Perhaps Dr. Smith and José Juan would hit it off, or perhaps José Juan would be able to get a good job at her son's workplace and get sponsorship through the job.

"Yes, I do know someone," Miguel told her. Pointing to her

lighter, he asked, "Dr. Sue, can I take your cigarette lighter and decorate it as I said I would?"

"Yes, take it," she said, handing to him, "Actually take it and swap it out for something else. I don't want it."

I looked up from the textbook to see her smash out her cigarette and then pick up her office telephone. "Josh, can you bring me a Coca-Cola. Would you all like one?"

"Yes, thank you," Miguel said.

Into the phone she asked, "Actually, Josh, could you bring three? Thanks."

A few minutes later a young man brought in three cold Coca-Colas for us.

Dr. Sue took a long drink and then said to Miguel, "You said your father practiced medicine in a little village in Mexico. Is that where you're from?"

"Yes, we were both born in the southern coastal area of Mexico. The Pacific side. I immigrated to Arizona in 1951, and Edgar came here in 1959."

"Tell me, Miguel, did your father die of cigarette abuse?"

"Yes, we think so."

"He developed a cough, like mine?" she asked.

"Yes, like yours. It got worse and worse with horrific unannounced coughing episodes paired with jetting blood. The uncontrolled coughing episodes frightened everyone, especially the children."

"Why didn't he stop?"

Miguel thought for a moment and then answered, "Everyone has a will within themselves. That will is meant to keep you alive and inspire those around you to also stay alive. He had no will power within himself. He gave up on himself."

Dr. Sue said, "Tell me, Miguel, why should I quit? I've tried to stop, but I couldn't do it. I don't think I have the will power to do it either."

Miguel said, "You are very wrong, Dr. Sue. Take a look at

yourself—you are a healer of people, so losing your life to this habit means many more brothers and sisters will lose their lives because you won't be there to heal them. Think of all the people on the brink of death or severe pain that will lead to death—that's where you come in. You can help these people even if you don't want to help yourself. It's a golden opportunity that you have, Dr. Sue. Don't lose it."

Miguel and the doctor locked eyes. It was his intense and soul-penetrating trademark eye contact.

After a few seconds, the doctor said, "This is incredible. Here I am, a doctor, and you, a silversmith, and I am having to listen to you about stopping smoking."

Miguel clarified, "But you see, it's not me telling you to quit. It is already your desire to quit, but it's your will that is weak. I'm only asking you to strengthen it a little so that you can continue to serve the people out there, that seek from you both inspiration and a demonstration of how important their lives are, both to them-selves and to their loved ones."

"Miguel, I don't even know how and why we started this conversation."

Miguel looked at her, again with his direct gaze, and said, "It was meant to be. Like you said, it makes no sense whatsoever to have me give you advice. After all, you are the doctor and I, a silversmith."

She said, "I hope Edgar is listening to our conversation because this conversation should be ever-lasting for him. If he can learn from it, it will help to make him a caring doctor."

I looked at both of them and smiled.

Pointing to the cigarette lighter that Miguel was still holding, she said, "Melt it and scrap it. I don't want it to be adorned in any way. But what I would like is to get to know you better. Let's have lunch together."

"Yes, I'd like that," Miguel replied.

"How about next week?" she asked.

As they were working out the time and location to have lunch, I was utterly mute. Thunderstruck by the mystical and mesmerizing influence of my older brother. The way he could infiltrate a person right to their very core and get them to tune into their purest self and access light, hope, and new beginnings.

In saying goodbye, Dr. Sue stood and addressed me, saying, "Edgar, you are lucky to have this man looking after you. You will be well protected forever. And I don't want to offend you all, but about your payment—you owe me nothing. The secretary told me you inquired about making payments towards my bill. Consider your bill paid in full."

Again, I was stunned and speechless, as was Miguel.

I spoke up, "But, Dr. Sue, we must pay you."

Miguel seconded.

"You already did. And, Edgar, remember what I said to you, just pass it along in your long-lasting career. I have no doubt you will remember our conversation."

Miguel hugged her and said, "Thank you."

I too thanked her for her generosity.

Miguel put the cigarette lighter in his pocket, and after shaking hands with everyone in the outer office, we departed. I should add that when we walked into the doctors' offices—both Dr. McFarland's and Dr. Sue's—Miguel shook hands with everyone in the office areas, even the water delivery person who happened to be making a delivery. Everyone seemed a bit perplexed at Miguel's gesture, but they all politely returned the handshake.

The next week when Miguel met up with Dr. Sue, he brought her a bracelet, a pendant, and a pair of earrings to match. They were silver (crafted from her silver lighter case) and adorned with turquoise and accented with gold. Sue and Miguel ended up becoming good friends.

About two months later, Sue and her son, David, met with Miguel and José Juan Bermudez. Dr. Sue convinced David to sponsor José Juan, and José Juan became a valued and longtime employee in David's business.

Dr. Sue Smith smoked her last cigarette the day Miguel and I met her in her office. About a year later when I accompanied Miguel to lunch with Dr. Sue, she was transformed. She'd gained some much-needed weight. Her face had changed from ashen-colored and wrinkled to firmer, shinier, and more vibrant. Her hair appeared fuller. Her eyes no longer appeared sunken and deep set in her skull. Perhaps most importantly, she seemed at ease, calm, and stable in the way she moved, talked, and listened. The nervousness and constant fidgetiness of the past were gone. It was like she was reborn.

———

From 1984 to 1986 while I was a member of the surgical staff at Scottsdale Memorial Hospital as a surgeon, I had the distinct and wonderful honor of assisting the great surgeon Dr. Jack McFarland.

———

Our brother Pedro, who became a highly skilled jewelry craftsman, ended up working two days a week at a jewelry shop in Scottsdale. As it was in the same area as Dr. Sue's office, they ended up going out to lunch together on occasion.

Over a lunch, Dr. Sue ended up telling Pedro, "When Edgar and Miguel came to my office that day, we must've talked for an hour or an hour and a half. Everyone on staff was stunned. They'd known me for a long time as someone always in a rush. Always hurried.

Someone who could never sit still, much less have a conversation of any length. They were very curious about what exactly we'd been discussing that got me to engage so fully. I never divulged anything about that conversation with my staff, but I want to tell you, Pedro.

"I expected that it would be a five-minute visit and then I'd let Edgar and Miguel know it was time for them to go—but that's not how it played out. Something unusual happened inside me when Miguel started talking to me. It's like I became transfixed. Magnetized by Miguel—his words, his manner, his very presence. I couldn't let him leave and didn't want him to. I even felt like I must have met him before. I still feel like that—like I've known him for decades. Maybe he was one of my patients? Maybe we sat together on a long flight and talked? I can't figure it out, but even though I know in my head that we've never met before, my heart tells me that he and I have known each another a very long time.

"And from that long conversation in my office to the friendship we've developed since, Miguel has somehow assisted me in revamping my whole life. I'm a new person—physically, mentally, and spiritually. It's hard to explain because it sounds so out there, but I wanted to tell you this, Pedro. As his brother, I figure that you understand that Miguel Hernández has an uncanny and breathtaking effect on people, at least on those of us fortunate enough to have our lives intersect with his."

Pedro was smiling and nodding his head as Dr. Sue said this to him.

When she finished speaking, Pedro responded, "Yes, it's true. Miguel is a marvelous mystery of a man."

Chapter 17

FOLLOWING THE PATH OF THE MOON

It was 1984. I was thirty-four years old, and Miguel was sixty-five. Though I was very busy as a surgeon having recently started my own private practice, I made it a priority to have lunch or dinner with Miguel several times a week. On this day, we were having lunch together.

After sitting down and ordering—meatloaf, lentil soup, and ice cream for dessert—Miguel then got up to wash his hands. I did so also. On our return, I sat at our table while Miguel approached the folks first at the table to our left and then at the table to our right.

I smiled as I watched their bewildered faces trying to figure out what this complete stranger wanted from them. Miguel simply shook each person's hand, introduced himself, and wished them an enjoyable meal. Oh, my brother—he was something else. Spreading his enigmatic and joy-filled presence to those around him as he'd been doing ever since I first met him so many years before.

When he sat back down with me, he first inquired about his namesake, my son Miguel, asking, "How is Miguel? I didn't see him today, and you know how terribly I miss him when a day goes by and I don't see him. I do miss him, and I will miss him."

I replied, "You 'will' miss him? What do you mean?"

"We can't live forever, Edgar," he answered.

"Well, rest assured, Miguelito is doing just fine."

"And Marisa?" Miguel asked.

"Marisa—as a healthy baby tends to do—is clinging to Lupe and doing well too. *Gracias a Dios.*"

"*Sí, gracias a Dios,*" Miguel seconded.

"What about you, Miguel? How are you doing? How's your blood pressure?" I asked.

"I'm doing well. My doctor is good and keeps after me to lose a little weight, and our meatloaf today won't be helping, but I'm doing well," he said. "Tell me about the patients you saw today."

"It's been a rough day at work, Miguel. There was a hit-and-run accident. Two elderly people were struck by a motorist, who then fled the scene," I told him.

"Will they survive?" Miguel asked.

"Unfortunately, they were killed instantly," I answered quietly.

When I saw Miguel's eyes tearing up, I asked, "What's wrong, Miguel?"

"You know—Phil," he said.

"Yes, I know, and I'm sorry to remind you of that horrifying event in our lives."

This is what Miguel and I were reminded of: twenty years earlier, in 1964, Phil, Miguel, and I went to the movies and saw *Flaming Star* with Elvis Presley and Dolores del Río. Afterwards, we walked to the old-fashioned Woolworth's department store in downtown Phoenix. We had a pizza and Coca-Colas.

Just after we exited Woolworth's, Miguel realized he'd forgotten a package inside. I ran back to the store to retrieve it, and Miguel followed. Phil continued on walking.

As Phil was crossing an alley, he got hit by a large dump truck. It killed him instantly. It was devastating for both of us. Absolutely devastating.

By 1964 Phil had finally found a community, steady work, close friends, and sobriety. He and Ernestina were considering marriage as well (and because Phil was killed, Ernestina had to get her green card through a work sponsor, the business owner who also sponsored Carolina and Juana).

All the silversmiths, the Lamberts, Nellie, Grace, Ernestina, Carolina, Juana, Charlotte, Ray Fasio—we were all numb and shocked at Phil's brutal and sudden death. It was a time of great sadness.

"Yes, Edgar, Phil's death was tough. It was very tough," Miguel said to me.

"Yes, Phil was a good brother," I responded.

"And six months prior to his death, Phil had Thomas, his accountant, do a will for him. Phil named me as his sole relative and assigned all his belongings and his bank account money to me. Honestly, I didn't want the money. Because Phil frequently helped out at that alcoholic rehab center where many Native Americans went for help, I donated all his money to them on Phil's behalf."

I said to Miguel, "Actually, I remember going to the bank with you and the lady from the rehab place. That was an incredibly emotional undertaking, seeing you show the people at the bank the will and then you giving Phil's hard-earned money to that lady. Miguel, you never fail to amaze me with your unlimited human kindness."

Miguel responded, "Edgar, it was a golden opportunity that Phil gave me. I was simply doing what Phil would've wanted me to do. And when I see Phil in the beyond, he's going to give me a hug and a handshake for seizing that unique opportunity and helping out the place that helped him so much."

Miguel and I then moved on to discuss the span of our relationship from the time I met him in La Mira in 1957 and when I came back to the USA with him in 1959 and over our twenty-five years together in Phoenix. We reflected on the many unique events that had taken place in our life together.

In this memorable conversation Miguel and I also talked about Santos Ortiz. I recalled, "I must have been four or five years old when I remember first encountering Santos Ortiz. Somehow Papá got ushered into a child's funeral, and since I was with him, I went too. I remember a little coffin and the overwhelming sadness of everyone. Then I saw a unique-looking man in white sackcloth clothing with a red handkerchief tied around his neck standing in the corner. He was playing a violin, but it wasn't melodies that sounded from those strings. He was making that violin cry and scream out the bottomless anguish that everyone was feeling. I was just a little kid, but Santos Ortiz and his heartbroken violin mesmerized me. Haunted me. I still get the chills recalling the memory."

A moment of quiet overcame both of us as we each reflected on the bewitching and melancholy violin playing of Santos Ortiz.

I pointed out to Miguel, "Did you know that when Mamá visited La Mira in 1973, she saw Santos Ortiz and spoke to him? Everyone estimated that he had been born in 1875, so when Mamá saw him in 1973, he was ninety-eight years old—and she made such a big deal about the fact that he didn't look any different than when she first met him decades earlier. It's like he truly was the magic man that people in La Mira accused him of being."

"Yes, Nena told me about that," Miguel responded, "And we heard that the last time anyone in La Mira saw him was in 1980, so that put him at one hundred and five years old. In 1980 people stopped seeing him around La Mira. His rustic dwellings suddenly empty. He disappeared, gone without a trace."

"What a mysterious man," I commented. "Growing up, the only person I ever saw him speak to was Mamá. She was the only one. Everybody else in the village treated him like he was a pariah, but Mamá always took care of him and showed him kindness. She told me that after you left, Santos Ortiz would mention your name to her. And that he called you '*hijo de La Mira*.' I thought that was interesting."

"That's amazing to me. Santos Ortiz and I never actually spoke to each other. I do feel like we communicated though and that he was aware of me, but we never actually spoke."

"What do you mean?" I asked.

"Okay, for example, the first time I recall encountering him was in 1929. I was ten years old."

I added, "So that would put him at fifty-four years old, correct?"

"Yes, that sounds about right," Miguel responded. "I was near the swift-moving Río Las Truchas when I first met him. He didn't speak but simply looked at me—right in the eye. It's a moment that's stayed with me over my lifetime. It was intense and chilling, but not frightening. We were close to the river, which was noisy with waves that crashed around the big rocks, but for some reason during that short span of a few seconds when we locked eyes, the roar of the river disappeared. It's like we'd stepped out of time or moved into a different space for those few seconds. Through our eyes we were communicating. We were connecting though we spoke no words. And after I took a breath and blinked my eyes—somehow Santos Ortiz was gone. He vanished—and that vanishing more than anything else spooked me."

I sat silent, taking in what Miguel revealed. After a moment, I said, "The way you describe it reminds me of how it feels when you exchange eye contact with me. You've always had an incredibly intense gaze when you look people in the eye. It's always felt to me like you were looking at my very soul, seeing my most honest and pure self."

Miguel smiled.

I continued, "I'll never forget when I was fourteen and you asked me to give the Stingray bicycle I'd won to Joselito. Oh my, Miguel, that was a huge ask. That was a hard one for me. But you looked me in the eye—and you applied your singular, stripping-to-the-bone gaze that pierced me right to the heart—that's what did it. That was what gave me the confidence, or rather—the grace—to let go of my desire for the bicycle. It's like you somehow empowered me to be my best self and share the one thing I had that would provide Joselito some needed joy and peace. It's a lesson that stayed with me."

"I've always believed in you, Edgar. I've always believed in your capabilities and your goodness. That's why I asked it of you at that time—because I knew you could and I knew how great it would make you feel. You know how I'm always encouraging you to seize those rare golden opportunities?"

"Yes, I know. And something I want you to know is that as a surgeon, I too aim to seize those golden opportunities, even though it sometimes drives the administrators batty," I said with a smile.

"What do you mean?" Miguel asked.

"Occasionally I encounter patients in dire need of surgery, but they don't have insurance and can't pay. Even still, I want to help them. This means I need to plead for fee adjustments with the hospital in order for them to get the surgery they need. Like make payment plans or place them in some type of special program that could assist them with their expenses. The hospital personnel have been very generous with my patients and helped me figure out ways to make it work. For example, the anesthesiologist and I can forgo payments for our services or substantially adjust our fees, just like Dr. Smith and Dr. McFarland did for us so long ago when I had my appendectomy. As I see it, just like that Stingray bicycle and Joselito, this is my way of giving the greatest gift I can with what I've been blessed with to patients in the greatest need. It's what you taught me to do through all you do for others—recognize unique opportunities and figure out ways to make them work."

Miguel grabbed my hand and told me with a smile, "I am so proud of you, Edgar. I always knew you'd be great. And even when I'm gone, I know you'll continue to pursue these golden opportunities."

I looked at him, puzzled, and then said, "That's morbid talking about 'when you are gone.' To me you are like Santos Ortiz—a man of mystery and spiritual significance. And just as he lived past a hundred, you will too."

Miguel chuckled, declaring, "I'm just a silversmith Edgar, who loves his family and all our brothers and sisters deeply. But there are more incidents with Santos Ortiz that I've never told you about. That I've never told anyone."

"Do tell me, Miguel. I'm all ears."

The Fiesta of the Virgin de Guadalupe occurs on December 12 each year. It is a day of major celebration in Mexico to commemorate how in 1531 Juan Diego Cuauhtlatoatzin, a Mexican indigenous peasant, saw a vision of the Virgin Mary who told him in his native language, Nahuatl, to build a church. When Juan Diego communicated this to the local Catholic bishop, the bishop asked for proof. A few days later Juan Diego saw a second vision of the Virgin Mary, and she provided him proof. She told him to gather roses from a certain nearby area and bring them to the bishop. The area was normally dry and barren, so when Juan Diego found roses growing there and brought them to the bishop, indeed, it was miraculous. But that's not all—when Juan Diego dropped open his long and loose sackcloth shirt, which he was using to carry the roses, and let them fall to the table, imprinted on his shirt was a perfect image of the Virgin Mary. To commemorate these miracles, a cathedral, the Basilica de Guadalupe, was built in that area, near Mexico City.

Ever since this event, Mexicans have revered and honored the Virgin of Guadalupe. On top of that, because she appeared to a poor indigenous Mexican man and spoke to him in Nahuatl, this miracle incited millions of indigenous people to convert to Catholicism when previously they had resisted. At that time most people practiced their own religions and viewed Catholicism with skepticism because it was the religion of the conquerors from Spain. It was Juan Diego's visions of the Virgin of Guadalupe that persuaded them to convert.

In the weeks and days leading up to December 12 and the Fiesta of the Virgin of Guadalupe, people all over Mexico make pilgrimages—walking, cycling, bearing torches—to honor this special day.

In 1931, around the time of the Fiesta of the Virgin of Guadalupe, Miguel, who was twelve years old, was at the church in La Mira. On that day he bore witness to one of the most moving and revered of penitential practices to honor the Virgin of Guadalupe. What he witnessed was an elderly woman who walked on her knees along the rock- and dirt-strewn road, up the church steps, and down the aisle until she reached the altar at the back of the church. Each step upon bloody step the old woman endured served as a ritual gesture to unite her with Christ's suffering. Each step she made acted as a public *novena*, or prayer, petitioning Christ and the Virgin Mary to hear her prayers and grant her a blessing. Perhaps she was praying for a loved one to return safely from a faraway trip or for a family member to be cured of a disease.

When she finally reached the altar, already on her knees, the old woman keeled over to lie curled on the church floor, bloodied, bleeding, and in agony.

That's when Miguel saw Santos Ortiz materialize from the church pews. He approached the woman and gently helped her to her feet. The front of her skirt, her knees, and her lower legs were pasted with blood, shredded skin, dirt, and gravel. Santos Ortiz wrapped one arm around the woman's small frame, and with his other he took her forearm. Slowly he guided her down the aisle to the church doors. She was weeping all the while.

As Santos Ortiz neared Miguel, he turned his head and locked eyes with the twelve-year-old. And just as happened when Miguel first encountered this hermit-bogeyman-mystic at the river two years earlier, as they held eye contact, the feeling of a cool wind surrounded him. A floating feeling came over him as well as a sense of utter calm. After a moment, the hermit's gaze shifted forward and to the ground, and he departed, carefully supporting the old woman and avoiding eye contact with those around him.

Miguel remained transfixed. Unable to take a step. Basking in the serenity of that sudden yet fleeting experience.

<hr />

It was 1935. Miguel was sixteen. He was accompanying our father who was going to treat a woman with a neck abscess as well as a serious dental problem. It was a follow-up visit.

She had first visited Papá at our house where he'd drained puss from the neck abscess and prescribed antibiotics and warm compresses. He was visiting her to drain the abscess once again and to see if he could access the problematic tooth.

As was usual, our father was smoking and downing copious amounts of liquor as he and Miguel walked to her mud-brick home. It was a cool afternoon with a slight breeze.

Miguel and Papá could hear the woman's moaning before they entered the tiny house. She was in acute pain. When they entered, her husband was present. He was pacing, and his face was contorted in worry and anger.

"Why is she hurting so much? You already treated her, but she's hurting! What have you done to her?" he questioned Papá.

Our father answered, "It's her tooth that's causing the pain. However, when she first visited me, I couldn't access the tooth because the abscess on her neck was so large and swollen. It had grown so big that she couldn't open her mouth wide enough for me to work on the tooth. That's why I treated the abscess first. Now that I see that the abscess has shrunken considerably, I'll be able to drain it a second time, and then I should be able to access the tooth and pull it. Afterwards, you'll see—she'll feel great relief."

"Ridiculous, outrageous! This so-called modern medicine. The witch doctor never made us wait so long. I knew we shouldn't trust you. What a waste! You're probably purposefully prolonging her agony," the man muttered, his rage increasing.

Our father did not comment but instead focused on the moaning lady, all the while smoking a cigarette and at times drinking a quick jolt of liquor.

Miguel helped by laying out all the instruments on the small kitchen table. Next he sterilized the instruments with boiling water, starting with the syringe. Once the syringe was sterilized, Papá injected local anesthetic into the woman's gums to decrease the pain.

Papá explained to her, "I'm going to stab the pocket of puss in the abscess on your neck to drain it. After that—we'll focus on the tooth. You'll feel much better shortly."

Because the husband was dramatically huffing and pacing the small room, creating an unsettling atmosphere for the wife and Papá, Papá suggested to him, "If you like, *señor*, you can go outside and wait until I'm done. Then I will call for your return."

After about two hours, Papá was finished.

The woman told him, "I feel much better. Thank you," but our father, who didn't like to be thanked, ignored her comment and continued cleaning up.

Miguel went outside to find the husband. He noticed that the sky had darkened, and the weather seemed to be changing fast. The sunny afternoon had disappeared and was quickly being replaced by darkness and ever-stronger winds. Thunder boomed and lightning struck in the distance. As it was January, the time of rains and hurricanes, this change in weather was not unexpected.

Though it had started to rain and the lightning strikes were moving closer, Miguel diligently continued looking for the husband, yelling out, "*Señor! Señor!* We're finished! Your wife is fine!"

The thunderstorm was gaining intensity, but still Miguel continued searching. After he moved farther from the house, some thunder cracked nearby, so near that Miguel felt afraid. As more and more lightning struck, Miguel could make out movement, like a cracking, zigzagging reflection of light off of a moving metal object, out in the distance in front of him.

For a moment, during the next lightning strike, the area around him was illuminated like it was daylight. Miguel then saw, several yards in front of him, a figure wearing white sackcloth clothing, a red handkerchief tied at the neck, and a straw hat. It was Santos Ortiz.

During the flash of illumination, Miguel and Santos Ortiz locked eyes. Santos Ortiz gazed into Miguel's eyes with great intensity. In a quick moment, it became dark again. Miguel found himself alone in the storm.

However, he felt different.

Despite the thunder and lightning, somehow Miguel's previous fears and worry were cleansed away. He felt a cool, then a warm and soothing feeling inside himself. The cold rain and darkness no longer felt threatening.

"*Mijo*! Time to go! Let's go!" Miguel heard his father calling.

Miguel carefully turned around so as not to slip in the mud and looked towards the house where he could just make out our father's striking silhouette with the smoke from his cigarette rising into the cool air as lightning illuminated his face and entire body.

Back at the house, the woman asked Miguel, "Where's my husband?"

He told her, "I was calling for him, but he didn't answer. I walked around looking for him, but I didn't see him either."

She told Papá, "Well, sometimes he can act a bit crazy and dangerous. He's probably just cooling off somewhere. God forgive him for what he said to you earlier. You've been kind and good to me and my family."

As quickly as the storm had descended, it passed. Our father told her he would see her again the next day to make sure all was well.

After they left, Papá commented to Miguel, "I can see that you got soaked. You must be freezing. Let's walk home quickly then."

However, Miguel assured him, "I feel fine. In fact, I feel great."

Papá raised his eyebrows to show his surprise.

The next morning before sunrise, a man knocked on the door and pleaded, "*Medico, lo necesito pronto, venga,*" which means, "I need you urgently."

Papá put on his coat, took a long drag from the cigarette he was already smoking, and off they went. Much to his surprise, the man was bringing him in the direction of the very house where he'd treated the woman the previous afternoon. However, they didn't stop at the house but proceeded to a barn located past it.

Near the barn, a crowd of people stood in a circle. When Papá infiltrated the circle, he found at its center a man lying in the mud. He was covered in mud and blood, and the mud around him was covered in blood as well. A machete was near him, embedded in the mud but its handle clearly visible.

When Papá crouched down next to the man, he realized it was the woman's husband. When the man realized that someone had crouched down near him, he started screaming and clawing at the mud. He was panicking.

Our father learned that the previous night, when the husband never returned, the woman went out to search for him. When she couldn't find him, she asked a neighbor for help. Finally, very late, they found him. He was in a state of confused shock and horror, and he was bleeding.

"Sir," Papá said gently, trying to calm him and bring him back to reality, "it appears that you have a slash on your head. I can clean it and fix you up very easily. Do not be afraid."

Someone from the crowd explained to Papá, "Earlier he told us that he was struck by lightning and at the same time a man hit him on the head. Something like that. But it's hard to make sense of what he's saying"

When the man calmed somewhat, several people helped him to his feet and walked him to his house. Papá advised his wife to first bathe him and then put him in bed, and then he would be ready to receive treatment.

Once the man was clean and in bed, Papá visited him.

"Let me see what is going on," Papá began. "Yes, you have a slash on your scalp. It looks like you got cut by a machete. Did someone cut you?"

"No, no," he responded, scared and gripping our father's hand. He then pulled Papá's head near him and whispered, "No, no, I don't know what happened. Yesterday evening, I sharpened my machete, and I was returning to the house to kill you because I was upset and I thought you were killing my wife."

Papá listened calmly, taking a drag from his cigarette and blowing the smoke up into the air. Papá said, "It will be okay. You will be okay. Tell me what happened."

The man, intermittently talking and crying, continued to whisper, "So, I sharpened my machete in the barn and went to the stream below for a cool drink of water and to think over what I was going to do. I decided to kill you. However, the lightning worsened. I was holding my machete and walking and waving it with rage as lightning lit my path. As I waved the machete in hot anger, a massive bolt of lightning struck, and it lit up the area around me. Everything appeared as clear as daylight. That's when I saw a man in front of me. He was standing there and staring at me. As I waved my machete at this interloper, I slipped and slid down the slope. And it was while I was sliding in the mud, that my machete cut my head.

"The whole thing happened very fast, but I swear that I saw a man as clear as I'm seeing you. Once I was down in the mud, I wanted to get up and continue with my plan. I tried hard to stand, but I couldn't. I felt paralyzed. For hours, I was paralyzed and stuck down in the mud, and all I could do was recall the image of that man with the red handkerchief tied around his neck."

———

Back to 1984 and our lunch together—Miguel continued, "As I see it, Edgar, Santos Ortiz saved my life and Papá's life that evening. And as you'll recall, that's not the first time he made a seemingly impossible appearance that saved me. Remember how after Danny stepped on that unique nail, we managed to remove his foot from the nail and free him?"

"Of course I remember," I answered.

"And next, remember how he somehow got a second wind and was able to lock me in a choke hold, and he was crushing my ribs and squeezing the breath out of me?"

"Yes, it was one of the scariest moments of my life," I said quietly.

"Something I've never told you or anyone, Edgar, is that when Danny was choking the air out of me, I looked up, and through the hole that was in the roof of our kitchen, I saw an image of Santos Ortiz. He appeared like an angel looking down on me. I also heard his haunting violin, crying and wailing. The tighter Danny squeezed, the more intense the violin bawled, but all this happened in a quick moment. Then, when Sam unexpectedly broke into our kitchen, Danny stopped attacking me.

"In reflecting on this, I've come to believe it was Santos Ortiz that saved me that night. Santos Ortiz somehow motivated Sam to unexpectedly and without precedent visit us that night at that exact moment. And, Santos Ortiz has to be responsible for that unique and impossible nail—four inches long with a brass head and steel shaft—that Danny stepped on. Because Danny stepped on that nail, he lacked the strength he normally had, which otherwise would've allowed him to break my ribs and seriously injure me or even kill me. I believe Santos Ortiz saved my life—and essentially he ended up saving Danny's life and Gwen's and Jimmy's too."

I looked at Miguel with wide eyes. He looked back at me, holding my gaze. After a pause, I then asked, "Why did you never share this with me before—about seeing Santos Ortiz and hearing that violin and your belief that he saved you?"

Miguel answered. "It's because you and Jimmy were already so afraid that I worried it would scare you more."

"It's a puzzle to me how Santos Ortiz keeps showing up in our lives," I commented.

"I agree," Miguel said, "I have no idea why the La Mira hermit has playedsuch a major and ongoing role in the Hernández family, but as I say—"

Before he could say it, I said it, "As you say, we shouldn't question miracles. Instead, accept them and thank God for them."

"Yes, indeed, Edgar. *Es verdad.*"

He and I both chuckled, and big grins spread across our faces.

Next I told him something that I'd never shared with him or with anyone before: the scorpion bite that happened when I was a child at the ocean with my grandfather. I confided to Miguel how during the ensuing seizures I too heard Santos Ortiz's crying violin.

Because scorpion bites are often fatal for small children, Miguel was incredibly jarred upon learning of this near fatal encounter. He actually began to weep and said, "Edgar, I'm going to tell you something that you should never forget." He wiped his tears and continued, "Edgar, we are here for a reason and that reason is not to live a long life. The reason we are here is to do something unique in life, something great, something that counts in life, that's for the good of all of us. God didn't let you die with that bite because you are destined to do something great. Truly, we are blessed to be here."

I smiled at my older brother and touched him on the shoulder.

He said, "Edgar, you are a surgeon, which is what you always wanted to do since you were six years old. You'd never worn tie-up shoes before you came to the USA, and now you are a surgeon. It's not by chance. It was meant to be. The strength from God to persevere is undeniable."

Then I admitted to him, "Miguel, you know sometimes I walk the halls of the hospital, and as I move between treating patients, I ask myself, 'How can this be—me, a surgeon?' I see myself as a little boy wearing *guaraches.* I only got my first pair of shoes at JCPenny's in 1959. All I can say is that it is thanks to you and the blessings from God that I am here."

Miguel smiled and gently repeated, "Remember, Edgar, you are here for a reason. Don't ever forget that."

We locked eyes. Intense, penetrating, a soul-to-soul connection through our eyes. Miguel's trademark eye contact.

"Edgar, do you remember when you got your green card, how I left mine with that nice gentleman, the American Consul?" Miguel asked me.

"Yes, I do, and I have never forgotten such an emotional event. He gave me the never-ending American dream!"

"Do you remember how I asked you to step outside, so I could privately talk to him?"

"Yes, very well," I responded.

"This is what happened—" Miguel started to say.

"But, Miguel, you told me what took place inside that office, and I am happy as to the outcome," I reminded him.

"Yes, but I never told you everything because you were young and I did not want to frighten you or confuse you."

"I do remember that you asked him to keep your green card and that you and I would return in a year with an update as to how I performed. So, what was it you did not tell me?"

This is what Miguel related.

The Consul felt hesitant about granting the green card. A part of him felt, as I was a child, I would be better off in Mexico with my mother rather than in the USA with a (in his eyes, at least) distant, much older half-brother.

As this was our third attempt at getting my green card and we'd put in so much effort, Miguel decided to go all out. He asked me to leave the office, so he and the Consul could talk privately.

The Consul's words were striking to Miguel. He explained, "I am totally responsible for everyone crossing to the USA. My signature clearly says that I, as the designated appointed American Consul, am totally responsible for each person legally crossing in the United States, including that young man outside. Young Edgar."

Miguel was stunned but agreed with him. It was a strong message.

To convince the Consul that he had my best interests in mind and that he sincerely cared for me and had no ulterior motive, Miguel proposed a deal. Miguel suggested that he hand over his own green card to the Consul. The Consul would hold onto the green card for one whole year. In a year's time, Miguel and I would return to give him a report of my life over that year, along with report cards and letters from other adult authorities. This way the Consul could decide if I had been progressing and living a positive new life in the USA or if I should return to my mother in Mexico.

The reason this was such a big deal is that Miguel would have to live for a year in the US with no green card. He wouldn't exactly be illegal, but he wouldn't have the identification necessary to avoid deportation if he got caught up in a raid. He would be vulnerable living in the USA without a green card. Because the green card was so important, it ensured that Miguel and I would return in one year's time to give him a progress report about my life and also to get back Miguel's green card.

The Consul was impressed by Miguel's proposal and agreed to it immediately.

At one point in their conversation, Miguel had grown so comfortable that he asked, "May I see that framed picture sitting on your desk, sir?"

"Yes, of course," the Consul said.

Looking at the woman in the photograph, Miguel commented, "This beautiful lady resembles you, sir."

"You think so?" the man asked.

Miguel smiled, looking into the Consul's eyes and locking eye contact with him for a few seconds. Then Miguel handed back the framed photo. As the Consul reached for it, Miguel noticed a small smile on his face, a noticeable change from the man's usual stern expression.

The Consul removed his dark framed glasses and noted, "Hmmm, Miguel Hernández, where have I seen you before? I feel as if we've met once in the past. Someplace, somewhere."

Daring yet polite, Miguel responded, "Yes, we've met before. I am sure it will come to you."

With their eyes again locking into a piercing eye contact, the man said, "Maybe when my mother died. Maybe at her funeral or after?" He knew Miguel was from Michoacán, Mexico, and not from the USA, yet he still said that.

"When did your mother pass?" Miguel asked.

"Oh, years ago . . . This is my favorite photo of my mother," he said indicating the framed photograph that Miguel had been looking at.

"Your mother is beautiful, sir," Miguel said.

"Yes. She died giving birth to me," he revealed and wiped his eyes. Then he went on to say, "You may think this is crazy but perhaps not—have you ever worked at a cemetery?"

"Maybe. I've had a variety of jobs here and there," Miguel answered.

Looking down for a few seconds then looking at Miguel, he said, "I seem to remember that you were with other men, maybe with a man wearing a red handkerchief around his neck. None of you said much. I was crying at the cemetery, and I was looking around, looking to find some kind of peace in my heart. I don't know, maybe it was a dream . . ."

He became emotional, and for a minute he did not say a word or dare to look at Miguel.

He again wiped his eyes, uttering, "A beautiful mother that died to give me life . . . I don't know what came over me. I am sorry I said those things to you. Maybe it's because it's been a long and stressful day for me. Sometimes I let my emotions make decisions for me when signing off on people seeking a better life. My signature to let someone cross is the most stressful hour of their life. Like for you, Miguel Hernández, and your young half-brother outside."

Miguel looked at him and again locked eyes with him.

The Consul smiled wider than before and said, "Thank you for listening to me. Miguel Hernández, you are a man of valor and uniqueness with your desire to bring all of your family to the United States. It's a long and hard road with many sacrifices. I know few men like you."

Miguel said, "You are noble. I see my plan as a golden opportunity to do something unique in life that will greatly impact my family members. We all should seek out such ambitious opportunities even though they aren't easy to pull off."

The Consul then signed my green card paper. He wrote a note on a second piece of paper. Then he stood up and shook hands with Miguel, saying, "That child outside will achieve the true American dream."

——◆◆◆——

With my eyes opened wide in wonder, I asked, "Miguel, he said that?"

"Yes, he did. And he was right about you, wasn't he?" replied Miguel, looking me directly in my eyes.

I smiled and hugged him, not realizing it would be our last hug.

Before we departed that night, out in the parking lot, Miguel said to me, "Oh—I meant to tell you that I came across a young man living behind the jewelry shop, Carlos. He's here illegally. I told him I'd help him find work and a sponsor. I wanted to start with you to see if you know of anything available at the hospital."

"Let me check. I'll give you a call," I replied.

——◆◆◆——

Late that night, Miguel Hernández, mystic, died.

Several hours after our meal, around midnight, he felt extreme pain in his chest, so he went to the ER. He ended up suffering a ruptured ventricular aneurysm, which means that a chamber in his heart burst. At that time, the chance of fatality from such a rupture was virtually one hundred percent. Miguel died in the hospital.

Miguel's death was a crushing blow to me, our family, his colleagues, and his many friends. It really crushed me and remains the greatest and most painful loss I have yet experienced. The one "comfort," if I can call it that, is that in the decades since his death, when I reflect back on that special final meal we enjoyed together, I realize that on some level Miguel knew that he was to die very soon. Several times in that meal—though it was very odd to me— he mentioned his passing.

I also find solace in recalling how even in our final meeting, he managed to remind me of his firm belief that, as he often said, "Each of us is here for a reason, and a long life is not always one of those reasons. It is what we accomplish in the time we are here." It's like, yet again, he was preparing me, strengthening me to summon the resilience to keep my eyes on the prize even in the wake of his imminent death. My older brother, my second father—yet again—put me before himself. Even in the hours before his death, he did all he could to assist, comfort, and build me up so as to lessen my ensuing grief by leaving me with those wise words. Again, he demonstrated his own propensity to self-sacrifice.

Just as happened in his life, Miguel's funeral brought together a multitude of people from a myriad of backgrounds to convene, mourn, commemorate, and celebrate him. Among the people at his funeral included the following:

- Everyone in the Hernández family, of course

- Miguel's silversmith friends and colleagues

- Grace, Nellie, and Sampson

- Ray Fasio—Miguel's first close friend in America, Korean War veteran, owner of a swamp cooler business, and sponsor of many of Miguel's guests

- William "Rex" Thompson—high-up immigration agent who provided Miguel with key assistance to help hardworking illegals get their green cards

- Jerry Johnson, Bonnie, and Bonnie and Gary's daughter Geraldine, who was now about twenty-one years old. Very sadly, Gary died of leukemia several years earlier.

- Frank Cooper, his wife, and their son, Anthony Miguel Cooper—in 1984 Anthony Miguel was twenty-five and in university studying for his architecture degree.

- Jimmy—an adult and a practicing physical therapist

- Ray Provencio—jeweler who sponsored Benjamín and friend of Miguel

One of the most moving parts of Miguel's funeral was when his godson, Sampson, then twenty-seven years old, spoke. Sampson spoke to Miguel in the Navajo language, delivering a Navajo wish for a safe journey. Here are his words, first in Navajo, and then an English translation:

> *Miguel shizhé'é ishi'nigíí dii j'įnh dóó ną́ą́sgóó*
> *nizhoni'go' oljééh do sin ya'ah'teyi'gii nih jééhyi'*
> *dii't'sa'go' bi'kééh yinąłdólee'h. Ho'zhóógo'*
> *niłchi'h dóó nalt'éhgóó, ałdóh bi'kééh yinąłdo.*

Báá'holzhiizhgo' ááhi'niildééhdi' gł'óódi'chi'h bił a'hinéédiikah'.

Miguel, my father, follow the path of the moon and the music of your own ears to the place of gathering, where we will all gather and feast with laughter. May the whispering spirit of the wind be kind and smooth in your travels.

Just as Miguel stood at our father's grave, so many decades before, to speak to him, something I did and still do is visit Miguel's grave to talk. Something I've talked to him about is one of our favorite shows, *The Rifleman*. It was set in the 1880s and told the story of a father and son, Lucas McCain (father) and Mark (son). They were from Oklahoma but ventured to New Mexico to start a new life there on a ranch after the death of Lucas's wife/Mark's mother. Every week Miguel and I would watch that show together in the little apartment above the jewelry shop. To me it seemed that in a way, we were watching a version of our own life, with Miguel as Lucas McCain and me as his son Mark, far away from where we were born and raised, relocated in a new territory that offered great opportunities but also obstacles. What was so interesting was that many of the episodes focused on the importance of giving people a second chance—which was also one of the Miguel's beliefs.

In one of our graveside chats, I confided, "I loved watching *The Rifleman* with you. Just like Lucas did for his son Mark, you taught me to be a man of stature, honesty, and integrity. And I remember how you would get upset when Lucas McCain was in mortal danger. I secretly loved it because I knew that when Lucas escaped and saved not only his own life but the lives of others,

Mark would run to his father and hug him. In turn, I too would hug you to celebrate the televised father-son victory. It was our victory, Miguel, and hugging you and getting to be raised by you was my life's greatest triumph. Miguel, I am a product of your sacrifice and victories. I love you, and I am forever grateful to you. You are remembered and loved."

Miguel Hernández
Photo taken 1952

The following are remembrances family and friends wanted to share about the mystical, enigmatic Miguel Hernández:

Jorge Hernández—Miguel's brother

As I have been meeting with my brother Edgar for breakfast, lunch, or dinner over the past few years as he has been writing his autobiography, our mother's biography, and now a biography of the greatest man who ever lived, it has brought me many emotional and tearful moments about

*how great it is to be related to Miguel Hernández.
Edgar's inspirational book is not just a testimonial
about our brother Miguel's life, but also it delivers
many messages to people as to how a life should be
lived. Miguel's generosity and his humble and deep
love for people are clearly and vividly brought to
life. When I read this book, I see clearly every bit of
Miguel. I believe those things I saw Miguel do were
mystical, and even just listening to Miguel would
give me goose pimples. My brother Edgar knew him
better than most of us. Miguel shaped Edgar into
becoming a unique person. Most people live a life
without sparks, but Miguel impressed all around
him with those unique things he did.*

*My most important recollection about his human
kindness was when he brought an abandoned baby
home in 1965. He stood his ground about finding a
good family for the baby. He wanted to find someone
who would nurture him. Edgar and I joked with him
about keeping the baby, but Miguel said he was going
to find a mother and father who would shape him
into a loving son and make him a respectable man. He
told me that when he decided on a specific family for
the baby that he would be accountable to that baby
beyond earth time when they would meet again and
that he did not want to disappoint that baby. He talked
about things that made you think beyond normal
thoughts and conscience.*

*When I became a jeweler, like Miguel, it was an honor.
I am a father, grandfather, and great-grandfather. I am
happy and proud to be called Jorge Hernández, brother*

to Miguel Hernández. I thank Edgar for writing this book. A book that brings Miguel Hernández, mystic, back to life for me and for everyone.

Pedro Hernández—Miguel's brother

My brother Miguel meant the world to me. He brought me to Arizona in 1954 to give me a future. I became a jeweler like him. He was my shining guiding light throughout all my life. There was not a single more talented jeweler than Miguel. He was the envy of many and at the same time a most respected man of the highest caliber. He was very sensitive to the needs of others and would rush to rescue those unfortunate brothers and sisters around him. He immigrated many people, too many to count.

He embraced and loved the USA and was always preaching that we must dominate the English language in order to compete in the fast-changing and challenging American society. He would say, "You must master the English language. It opens the doors to success." I never saw anyone in my life do what my brother did, bringing all of us to the USA, and still he managed to help dozens of other unrelated people immigrate.

Blanca Rojas—Miguel's niece

My experience with Tío Miguel goes back to when I was a child in Mexico. He was like a second father to me. He was always kind, funny, and caring with everyone, and especially with his nephews and nieces. He was a great role model to us all.

During my early years in Phoenix, Arizona, in the early 1960s, it was not uncommon to see my uncle extending a helping hand to those in need. He would help someone find work or a place to live, whether they were relatives or friends. He seemed to be particularly concerned with people with immigration issues and would do whatever he could for them. He always wanted everyone to improve their quality of life. Tío Miguel impacted our entire family in a positive way, and we miss him dearly. Thank you, Tío Miguel!

Daniel "Boli" Hernández—Miguel's nephew

My Uncle Miguel brought my sister Blanca, my brother Luis, and me from the town of Arteaga, Michoacán, to the city of Nogales, Sonora. We lived there nearly two years until we collected the necessary papers to immigrate to the USA. Tío Miguel, as we all called him, was constantly helping relatives and friends who wanted to live in the USA to legally reach their goal. He also helped many of those who were living in the USA illegally to achieve legal residency. He helped in finding sponsors for some to increase their chances of becoming legal residents. He was always encouraging his family and others he helped to reach their full potential. I believe he would be proud to see the results of his efforts. My sister, my brother, and I all became naturalized citizens of the United States and raised families. Sadly, my brother Luis passed away in 1997. His children and grandchildren, as well as my sister and I, along with our respective families, live very productive lives. I am forever grateful to Tío Miguel for putting me and many others in a position to improve our lives.

Raymond Provencio—a jeweler and friend of Miguel

One of Miguel's guests, Benjamín, lived with me and my family for three months. He came from Oaxaca, Mexico, but worked in Mexico City setting diamonds onto platinum (white gold) or yellow gold. Metal is quite hard, so it requires great dexterity to manually set diamonds onto metal. To do so requires the use of a sharp tool that carves slivers of metal to fold over the diamonds to secure them in place. Because the Lamberts' jewelry artisans worked only with silver and turquoise, they could not hire Benjamín unless he was retrained. He was doing part-time work in a jewelry store when Miguel met him and connected him with me. Because I worked for a diamond jewelry chain store in Scottsdale, I got him a job and got the owner of the store to sponsor him. Miguel guided Benjamín through the green card process and helped the owner with everything required to sponsor Benjamín.

Ray Fasio—Miguel's longtime friend

I met Miguel Hernández in 1951 after I returned from the Korean War where I worked in the aviation department. From the first time I met Miguel he talked about someday bringing his family to the USA. In 1954 I accompanied him to Mexico when he brought Pedro and Olivia to Phoenix, Arizona. I knew him till his death thirty-three years ago when he passed away in 1984. It was a sad day for not just me but also for many people who knew him.

I worked with many people he helped immigrate. His concern for people going through bad times was clear. He personally helped, to my recollection, over sixty people get their green cards. He was concerned about those here in the USA illegally. He was concerned about their futures and their families' futures. He wanted to change and better their lives. He was a strong advocate. He wanted them to learn English to better compete here in the USA. His vision for what he did was most unique and impossible for anyone else to do. He was beyond human.

———

Miguel, mystic—you are remembered and loved.

ACKNOWLEDGMENTS

I would like to thank my sisters—Surama, Lupe, Asunción, and Reyna—and my brothers—Pedro, Jorge, Manuel, Salvador, and José Ángel—as well as Daniel "Boli" Hernández—for their valuable information, which was essential for the preparation for this book about our brother Miguel. I would like to thank my wife, Lupe, for encouraging me to write this book and my sons, Miguel and Carlos, and my daughter, Marisa, for their further encouragement.

Mr. Ray Fasio, the only living non-family friend who met Miguel in 1951/52—I thank him for his valuable information about Miguel.

Thank you to Carol J. Benally, RN, MSN, for her advice on Navajo writing, translating, and culture. Her recommendations have been invaluable.

I'd like to thank Shanna Hardman for her steadfast support in helping transcribe my manuscript.

I would also like to thank Denny's diner, both the branch in Tempe, Arizona, and the one in Chandler. Over the years I've spent hours at these two Denny's writing my books. The waiting staff at both are exemplary. They left me alone to concentrate on my writing but always kept my mug full of nice and hot coffee—and even added cream and sugar, so I wouldn't have to interrupt my writing to do so. Thank you to those two Denny's.

ABOUT THE AUTHOR

E dgar H. Hernández, M.D., M.S., F.A.C.S., lives in Tempe, Arizona. In addition to being a proud husband and father, he is now a happy grandfather of six granddaughters from the ages of 3 to 19 years and a grandson who is now a year old, and expecting twins: a boy and girl.

For over thirty-four years he has been a surgeon in private practice. Additionally, he has served as chief of surgery, chief of staff, and member of the board at Chandler Regional Medical Center in Chandler, Arizona.

For over 20 years, Dr. Hernández has practiced general surgery. In the last fourteen years, Dr. Hernández has dedicated himself to the field of breast surgery. He cares for women with minimal to devastating breast cancers. Recently, Dr. Hernández joined the Ironwood Cancer and Research Center, a renowned oncology center in Arizona. He is a diplomate of the American Board of Surgery, a fellow of the American College of Surgeons, and a practicing oncoplastic breast surgeon.

Over the course of his career, Dr. Hernández has worked with charitable groups and various foundations. He has led and participated in many mission trips to Mexico to perform surgeries, teach and train Mexican surgeons, and bring medical equipment and supplies to underfunded Mexican hospitals. In 2000, the Phoenix Hispanic community awarded him its "Humanitarian Award" for his mission work in Mexico. In 2011, Dr. Hernández was named "Man of the Year," a humanitarian distinction, by Fresh Start Women's Foundation of Arizona for his treatment of uninsured women in need of surgeries for breast disorders, including breast cancers. The Desert Cancer Foundation of Arizona also honored Dr. Hernandez with a humanitarian award. South Mountain Community College of Arizona selected Dr. Hernández to speak at their 2017 commencement ceremony. He also gave the keynote speech at the Fourth of July 2018 Naturalization (Citizenship) ceremonies in Phoenix, Arizona.

1957: Edgar (on right) meets Miguel for the first time

1954: Ray Fasio (front row right), with Pedro, Chucho, Surama, and Papa

1963: Olivia with Miguel's 1957 Ford Fairlane in background

1964: Guests in front of the 7-bay garage

2019: Jorge working at his jeweler's bench

2019: Sam's convenience store

2019: Ray Fasio (age 84)

9 781732 173651